OUR FIGHT HAS JUST BEGUN

Our Fight Has Just Begun

HATE CRIMES AND JUSTICE IN NATIVE AMERICA

CHERYL REDHORSE BENNETT

THE UNIVERSITY OF
ARIZONA PRESS

TUCSON

The University of Arizona Press
www.uapress.arizona.edu

ISBN-13: 978-0-8165-4168-3 (hardcover)
ISBN-13: 978-0-8165-4167-6 (paperback)

Cover design by Leigh McDonald
Cover photo: Bob Fitch Photography Archive, Department of Special Collections, Stanford
University Libraries
Typeset by Sara Thaxton in 10.25/15 Minion Pro with Cutright WF, Altivo, and Helvetica Neue LT Std

Publication of this book is made possible in part by the proceeds of a permanent endowment
created with the assistance of a Challenge Grant from the National Endowment for the Humanities,
a federal agency.

Library of Congress Cataloging-in-Publication Data
Names: Bennett, Cheryl Redhorse, 1978– author.
Title: Our fight has just begun : hate crimes and justice in Native America / Cheryl Redhorse Bennett.
Description: Tucson : University of Arizona Press, 2022. | Includes bibliographical references and
    index.
Identifiers: LCCN 2021038742 | ISBN 9780816541683 (hardcover) | ISBN 9780816541676 (paperback)
Subjects: LCSH: Navajo Indians—Crimes against—Four Corners Region. | Hate crimes—Four
    Corners Region. | Racism—Four Corners Region. | Four Corners Region—Race relations.
Classification: LCC E99.N3 B46 2022 | DDC 305.8009792/59—dc23
LC record available at https://lccn.loc.gov/2021038742

Printed in the United States of America
♾ This paper meets the requirements of ANSI/NISO Z39.48-1992 (Permanence of Paper).

This book is dedicated to the Native American victims and survivors of hate crime.

Contents

Preface

> The fight has only begun and we are prepared spiritually with human
> dignity, to carry on our fight in all avenues that we consider necessary in
> order to be heard—not as militants or as fanatics, but as human beings,
> as Navajos.
>
> —Larry Emerson for the Coalition for Navajo Liberation, *Navajo Times*, 1974

As a Diné and Numunuu woman from Diné Bikayah (Navajo land) I
am no stranger to race, racism, and hate crime. I experience racism
daily as a citizen of the Navajo Nation, and I also experience discrimination daily as a woman of color. Growing up, I often thought I was overan-
alyzing racism and discrimination. Yet some of my experiences reveal how
racism is embedded into the fabric of our culture. This book is about race,
racism, and bias-motivated hate crimes committed against Native Americans in the Four Corners.

I grew up in the small community of Kirtland, New Mexico, near the reservation border town of Farmington. The San Juan River, which lies south of
Kirtland, is the only physical boundary separating Kirtland from the Navajo
Nation. Farmington is part of the Four Corners region, where the four states of
New Mexico, Arizona, Colorado, and Utah meet. The town lies within a valley,
and sharp jutting mesas and vast desert wilderness surround the town, where
three rivers meet. Navajo people, or Diné, call Farmington Totah, which translates as "three waters." Farmington is a blue-collar town, with a predominantly
white population among Native American and Hispanic peoples. Farmington,
nestled within the Republican stronghold of San Juan County, is a conserva-
tive hub in the otherwise Democratic state of New Mexico. The Navajo Nation
is close to Farmington: at the southern edge of the town, just across the San

Juan River, is the Navajo Nation's northern border. Farmington's place just eighteen miles west of the Navajo Nation's western border locates it nearly within the Navajo Nation and qualifies it as a reservation border town. When whites settled the area after 1866, the river became the boundary between traditional Navajo farms and new white settlement. But this area is traditional Diné territory regardless of settlements and boundaries. It is Diné Bikeyah, Navajo homeland since time immemorial.

The first time I remember experiencing racism was when I was four years old. In 1982 my mother, sister, and I were shopping at the brand-new Animas Valley Mall in Farmington. We wandered around the mall, feeling excited about the stores and junk food at the food court. I felt fearful as we approached a group of white teenage boys congregated in the walkway. One blond white teen stared at me menacingly, then suddenly screamed at me. The group of white teens laughed uproariously. He had tried and succeeded in frightening me, a small child, which was a typical "game" that white teens played to show dominance. My mother reported the incident to the white security guards, but they made excuses for the racist bully and said he was just playing a prank. I remember being confused about what had happened, but even at such a young age I knew this wasn't acceptable behavior. This was the first of many such incidents I experienced growing up in Farmington and the Four Corners.

Twenty-five years later, in October 2007, I walked around Dillard's department store in the same Animas Valley Mall. I was taking a break from the hospital after my father was rushed to San Juan Regional Medical Center in Farmington with a serious head injury. A white saleswoman trailed close behind me and periodically asked if I needed assistance. I was on my cell phone, updating my sister about my father's condition. I remarked to her, "Wow, customer service here is really great." As I said those words aloud, I realized why I was being followed: I was being racially profiled. The white, overattentive saleswoman was not there to offer me service. She was there to spy on me, to watch me, to let me know that I was unwelcome. Her behavior is another form of dominance and a continued a pattern of racism I have experienced since childhood.

In another incident, my sister and I were in the San Juan Regional emergency waiting room. A Navajo trans woman, "Jamie," had just been released from the emergency room. She came and sat down with us and without fear told us her story. She said she had tried harming herself and admitted that she was an alcoholic and in and out of jail and rehab. Though her story was sad, she had a wry sense of humor. She made us laugh despite all of our unhappy circumstances. We shared humor that Native people rely on in difficult times but that may seem self-deprecating to outsiders. "I hope your dad recovers," Jamie said, then she disappeared on foot onto the streets of Farmington at dawn. I was concerned for her after she left. She had just tried to harm herself. *Why was she released?* I thought. *If she were white would she be getting better health and psychological care?* I began to question the system that allowed Jamie to continue untreated, which is motivation for this study.

During my father's hospital stay, I began critically analyzing racism and racial violence in the Four Corners, specifically when my family interacted with the hospital staff, doctors, and nurses. The doctors and nurses spoke to us with scorn and were neither supportive nor caring, efforts on their part to show their racial superiority. At times my father's caretakers were irresponsible. One memorable moment of their negligence and maltreatment was when nurses and orderlies dropped him to the floor while moving him from his bed after his neurosurgery! If we had not assertively advocated for his care, he would have been treated much worse.

At this point in my life, I had been living away from the Four Corners for nearly ten years. As a student and young professional, I lived on both the East Coast and West Coast and attended school at UCLA. After such a long absence, the racism in Farmington felt magnified, unmistakable, when I returned.

I formed the foundations of the intellectual concepts I develop in this book during this time, as I reacquainted myself with my home as a professional and scholar. I have been developing the concepts in this book for more than twenty years, but the root problems have been around far longer. And although I spent more than thirteen years conducting my research and data collection and analyses, my work is not done. This book is an academic work as much as it is a personal endeavor for justice. In particular, my motivation to research hate crimes in Indian Country was spurred and shaped by one incident.

On the night of May 29, 1998, twenty-one-year-old Pernell Tewangoitewa (Navajo and Hopi) met with friends at a sports bar in Farmington. Gators Bar and Grill was popular with the younger crowd, and one of the few places in Farmington that occasionally played alternative and metal music. The bar was small and dark. The place reeked of vomit, cigarettes, and cheap whiskey. But a few times a week, it offered a haven for those who were considered outsiders in straitlaced, white-bread Farmington. Pernell and his friends were regulars at Gators.

Later that night, Pernell drove a station wagon that belonged to his sister, Brooke Milligan, out of the parking lot of Gators, following Milligan and her boyfriend. Milligan saw that Pernell was driving close behind her down the dark streets of Farmington, but after a few miles his car vanished. Pernell Tewangoitewa never made it home that night and was never seen or heard from again.

Three weeks later, an oil field worker found Milligan's station wagon in a wash five miles northwest of Farmington in a desolate area known as "the Glade," or Chokecherry Canyon. The Glade was a party spot for local white and Hispanic youth. The car had been deliberately burned, so severely that there was nothing left but the frame. San Juan County Sherriff's Office called Brooke Milligan and instructed her to tow her car. Milligan asked the police if they had been able to locate her brother, who was still missing. The family had tried to report him missing several times to the Farmington police, but police never filed a missing person report. The Farmington police assumed he was another "drunk Indian" and did not take his disappearance seriously. But his disappearance was unusual because Pernell had recently secured a new job as a hair stylist and was scheduled to start work shortly after his disappearance (New Mexico Advisory Committee to the U.S. Commission on Civil Rights 2005). The San Juan County sheriff did not immediately investigate. Milligan and family members were left to conduct their own search of the area on June 19, 1998, "and felt that police were overlooking a crime scene." In the weeks after his disappearance, I saw his elder sister Ramona Tewa at the local mall. She conducted her own search for Pernell. She frantically distributed missing-person flyers and desperately asked people if they had seen her brother or knew anything of his whereabouts.

As of 2021 Pernell is still missing, and his disappearance remains unsolved (J. Mills, "Botched New Mexico Murder Case Draws Eye of U.S. Civil Rights Commission," *Indian Country Today*, February 5, 2002). In an announcement, police stated that because he has been missing for such a long time and because his family has not heard from him in twenty-one years, they are treating his disappearance as a cold-case homicide. His case garnered some attention periodically through the years, but frustratingly no development has been made, and his family has been left with unanswered questions. This unsolved case has haunted me throughout the years and is my motivation to write this book.

I think of Pernell often when I return home to the Four Corners. Pernell was my classmate, a friend of my sister, and part of a group of high school friends who considered themselves "alternative." They organized Farmington's only raves and were part of the town's alternative music scene. Much later I would learn that many in this group were primarily LGBTQ and couldn't come out in oppressive Farmington. I remember Pernell as a fun-loving, kind person who was always laughing.

At Ramona Tewa's relentless urging, the botched investigation into Pernell's disappearance drew attention in 2002 from the New Mexico Advisory Committee to the U.S. Commission on Civil Rights, which held a series of hearings in Farmington. She traveled from Georgia to testify before the committee, stating emphatically: "My brother, Pernell Tewa, has been missing since May 1998. It took five attempts to file him missing. He was deemed a wandering drunk Indian. The officer told me to go out and look in the bars and the streets and, on the reservation, because that's where they usually end up. (My brother) was driving a car that was found burnt out in Chokecherry Canyon. The vehicle was later lost by the department. I later found it at a local salvage yard. The case is still unsolved" (New Mexico Commission on Civil Rights 2005, 17).

Her testimony was met with applause from the audience. Even though it was not determined whether Pernell's disappearance was the result of a hate crime, what is certain is that law enforcement's mishandling of the case was negligent, and to his family it was discriminatory. Pernell's case follows a trend. Overwhelmingly, police fail to take cases involving missing Native American persons seriously and instead blame the missing person, pointing to their "risky" lifestyle. Additionally, reservation border town police are viewed with skepticism by many Native people (Perry 2008, 94). In some cases, law enforcement are perpetrators of crimes against Native Americans, which may be a reason why they are reluctant to investigate crimes (Bennett 2018). There have been several police shootings of Navajos and Native Americans in Farmington (chapter 6). In one instance, a Farmington police officer was accused of raping a Navajo woman (Bennett 2018). Native Americans disproportionately experience violence from police, and in particular Navajos experience police brutality and killings in Farmington (Jerome 2007).

The stories I share within this book expose a pattern of racial violence in the Four Corners that has been ongoing since colonization. Pernell's story follows an infuriatingly common pattern of racism, discrimination, and marginalization that Native Americans face in the modern justice system, and it is time this pattern is exposed. Yes, this book is about hate crimes perpetrated against Native Americans in Farmington and the Four Corners, but it is also about lighting up the darkness and paving a way for hope and change.

Note on Terminology and Names

The terms *Native American*, *American Indian*, and *Indian* will be used interchangeably throughout this text. The terms *Native American* and *Native* are more inclusive and are considered more modern terminology. American Indian will primarily be used when discussing specific laws and legal status. The preference is to name a person's Native nation when possible. *Navajo* and *Diné* are also used interchangeably. *Navajo* is used specifically in reference to the Navajo Nation's government. The term *Native nation* is preferred over *tribe*.

I prefer the terms *unsheltered relative* and *unhoused relative* for Native people who may reside on the streets over the terms *inebriates* or *homeless*, which are used in some reports. The term *unsheltered relative* was developed by mutual aid organizations such as Indigenous Action. It is considered a more respectful phrase that honors the fact that Native peoples are not in fact homeless on their aboriginal lands, even though they may not have access to a traditional house or shelter.

I do not use the full names of survivors and victims of hate crimes, especially victims of murder. It is against Navajo tradition to speak of the deceased. I have also changed the names of interview participants to protect their identities and privacy. I do use the full names of perpetrators who were identified in local newspapers, as their names are a matter of public record.

Acknowledgments

I would like to express my gratitude to the survivors of hate crimes and racism who bravely and freely shared their stories with me. I hope I have honored your narratives. I also want to thank Tiis Tsoh Sikaad Chapter House officials and members, the Northern Agency Council, and the Navajo Nation Human Rights Commission and staff, who in 2011 supported the seed of this undertaking when it was a dissertation project. Their supporting resolutions allowed me to gain approval from the Navajo Nation Institutional Review Board. I am grateful to the Navajo Nation Institutional Review Board for its approval, support, and encouragement.

Thank you to the late Dr. Larry Emerson, who encouraged me to embark on this research and gave me sound advice. I also want to thank Duane "Chili" Yazzie for sharing his stories and perspective with me and demonstrating the true meaning of leadership. Thank you to my former professors and mentors for all their support: Dr. Mary Jo Tippeconnic Fox, Dr. Patrisia Gonzales, Dr. Raymond Austin, and Professor Eileen Luna Firebaugh.

Thank you to the collections of the Stanford Libraries and the Bob Fitch Photography Collection for use of photographs of the 1974 marches. Also, thank you to the Farmington Museum for use of archival *Daily Times* photographs. And a big thank you to everyone at the University of Arizona Press.

Finally, I want to thank my family: my mother, father, sister, and nephew, for their unwavering support and encouragement throughout this whole process. They always believed in this research. Also, a special thank you to my husband and children. They sacrificed the most while I was mired in rewrites and edits, during a pandemic no less. I could not ask for a more supportive team.

OUR FIGHT HAS JUST BEGUN

Introduction

This book comes at a time when hate crimes and racial violence have drastically increased in the United States, resulting from an intensification in racist rhetoric in politics. The current racial climate in the United States has been compared to that of the 1960s, during the height of civil unrest. In 2020 and 2021 we have seen ever-increasing racism, hate crimes, and police violence against people of color (Southern Poverty Law Center), and hate crimes against Asian Americans have increased during the COVID-19 pandemic (*Los Angeles Times*, March 17, 2021; *Los Angeles Times*, March 5, 2021). I believe the time has come to dismantle all racist systems in the United States.

Today we witness in near real time as white people brazenly attack people of color. In this age of video recording and social media, we can see the extent to which people of color in the United States face everyday racism, hate crime, and white terrorism. Video and social media are mechanisms that previous generations did not have to document hate crimes. We are also able to bear witness to the police killings of Black Americans and other people of color. The deaths of Black Americans have ignited a movement for racial justice and demands for change (Khan-Cullors and Bandele 2018). This movement needs to extend to Indian Country as well.

As I authored this introduction, the United States was on the eve of another election. Scholars in my circle who study race and hate crimes were not surprised by the rise in hate incidents during President Donald Trump's time in office. We were also not surprised by the violent response from white terrorists after Donald Trump was defeated in the 2020 election. We will never forget that on January 6, 2021, the United States Capitol was stormed by white supremacists emboldened and encouraged by President Trump. The insurrection at the Capitol hearkened back to the rhetoric displayed during a Unite the Right rally in Charlottesville, Virginia, in 2016, as well as other events that defined Trump's legacy of hate. Since 2016 reports of hate crimes have increased throughout the nation, and it appears that such incidents will continue to increase unless something is done to stop them (https://ucr.fbi.gov/hate-crime/2019). This Trump era has been an overwhelmingly challenging time to be a person of color and a hate crimes scholar, but we know that our work has only begun.

American Indian scholars are typically not rewarded for exposing America's mistreatment toward American Indians. We are often labeled as radical threats to America's system. But we are not going away, and neither is our work. My work also speaks against a system that has steadily marginalized American Indian scholars and their scholarship. The primary goal of this book is to expose, examine, and investigate bias-motivated hate crimes perpetrated against Native Americans.

Hate Crime and Hate Speech in America

Hate crime may include crimes against people or property, and the FBI classifies race-bias-motivated hate crimes against Native Americans as being "anti–American Indian/Alaska Native" (https://ucr.fbi.gov/hate-crime/2019). In the cases I examine in this book, the most common crimes against Native people are threats of violence, assault, and murder. I define and examine these common hate crimes against Native Americans in chapter 1.

News outlet ProPublica began recording hate crimes as part of its Documenting Hate Project after noticing an escalation in 2016 during the Trump administration. The Documenting Hate Project assessed that there was scant documentation of hate crimes against Native Americans, that the available data from the FBI and law enforcement is flawed and lacking, and that more data collection and investigation in this area is acutely needed.

In 2019 *Huffington Post* contacted me and inquired about hate crimes against American Indians (C. Mathias, *Huffington Post*, December 23, 2019). I was able to provide data that the Documenting Hate Project could not. For example, in my research I have documented hate speech in which Native Americans are told to "go back to the reservation." This type of hate speech against Native Americans has also been documented in hate crime scholar Barbara Perry's (2008) book *Silent Victims*, but it is a common tactic for intimidating all people of color.

For example, on July 14, 2019, President Trump tweeted a call for three women of color congresswomen to "go back" to their "crime-infested places." His words encouraged the same type of hate speech and hate rhetoric that racists use against Native Americans. Hate speech, racial slurs, and racist attacks have been reported and recorded more frequently during the Trump administration, and evidence shows that such actions will continue to plague America's culture unless confronted (Hswen et al. 2020; Bazian 2019; Gantt Shafer 2017).

Another example of hate speech against Native Americans occurred recently, when Karina Rodriguez, a young Indigenous woman in Phoenix, was told to "go back to Mexico" by an older white woman, Tamara Harrian (J. Bowling, *Arizona Republic*, June 9, 2020). The incident was filmed by a bystander, and footage shows Harrian appearing to grab and shove Rodriguez. Rodriguez slapped Harrian in self-defense in what was described online as "the slap heard around the world." Rodriguez received an outpouring of support and encouragement for her courageous resistance, yet these types of incidents became the norm in 2020. White supremacists and white terrorists were emboldened with the rhetoric coming from the White House, and now every community of color has witnessed their share of racists incidents displayed for the world to see (Matias and Newlove 2017; Silva 2019; Stein and Allcorn 2018).

It has become apparent to the world that hate crimes, racial violence, and racism are not relegated to America's past, and recent white supremacist demonstrations prove that hate in the United States is incessant (Blout and

Burkart 2021). On August 11, 2016, white supremacists brazenly marched with torches during the Unite the Right rally in Charlottesville, Virginia. They yelled hateful phrases like "The South will rise again!," "You will not replace us!," and "Hail Trump!" (Feola 2021). Shortly thereafter, in Sturgis, South Dakota, teenagers spray-painted a swastika and the words "Go Back to the Reservation!" on a car that represented an opposing football team from the Pine Ridge Reservation. In June 2019 a Native American man's rental home in Butte, Montana, was vandalized with hate speech that read, "go home, prairie n——r." The incident was investigated as a hate crime (M. Vincent, *TCA Regional News*, June 16, 2019). In an incident in Rapid City, South Dakota, white spectators poured beer on Native American children at a sporting event ("Police ID Suspect" 2015). These are not isolated incidents but just a sample of the types of hate crimes perpetrated against Native Americans in recent years. But even amid its rise, racial violence has largely been hidden or forgotten, particularly regarding Native Americans.

Our Fight Has Just Begun

Our Fight Has Just Begun is an attempt to shine a spotlight on racial violence and uplift the stories of Native American survivors and victims, specifically in the Four Corners. Racial violence in the Four Corners began, as it did almost everywhere in the United States, with the arrival of Euro-American settler colonists. Colonization was spurred on by Indian-hating ideology and subsequent massacres and racial violence (Cook-Lynn 2001). The historical forms of racism and racial violence continue.

Racism is so entrenched in this region that Farmington has been dubbed the "Selma, Alabama, of the Southwest" (Barker 1992). In 1974 Navajo activists marched in the streets of Farmington to protest the murders of three Navajo men by white teens. One protester, a Navajo woman with her child, held a sign that read "Our Fight Has Just Begun." Most of these stories of racial violence and hate crime perpetuated by whites in the Four Corners have not been told, which is why the message of that protest sign remains relevant today.

Our Fight Has Just Begun documents these incidents and untold stories to expose the hate crimes that have been committed against Navajo (Diné) people and Native Americans by whites in Farmington and the greater Four Corners region. My hope for this research and book is to bring about awareness and change, to call for action and justice. The history of the Farmington area is violent, and racial tension has been prevalent for hundreds of years, but whites continue to perpetuate violence against Navajos. These hate crimes stem from a long-held culture of hate between Native Americans and whites (Cook-Lynn 2001; Perry 2008). This book seeks to explore the extent of the region's history of hate by answering a few fundamental questions: What types of hate crimes have been perpetrated against Native people in Farmington and the Four Corners? How have hate crimes in Farmington impacted the lives of Native Americans? How have survivors responded to hate crimes? For far too long, this topic has been whispered about and hidden. It is an urgent, important topic that deserves and demands attention after being ignored for so long.

The available data regarding hate crimes committed against Native American peoples is very sparse. Only one academic book, *Silent Victims* (2008), has been published on this topic, and its data was derived from a 1999 study. Until my study, which was in part completed in 2013, no academic research had been produced by a Native person to provide an insider's perspective on the violence. I provide a Native perspective that has also been marginalized, ignored, or deliberately hidden. As a Navajo researcher, I follow a decolonized paradigm, making my perspective especially unique and valuable to this topic, which seeks to "rewrite" and "reright" our stories and histories (L. T. Smith 1999). "Indigenous peoples want to tell our own stories, write our own versions, in our own ways, for our own purposes. It is not simply about giving an oral account or a genealogical naming of the land and the events which raged over it but a very powerful need to give testimony to and restore a spirit, to bring back into existence a world fragmented and dying" (L. T. Smith 1999, 28). This book uses a mixed-method approach, but it also employs some Western methods. Decolonized research does not have to be a "total rejection of all theory or research or Western knowledge." Instead, it is about "centering our concerns and world views and then coming to know and understand theory and research from our own perspectives and for our own purposes" (39). Using these approaches, I explore and interrogate racism against Native Americans, hate crime, and race relations in border towns.

Hate crime research is significant to Native communities but is reflective of larger problems regarding race relations in the United States. The stories in this book divulge how the justice system has largely failed Native American victims of hate crime and racial violence and how little improvement in race relations has been made throughout the years. This book is about survivors and victims whose stories are at times horrific and gruesome, but above all this book is about hope. In the face of racism and violence, the survivors are still hopeful that with the sharing of their stories, race relations can improve.

Native American Hate Crime Research

Barbara Perry's (2002, 2005, 2008, 2009b) groundbreaking longitudinal research focused on three parts of the United States: Montana, the Southwest, and the Great Lakes. Though her work was seminal, Perry does not provide the Native perspective on these crimes, which views racial violence as a mechanism of power embedded within systemic racism. Furthermore, she does not address Native nations' response to racial violence in reservation border towns, and she focused the majority of her book *Silent Victims* on the hate crimes against Native Americans that have taken the form of microaggressions and "bias incidents," rather than "bias crimes" (Perry 2008, 77). While bias incidents and microaggressions are notable, I base my analysis in a non-privileged position, focusing on a wider range of hate crimes, including the most violent types. Perry's data was gathered in 1999 and is now dated, even though the topic remains relevant. And while her analysis is important, it lacks a Native perspective, which I believe is imperative to racial justice research. Additionally, I have chosen to take the approach of a regional study, focused only on the Southwest and Farmington. Hate crimes perpetuated against Native Americans across the country have many similarities, but stories from the Four Corners and Farmington provide an excess of information that warrants a focused investigation.

Hate crime literature in general is extensive, but most studies do not address the unique position of Native American victims, jurisdictional issues in prosecuting crimes, and the lack of reporting by victims (Kelly and Maghan 1998; Perry 2001). Also extensive are historical accounts of the genocide perpetrated against Native Americans during the colonial era and into the early twentieth century. These studies, however, do not address racial violence committed in the twentieth century and the present (Stannard 1992; Pearce 1988; Slotkin 1973; Drinnon 1980; Berkhoffer 1978). The body of historical research that focuses on violence against American Indians provides valuable insight but does not address the current hate crimes and racial violence perpetuated regularly against Native American populations. I believe there is a strong connection with the history of violence against Native Americans and the current high rates of hate crimes, and other scholars agree. Petrosino (1999) contends that hate crimes in fact began with the genocide and assimilation of Native Americans; Perry (2008) argues similarly.

Journalist Rodney Barker's (1992) *The Broken Circle* chronicles the 1974 murders of three Navajo men by three white teenagers in Farmington. *The Broken Circle* is a work of creative nonfiction, with no academic analysis. The book is flawed by a salacious depiction of Navajo religion but provides valuable interviews and documentation of the murders and the events leading up to them. Native Americans and whites in Farmington accused Barker of exploiting painful and embarrassing past events for his own personal gain. His book, which I discuss further in chapter 4, provides a useful source of information on the history of racial violence in Farmington considering continued racial violence. Lisa Weber Donaldson's (2006) dissertation offers compelling investigation and analysis of white violence in Farmington. However, her research draws heavily on Barker's work and sociological frameworks to explain white violence, without a Native perspective.

Two Native American scholars tackled the difficult task of writing about racism against Native Americans. Elizabeth Cook-Lynn is an American Indian studies scholar and novelist who, with her book *Anti-Indianism in Modern America* (2001), trailblazed a body of literature dedicated to exploring anti-Indianism and advocating for sovereignty of Native nations (discussed further later in this chapter). Dean Chavers's *Racism in Indian Country* (2009) offers a general discussion of racism as it relates to Native

Americans. Chavers discusses the incidents in Farmington and provides an overview of the socioeconomic exploitation of Native Americans in reservation border towns. However, he offers little analysis beyond documentation of different incidents of racism and racial violence. His text is valuable in that it starts a conversation and about racism against Native Americans and provides a Native perspective.

Though the literature about racism against Native Americans in general is sparse, a growing body of research in public health focuses on racism as it relates to health disparities. Particularly, Gonzales and colleagues (2021) examined discrimination among American Indians and Alaska Natives as part of a diabetes research project. Though these are important contributions, research about everyday discrimination, racism, and hate crimes against Native Americans remains scarce.

Anti-Indianism and Historical Studies

Elizabeth Cook-Lynn's collection of essays *Anti-Indianism in Modern America* (2001) argues that the formation of the United States was established on racist ideology and hatred for Native Americans. In this critical examination of race and "anti-Indianism," she examines hate crime in South Dakota in a thought-provoking essay and calls for Native American scholars to research and write about hate crimes. Cook-Lynn's analysis of anti-Indianism is especially important as she is among the few Native American scholars who have interrogated the concept. This book draws from and builds upon Cook-Lynn's definitions of anti-Indianism.

In order to understand twentieth- and twenty-first-century hate crimes against Navajos perpetrated by whites in Farmington, it is essential to consider and analyze the historical conflict between Navajos and white settlers who colonized Farmington and surrounding areas. The Navajo people are among the most studied and written-about groups of Native Americans; numerous texts have been written about Navajo religion, society, and history, though only a handful were written from the Navajo perspective. Furthermore, few studies and published histories have focused on the Four Corners region and the Farmington area. Previously, academics and those interested in Navajos focused their attention on the western and central regions of the Navajo reservation.

Garrick Bailey and Roberta Glenn Bailey (1982), historians who studied the eastern regions of Navajo land, offer a rare history and describe the occupations of Navajos in and around the Farmington area. Other scholars have studied the relationships between the settlers and the Navajos in the Farmington area and larger San Juan County region, but from a white perspective (Bailey and Bailey 1982, 1986; McNitt 1990; McPherson 1988; Furman 1977; Spicer 1962). The texts are still important in that they provide a historical reference for the violent atmosphere created by the settlers in Farmington and in the larger San Juan County region. The texts by Bailey and Bailey in particular discuss the violent confrontations and battles for land and resources between the Navajo and the settlers. These texts often characterize Navajos as the instigators of conflict, but this perspective is obviously biased and contradicts Navajo oral history narrative and facts. Whites were the foreign invaders to Navajo land and the root cause of conflicts over the land.

Navajo perspectives on Navajo history are rare, which is why it is important for scholars of Navajo history to privilege them. They build a solid Indigenous foundation that other histories and historians rarely duplicate. As a Navajo scholar, I recognize that Gus Bighorse's history of the Farmington area and San Juan Valley is crucial to the studies in *Our Fight Has Just Begun.* In *Bighorse the Warrior* (1990), Bighorse's granddaughter narrates his memories of the historical Navajo homeland in Farmington and the encounters with whites. His narrative is essential to understanding the history of race relations and hate crimes perpetrated against Navajos. I chronicle these events in chapter 3, which connects this history with the twentieth- and twenty-first-century hate crimes perpetrated against Native peoples.

Data Collection

For this study I collected and analyzed five types of data: historical documents and records, government reports, newspapers, Internet forum posts, and qualitative interviews that I conducted. A portion of this book is dedicated to documenting the history of settler occupation and the detailing the history of hate crime in the Four Corners. Another significant portion analyzes the unique type of racism directed toward American Indians. This racism is based on experiences that no other people of color or ethnic group endured, such as the loss of aboriginal land.

As a multidisciplinary American Indian scholar, I utilize multiple sets of content analysis through detailed evaluations of newspapers, Internet forums, and interviews. The body of published research and the current literature regarding hate crimes and racism in mainstream media is sparse, so I expanded my scope to explore other resources. I was able to create and re-create lesser-known methods by examining studies that evaluated hate speech online (Gerstenfeld et al. 2003; Glaser et al. 2002) as well as other studies that examined racism pertaining to media representations of Native Americans (Hill 2008; Flaherty 2013; Steinfeldt et al. 2010).

My background as an American Indian studies scholar enabled me to explore more deeply and find valuable resources essential to this book. For example, my expertise and training as a scholar of federal Indian law and policy, tribal sovereignty, and jurisdiction allows me to evaluate documents such as the U.S. Commission on Civil Rights reports from 1974 and 2005 from a unique perspective. These reports were compiled from testimony gathered in two hearings thirty years apart. The 1974 report was created in direct response to the murders of three Navajo men, and subsequent marches that were coordinated by the Navajo community. The reports include testimony from community members, Navajo and non-Navajo, about racial incidents, discrimination, and Farmington's problems with racism. This testimony is most useful to my research. The *Farmington Report* (2005) provided full transcripts from the hearing, but full transcripts were not available for the 1974 report. However, the reports are not comprehensive and provide no analysis on their own. Through my analyses, I fill this gap.

In 2005 the U.S. Commission on Civil Rights revisited Farmington and conducted new hearings. This newer report discusses the "improvements" that have been made within the community of Farmington during the thirty years since the 1974 report. The 2005 report discusses racism as now being "covert" instead of openly obvious, or "overt," as it had been in 1974. The commission claimed to be following up on the incidents of 1974. However, the commission itself did not mention the ongoing racial incidents throughout the ensuing thirty years; rather, the victims' families disclosed the ongoing racial violence within their own testimony. The commission's inaction is crucial to the current situation in the area. I reexamine important testimony from both reports in chapters 4 and 5. Both reports provide a historical reference point for the current issues of racial violence, while my analysis interrogates the culture of racism.

Newspaper articles provide an untapped resource for documenting racial attitudes. I analyzed Farmington *Daily Times* news stories and editorials from 1974, during the Chokecherry Massacre and ensuing trial, and used a content analysis model to track and identify racial attitudes in these pieces to illustrate the racial climate at the time. In 2011 I was fortunate to gather more than 2,800 Internet posts from the now-defunct website Topix.com, which I analyzed employing the same content analysis model. Themes emerged from my intense and extensive analysis from the content of these varying sets. These included racist stereotypes that characterized Navajos as dirty, stupid, drunks, living off government handouts, or having special privileges such as receiving money from the federal or tribal government; racism referencing historical events; and adamant denials of racism by whites. Upon data review, I found that these themes directly correlated with the qualitative interviews I discuss in detail in chapter 8.

The Stories of Survivors

As an advocate of human rights, I believe it is crucial to amplify the voices of those who have been ignored, marginalized, and made victims of injustice. Therefore, I dedicated a significant amount of time and energy to collecting qualitative data through in-person interviews with survivors. The process of collecting the qualitative data from this research project is a story of accomplishment in itself. The results proved to be extraordinarily valuable to my research and the goals of *Our Fight Has Just Begun*.

Growing up in the Four Corners, I often heard stories about acts of everyday discrimination and racial violence. As a Navajo and member of the Four Corner community, I knew these stories existed, but it proved difficult for me, even as an insider, to get people to talk about racial violence and hate crimes. Nonetheless, it was important to include qualitative data through interviews in this book because the voices of victims and survivors are of the utmost importance in achieving justice and change. The recruitment process was very slow and difficult at times. Even though the project garnered immediate interest and support on social media, many initially interested parties did not follow through with the interview process. The most successful recruitment approach proved to be advertisement flyers posted at chapter houses, convenience stores, and grocery stores around the northern region of the Navajo Nation and in Farmington. Some participants were identified and recruited through referral and word of mouth. I received no direct criticism toward this project. If people were not interested in participating, they simply did not respond to the advertisement or requests.

As a Native scholar in American Indian studies, I designed a qualitative research agenda that best fit the goals of *Our Fight Has Just Begun* while meeting the standards set by mainstream disciplines in the academy. One of the most significant accomplishments in my qualitative research agenda was obtaining approval to conduct interviews through the Navajo Nation Institutional Review Board (IRB), which was a long and arduous process, but I am sincerely grateful for the board's guidance and support of my research. Part of the IRB procedure included approval from the Tiis Tsoh Sikaad Chapter House, the chapter in which I am a registered member. Navajo Nation chapters are the local form of governance for communities, and I am thankful for the support of my chapter house. The IRB procedure also required me to gain approval from the Northern Agency Council, which is composed of twenty chapter houses in the northern region of the Navajo Nation. I am humbled that the Northern Agency Council approved my research proposal and thankful that the council agreed that my research is important to the health and well-being of the Navajo people of the northern agencies. In 2011 I was fortunate to gain support for my research from the Navajo Nation Human Rights Commission (NNHRC) through a supporting resolution. I am thankful that the NNHRC approved my research. As required by the IRB process, I formally presented this project to each entity, and I was proud to gain unanimous support from each one to move forward. Without their support, I could not have acquired the testimony of survivors.

Six survivors of hate crimes participated in this study. All are adult Navajos who experienced hate crimes in Farmington, New Mexico, or are adult family or friends of victims. Participants were from a variety of backgrounds, including college students, professionals, and members of the communities surrounding Farmington in the Four Corners. The interviews enabled me to create a complete narrative about hate crimes through the Navajo experience and through Navajo perspectives (chapter 8). As a Native scholar, I found that approaching this research via a multidisciplinary and mixed-method approach yielded the best results. I could not have accomplished the goal of the book had I limited my research methodologies.

The Chapters

Each chapter title is borrowed from protest signs from the Bob Fitch Photography Collection or quotes from community members. Chapter 1 explores the definition of hate crime and the definitions I utilize that are specific to Native Americans. *Hate crime* is a legal term, but I seek to demonstrate that hate crime is different when perpetrated against Native Americans and so must be defined distinctly. I expand the limited legal definition to fit Native American survivors and victims. Chapter 2 explains theories of race and racism to explain the root causes of hate crimes and to explain how hate crimes can thrive and even be encouraged in certain climates.

Chapter 3 analyzes the historical conflicts between Navajos and whites, beginning with the Spanish, then examines Navajos' relationship with Americans. This chapter focuses on Navajo-white relations, primarily the conflict in the Four Corners region. The history in this region is one of boundaries. The chapter explores the history of the region as a Navajo homeland first, then of the fight for and dispossession of the land that is now occupied Farmington. In chapter 4 I provide a history of the 1974 Chokecherry Massacre, when three Navajo men were brutally tortured and murdered by white teenagers. This era is often referred to as a volatile period in Farmington that ignited Navajo activism. The focus of this chapter, however, is not to rehash the murders but to focus on the responses of both the Navajo and white communities of Farmington.

In chapter 5 I document and analyze the hate crimes committed since 1974 in Farmington. Despite the city's denial and downplaying of racial violence, hate crime in Farmington continued long after the notorious Chokecherry Massacre. In fact, the most extreme hate crimes continued in the form of murder and torture. The mainstream local media did not bring attention to the crimes, but the Navajo community developed a response as a result of hate crimes that occurred in 2000. Chapter 6 focuses on the return of the Civil Rights Commission to Farmington in 2005 and the state of race relations in Farmington and the Four Corners at that time. Chapter 7 continues to document the hate crimes that occurred after the *Farmington Report* (2005) and the steps the Navajo Nation took to combat hate crimes. I also document and analyze hate speech in Farmington's online Topix forum. Chapter 8 centers the interviews with individuals who experienced hate crime. This chapter focuses on the themes and impacts of hate crimes, racism, and discrimination in Farmington. The dominant narrative in Farmington and the Four Corners is that hate crime and discrimination have "improved." However, my interviews with survivors demonstrate that though on the surface race relations may have improved, white supremacy and systemic racism in Farmington is entrenched. In chapter 9, I provide concluding discussion, including of remedies and interventions that can be implemented by Native nations, Native people, and communities.

The ideas in this book have been developed over thirteen years of research and data collection, which initially began as dissertation research, then expanded to include violence against Native women (Bennett 2013, 2018). From 2010 to 2013, I presented preliminary findings of this research at national American Indian studies conferences and at universities. I have presented my findings since then across the country. When I first planned to research hate crimes, I wanted to study hate crimes perpetrated against Native Americans throughout the entire United States. Due to time limits and overwhelming data collection in the Four Corners, I narrowed the scope; data from the Four Corners alone would be enough for more than one book. I am now working on a national data collection project that will include hate crime statistics and narratives, as there is still a critical need for research about hate crimes perpetrated against Native Americans. With some hate crime cases, I relied on news stories but was diligent in verifying events and case outcomes. Any mistakes in the accuracy of dates and events are my own.

This book seeks to fill a void in the literature and research about hate crimes perpetrated against Navajos and Native peoples, not only to explore the effects of these crimes on their Native victims, but to propose ways of ameliorating the racial conflict between the Native people and their non-Navajo neighbors. I analyze how groups promoting racial justice, such as the Southern Poverty Law Center and the Anti-Defamation League, have dealt with hate crimes. Other Native nations can also look to this study for their own hate crime issues, as this problem affects not only the Navajo Nation but many other tribes in the United States and Indigenous and marginalized groups around the world.

This book was difficult to write at times. Within are stories that weigh heavy, of victims of atrocious hate crimes and hate speech. Most surprising, however, was that these hate crimes remain largely unknown. The cycle of racial violence keeps repeating itself, not only in the Four Corners but in the United States. This book documents hate crimes against Native Americans and analyzes them in the hopes of raising awareness, not to stir up controversy or reawaken resentment and animus toward whites, but to honor the victims and survivors. Only when we fully comprehend hate crime in the United States and reconcile with the racial intolerance can we begin to move forward toward justice.

one

"Fight for Justice"

Defining Hate Crime against Native Americans

The phrase *hate crime* is formidable. It demands attention, evoking images of Emmett Till, Matthew Shepard, James Byrd Jr., and civil rights martyrs. Though the term and subsequent laws are relatively new, hate crime and racial violence have been a part of United States history since colonization. Hate crime itself has become a controversial topic, though strides have been made by lawmakers and advocates to improve hate crime laws in combating racial violence. In the current culture of the United States, there are elements and players who have power to marginalize and erase the existence of current hate crimes, similar to how America's history of hate crimes has been marginalized and erased. Time is overdue for hate crimes in America to be exposed for what they are and how destructive they have been to people of color.

In 2019 Nick Sandmann, a white male teen, was filmed by onlookers wearing a red "Make America Great Again" baseball cap as he stared down Omaha elder Nathan Phillips. This now-infamous confrontation after a protest at the nation's capital quickly went viral. The world saw firsthand how a lone American Indian veteran stood and sang amid a crowd of young white students who mocked and jeered him. At first, this incident was viewed as a clear case of blatant racism and harassment and possibly hate crime, but as the world watched, more videos surfaced that depicted Nick Sandmann and his fellow classmates as the victims. In a dramatic turn of events, Nathan Phillips was vilified because of the racist stereotype of Native American male aggression.

On January 7, 2020, Sandmann was vindicated when CNN reached a settlement with him in a defamation lawsuit he had filed against the network. Sandmann also filed lawsuits against the *Washington Post* and NBC Universal, claiming that he was defamed and bullied as a minor by the news outlets. In January 2019, within the same period as the Sandmann incident, Jussie Smollett, a Black and openly gay actor, was accused of fabricating a hate crime. The Sandmann incident combined with Smollett's fabricated hate crime inflamed right-wing skeptics, who already claim that most hate crimes are faked (Gomez 2019). Both widely publicized incidents make it even more difficult for victims of hate crime to report incidents to police and potentially achieve justice (Pezzella et al. 2019).

Discussion of hate crimes, race, and racism increased in 2016, during Donald Trump's presidential campaign and eventual election. Trump spewed derogatory rhetoric about Muslims and Mexicans, Blacks, and other people of color, in turn condoning hate speech. I recall that shortly after the Nick Sandmann incident, the Tempe campus of Arizona State University was littered with flyers with Sandmann's image and the phrase "Make American Great Again." Whoever placed the posters on the university's campus sought to send a message of hate to minority students and faculty. The poster incident linked the Sandmann confrontation to a wave of hate speech and right-wing propaganda appearing on university and college campuses throughout the country. Such vicious but seemingly harmless acts are the roots of hate crimes. Since then, we have entered an era in U.S. history in which hate crimes have become further politicized and out of control. Correspondingly, this wave has been met with fierce resistance led by people of color, and this time they will not stop until racism is defeated.

Native Americans are equally part of the movement to end racism, seek justice, and bring forth practical solutions to the disease of racism. This movement, like the movements led by other peoples of color, demands that Native scholars provide an intellectual foundation and advocate for change. While researching and writing about violence against Native women

(Bennett 2018), I recognized that using the phrase *hate crime* in certain cases of violence against Native women could more effectively demand attention to the problem and possibly pursue a path to seek justice. It was a natural progression for me as a Native woman scholar of hate crimes, violence, and crime in Native communities to make this connection. Thus, by the definition of *hate crime*, crimes against Native women meet two legal criteria, which I explored elsewhere (Bennett 2018) but must highlight again, as it is crucial that scholars and advocates understand and use appropriate terms. Using the term *hate crime* contextualizes the way we as Natives see violence committed by racists and bigots.

Hate Crime Laws

The discipline of American Indian studies extends to legal studies, including concepts such as tribal sovereignty, jurisdiction, and tribal law. However, American Indian studies seeks to analyze legal studies from American Indian perspectives, primarily by evaluating the impacts of law and policy on tribal nations and individual Indian persons. Most studies involving Native Americans and race center on the historical development of federal Indian law (Getches et al. 2017; Williams 2005). Hate crime laws have rarely been evaluated through a Native American perspective, but such an evaluation is critical.

The first federal statute created to protect the rights of individuals was the Civil Rights Act of 1968, which sought to protect individuals' participation in federally protected activities such as voting and attending public school. This law was an important culmination of civil rights activism, but it did nothing to address race-bias-motivated crimes. In order to track hate crimes, the Hate Crime Statistics Act was passed in 1990, which required the attorney general to collect data "about crimes that manifest evidence of prejudice based on race, religion, sexual orientation, or ethnicity" (Uniform Crime Reporting). This was then tasked to the FBI and its Uniform Crime Reporting (UCR) program, which compiles national hate crime data annually. All law enforcement organizations in the United States are required to submit their data to UCR each year that they have reported hate crime.

President Barack Obama signed into law the most significant piece of hate crime legislation, the Local Law Enforcement Hate Crimes Prevention Act of 2009, also known as the Matthew Shepard and James Byrd Jr. Act. It had previously been introduced in Congress in 2007 and was the first federal hate crimes law. Matthew Shepard's family spent years advocating for federal legislation that included provisions for hate crimes based on sexual orientation and gender. Most states have their own hate crime law, but Wyoming did not when Matthew Shepard was murdered there in 1998. Nonetheless, in some limited cases, federal hate crime laws can be used when states do not have their own.

When passed in 2009, the Matthew Shepard and James Byrd Jr. Act expanded the funding and investigative capabilities of federal officials for aiding their local counterparts. The law defines hate crime as "a traditional offense like murder, arson, or vandalism with an added element of bias. For the purposes of collecting statistics, the FBI has defined a hate crime as a 'criminal offense against a person or property motivated in whole or in part by an offender's bias against a race, religion, disability, sexual orientation, ethnicity, gender, or gender identity.'"

Despite the improvements in defining, codifying, and expanding the definition of hate crime in federal statutory law, American Indians have faced different challenges when confronted with hate crimes. One of the major concerns for crime in Indian Country has been jurisdiction. Jurisdiction over crimes committed on American Indian reservations is very complicated. Additionally, I found that most hate crimes against American Indians are committed on non-Indian land. For those reasons it remains to be determined what effect this law will have on Native nations and communities (chapter 9).

Currently, forty-seven states and the District of Columbia have hate crime laws, but legislation varies from state to state. The state laws mostly offer penalty enhancement, meaning that there is an additional penalty for targeting someone because of race, gender, disability, and other protected classes. New Mexico finally adopted hate crime laws in 2003. Before 1999, New Mexico governor Gary Johnson vetoed hate crime bills twice. Democratic state representative and Navajo Nation member Ray Begay supported the legislation, especially after a former skinhead was convicted in the assault of a Navajo man (chapter 5). New Mexico law defines hate crime as "noncapital felonies, misdemeanors or petty misdemeanors committed because of the victim's actual or perceived race, religion, color, national origin, ancestry, age, disability, gender, sexual orientation or gender identity."

Three states do not have hate crime laws: Arkansas, South Carolina, and Wyoming. Wyoming has a large population of Native people, in particular Arapaho and Shoshoni tribal members of the Wind River Reservation. On July 18, 2015, two hate crimes were perpetrated against members of the Arapaho tribe. After a white man opened fire on two Arapaho men in a treatment center (S. Tory, *High Country News*, August 11, 2015), tribal leaders noted the need for hate crime laws in Wyoming.

At least thirty-one states do not have comprehensive hate crime laws that address crimes related to gender. In 2002 F.C. Martinez was the victim of a hate crime in Colorado, which did not have hate crime laws that included gender-bias-motivated hate crime. Hate crimes mostly are under the jurisdiction of the state, and that is why it is important to have sufficient legislation at the state level (Anti-Defamation League).

Defining and Redefining Hate Crime

American Indian studies also relies on other disciplines to define and redefine concepts that apply to Native Americans, even though these concepts have not been directly connected to those disciplines. Rarely do American Indian studies scholars study hate crimes, but if they do, they must build theoretical foundations based on concepts and definitions from across disciplines. This process is challenging but yields the best results when bringing Native Americans to the forefront of ongoing discussions of race and hate crimes.

In addition to the legal definitions of hate crime, sociologists and criminologists have developed definitions over the years. Perry (2008, 2001) has defined hate crime as a "mechanism" to keep the colonized under control. She explicates further that hate crime "does not occur in a social or cultural vacuum, nor is it over when the perpetrator moves on. Hate crimes must be conceived of as socially situated, dynamic processes involving context and actors, structure and agency" (Perry 2008, 11). Perry (2008) also included "hate incidents" within her analysis and definition.

Hate crime reaffirms boundaries; for American Indians, it affirms that Native peoples are not welcome off-reservation and in white spaces. Thus the anthem of border town racists, "go back to the reservation!" becomes a mechanism to maintain the settler-colonial hierarchy.

I expand on Perry's definition to account for more components related specifically to Native Americans. The way hate crime impacts Native people is unique, and it is important to reinforce the fact that hate crime sends a violent message of unwelcome to the victim and the victim's social group when they go outside a perceived boundary. Hate crime is an offense not only against an individual but against the entire victim's group (Anti-Defamation League 2018; Perry 2008).

Additionally, in analyzing hate crimes I employ the Anti-Defamation League's Pyramid of Hate (fig. 1; 2018), which shows how discrimination and bias can lead to violence and in some case, genocide. In the case of Native American hate crimes, my research shows a pattern of hate speech and racist stereotypes directed toward Navajos. Unchecked racist stereotypes and hate speech can and do lead to violence. In the next sections I also categorize hate crimes further to include different types of hate offenses.

Reporting Law Enforcement Statistics of Hate Crimes against Native Americans

In 2018 there were 194 documented incidents (single incidents may involve multiple victims) against American Indians and Alaska Natives in the United States, with a total of 209 victims of hate crimes reported to law enforcement agencies (https://ucr.fbi.gov/hate-crime/2018). Most of the hate crimes reported in the UCR data were cases of simple assault and larceny or theft. The fifth-highest motivator of nine categories was anti–American Indian bias. In all categories of bias motivation by race and ethnicity, most offenders were white.

Also in 2018, in the Four Corners, New Mexico reported 34 total hate crime offenses, Arizona 211 offenses, Colorado 176, and Utah 36. In New

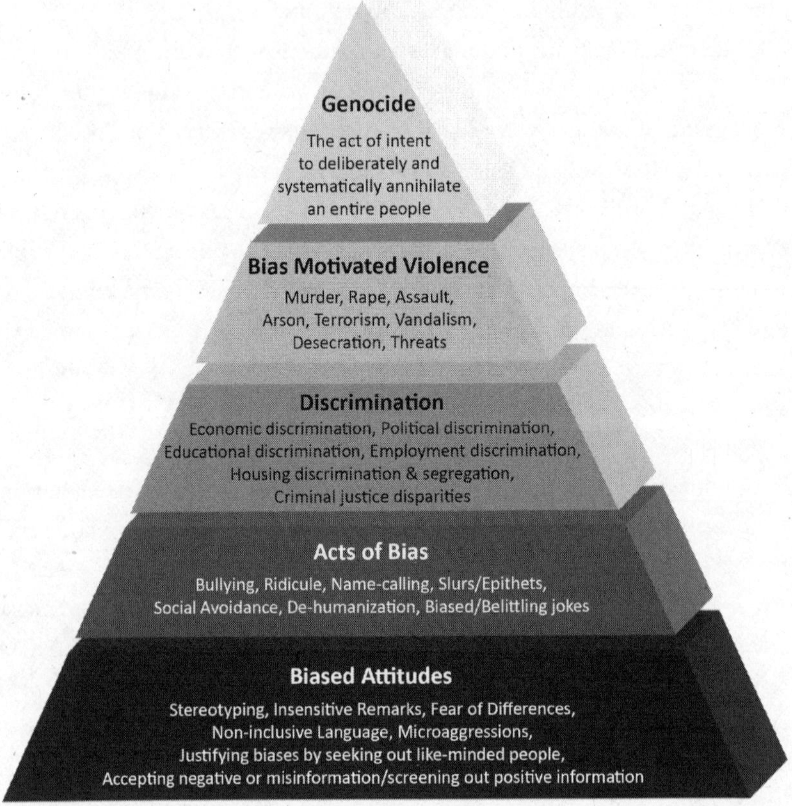

Chapter One

Genocide
The act of intent
to deliberately and
systematically annihilate
an entire people

Bias Motivated Violence
Murder, Rape, Assault,
Arson, Terrorism, Vandalism,
Desecration, Threats

Discrimination
Economic discrimination, Political discrimination,
Educational discrimination, Employment discrimination,
Housing discrimination & segregation,
Criminal justice disparities

Acts of Bias
Bullying, Ridicule, Name-calling, Slurs/Epithets,
Social Avoidance, De-humanization, Biased/Belittling jokes

Biased Attitudes
Stereotyping, Insensitive Remarks, Fear of Differences,
Non-inclusive Language, Microaggressions,
Justifying biases by seeking out like-minded people,
Accepting negative or misinformation/screening out positive information

FIGURE 1 Anti-Defamation League's Pyramid of Hate

Mexico, out of 110 reporting law enforcement agencies, only 3 submitted their data. Those agencies were in Albuquerque, Belen, and Bernalillo. There are three main problems with this data. First, the data regarding American Indian victims of hate crime is rather unclear in that the UCR does not list hate crimes against American Indians by state, making it difficult to determine hate crimes in reservation border towns. Second, these incidents only reflect the hate crimes from participating agencies that report to the FBI. Participating agencies vary from year to year and may not include tribal agencies. Such unreliable data makes it more difficult to discern hate crime locations. Third, I uncovered a gross discrepancy within Farmington's hate crime data: in 2018 the Farmington police had not submitted any data to the

UCR since 2010. Others have noted extensive problems with the UCR data as well (Silverman 2009). This third discrepancy required a much closer evaluation than the others.

Hate crime statistics are unreliable and difficult to determine (Silverman 2009). Because some agencies do not submit their data to the UCR, in 2017 the Documenting Hate Project began collecting its own data from police departments. The Farmington Police Department did submit data to the Documenting Hate Project from 2010 to July 2017. The Documenting Hate Project requested the following information:

> Any database or other records of hate crimes or crimes evidencing bias of race, color, ancestry, ethnicity, religion, gender, gender identity, sexual orientation, national origin or disability reported to or investigated by your agency since Jan. 1, 2010, including where available, but not limited to: the incident number, date of the incident, whether the crime was against individuals or a business / property, number of victims, race or ethnicity of the victims, gender of the victims, the offense classification, the location of the incident, the bias motivation (anti-black, anti-Muslimism, etc.). (Documenting Hate Project)

The data was made accessible to the public, and I was able to acquire and review it. Neither the Farmington police nor Documenting Hate Project provided any definitions for bias motivation, making it near impossible to discern what they consider "anti–American Indian."

The incidents that the Farmington police shared with the Documenting Hate Project are staggering (table 1). The Farmington police reported thirteen hate crimes involving an American Indian either as victim or offender. Of the total forty-four incidents of hate crime reported to Documenting Hate, seven are reported as anti–American Indian.

Abnormal is that four hate crimes are listed as an anti–American Indian hate crimes perpetrated by an American Indian. It is unclear how the Farmington police made this determination. This is the first time I have seen bias-motivated by race hate crime reported with both the victim and offender being of the same race. I would not classify such incidents as hate crime without there being an additional bias present, such as anti-gay. American-Indian-on-American-Indian, anti-Indian hate crime does not fit within any legal

TABLE 1 Hate Crimes Involving Native Americans in Farmington

Year	Type of Bias	Victim Race	Offender Race	Offense Type
2010	Anti–American Indian Anti-lesbian	American Indian American Indian	American Indian American Indian	Assault Assault
2011	Anti–American Indian Anti-homosexual	American Indian American Indian	American Indian American Indian	Assault/Battery Sexual Offense
2012	Anti-homosexual	American Indian	American Indian	N/A
2013	Anti–American Indian Anti–American Indian	American Indian American Indian	White American Indian	Shoplifting Child Abuse
2014	Anti-religious	American Indian	American Indian	Breaking and Entering
2015	Anti–American Indian Anti–American Indian Anti–American Indian	American Indian American Indian American Indian	White N/A American Indian	Weapons Violation Traffic Violation Assault/Battery
2016	N/A	N/A	N/A	N/A
2017	Anti-white Anti-trans	White American Indian	American Indian American Indian	Assault/Battery Assault/Battery

Hate crimes data from the Documenting Hate project, https://www.muckrock.com/foi/farmington-22237/propublica
-hate-crimes-data-farmington-police-42540/#comm-425616

definition of hate crime and creates the false portrayal that American Indians in Farmington are primary perpetrators of hate crime. Also, Farmington police reported to Documenting Hate an instance of child abuse as a hate crime, which does not fit within any state or federal definition. Obviously, more information is needed about why Farmington police categorized these incidents as hate crime and whether hate crime charges were filed in any of them. The department did not answer my request for more information. We are left with more questions than answers, including why none of this information was reported to the UCR.

The Uniform Crime Reporting Program collects data on anti-white hate crimes. But as mentioned, the main perpetrators of hate crime in the United States are white males. In my research, I have not uncovered any instance of anti-white hate crime committed by an American Indian person.

The Farmington Police Department was the only law enforcement agency in the Four Corners region that submitted hate crime information to the Documenting Hate Project. Other border towns such as Cortez, Colorado, and Aztec and Gallup, New Mexico, did not participate, which further demonstrates that many factors contribute to the difficulty in obtaining accurate hate crime data. In this instance, there are three: first, victims' reluctance and refusal to report (Pezzella et al. 2019; Perry 2008); second, the police's reluctance to investigate and even investigating officers' disbelief of victims who do report; and third, as seen with the Farmington data, officers' unclear understanding of what hate crime and bias-motivated crime are. Farmington Police did submit data to UCR in 2019 and documented one hate crime that was bias-motivated by religion.

Native American Hate Crimes Classification

Because of the lack of a good definition, I have created a categorization of hate crimes committed against Native Americans. Within my classification system, I differentiate between types of hate incidents, which are more difficult to track, and serious assaults that can be classified as crimes. My new categorization is based in part on the FBI categorization in the UCR reports. This categorizing does not lessen the impact of hate crimes that are nonphysical; rather, it broadens the definition to include more types of incidents that tend to be marginalized or ignored. The analyses of hate crimes committed against Native peoples previously had not focused on more violent types of hate crime that have resulted in death.

I categorize hate crimes against Native Americans under five levels. **Level 1** includes crimes against property, such as robbery, burglary, larceny, motor vehicle theft, arson, and destruction, damage, and vandalism. **Level 2** includes threats of violence, intimidation, and hate speech. **Level 3** includes simple assault. **Level 4** includes rape and aggravated assault. **Level 5** includes murder and nonnegligent manslaughter. I include both nonphysical and physical hate crime because both exist within the climate of Indian hating prevalent in reservation border towns. All levels in this definition can be used by watch groups to document and identify hate crimes.

Loyola law professor John T. Nockleby (1994, 2000) defines hate speech as "any communication that disparages a person or a group on the basis of some characteristic such as race, color, ethnicity, gender, sexual orientation, nationality, religion, or other characteristic." Currently hate speech is not illegal and has been upheld as freedom of speech. However, I include hate speech in my definition of hate crime because it causes harm and incites terror (Nockleby 2000). Hate speech has also been determined to be a precursor to more violent types of hate crime, including assault and murder (fig. 1).

Unlike hate speech toward other marginalized groups, hate speech toward Native Americans may reference historical incidents, massacres, or events and is meant to terrorize the individual first, then the entire group. Common hate speech toward Native Americans includes phrases that reference historical genocide and wars, like "get over it," "you lost the war," "go back to the reservation." It also includes racist stereotypes and chants associated with sports teams, like the chants and dances done at Washington football games or Cleveland Indians games.

Words have more significance to many Native Americans than they may to English-speaking whites and mainstream Americans, making hate speech toward Native Americans especially harmful. In Navajo, words have power, and speaking has the same impact as acting (Austin 2009). Although I did not give it its own category, some participants in this study discussed microaggression, which has been defined as "the everyday verbal, nonverbal, and environmental slights, snubs, or insults, whether intentional or unintentional, which communicate hostile, derogatory, or negative messages to target persons based solely upon their marginalized group membership" (Sue n.d.). An example of frequent microaggression is telling Native American professionals that they don't look like doctors, lawyers, or professors. Microaggression can also include subtle comments about appearance, Native language, skin tone, and living on the reservation (Drywater-Whitekiller, 2017).

"Indian Rolling": The Native American Lynching

The term *Indian rolling* was popularized in the 1970s to describe the phenomenon of white youths assaulting and robbing Navajos and Native people, primarily in Farmington (Barker 1992). Indian rolling was known among Native Americans in the western United States as a hate crime against them by whites. This common type of hate crime has continued to be an injustice for Navajos in Farmington because the crimes often go unpunished. I have noted similarities between Indian rolling and the lynching of people of color, namely Black Americans (Rushdy 2012). Definitions of lynching vary, but most scholars agree that lynching is typically perpetrated by groups of people after a perceived transgression or alleged violation. In particular, there are similarities between Indian rolling and lynching in the twentieth century (Donaldson 2006).

My definition of *Indian rolling* is bias-motivated assault against a Native American in a border town. In its most mild form, Indian rolling includes only robbery, where inebriated Native Americans are rolled over and robbed of money or belongings. In many cases, Indian rolling also includes physical assault, and in the most serious cases it has escalated to murder, torture, and disfigurement, such as in the Chokecherry Massacre. The victims' so-called transgressions, the purported "reasons" for the attacks, were intoxication and simply being an "Indian."

Indian rolling ranges from level 4 to level 5. In all the cases I have analyzed, perpetrators of Indian rolling are white males under the age of twenty-five, and much like with lynching, most Indian rolling is perpetrated by two or more attackers. Indian rolling is viewed as "sport," a "rite of passage," and a thrill-seeking crime (Barker 1992; Donaldson 2006), and perpetrators are said to derive some sort of pleasure from the attacks. There is an element of entertainment and fun derived from the lynching. The white community condones the attacks by ignoring them.

Reservation Border Towns

The majority of the hate crimes examined within this book occurred in reservation border towns. I define reservation border towns as predatory towns economically profiting off Native peoples yet excluding them from the community: "Border towns are places where whites can 'get away with' harming American Indians. American Indians are viewed as a disposable population or annoyance" (Bennett 2018). Reservation border towns are known as places of racial tension between whites and American Indians, and in fact they have long histories of violence against Indians, since these were typically the first white settlements on Indian lands. They also represent the broken system that has subjected Indian nations to paternalism and dependency, which has in turn made these towns centers of rampant economic exploitation, discrimination, and corruption. In some areas, Native people refer to entire states as border towns, meaning that the whole state espouses Indian-hating ideology and has a history of systemic racism and exploitation (Bennett 2018; United States Commission on Civil Rights n.d.). Border towns and their cultures of racism are a stark reality for both Native Americans and whites.

My Comanche father grew up in West Texas in the 1950s, when it was common for whites to post signs in stores and bars that read, "No dogs or Indians allowed." Similar signs across the western United States simply read, "No Indians allowed." Native people have told me that such signs were common in Montana and South Dakota border towns, such as in a bar called Jim Town on the northern border of the Northern Cheyenne Indian reservation in Montana. This type of sentiment and historical phenomenon is the embodiment of the way Native peoples continue to be viewed and treated in border towns (Wyoming PBS 2018).

Lumbee scholar Dean Chavers (2009) explains that border towns profit from the American Indian people who conduct business there. Gallup, New

Mexico, a reservation border town to several Native nations, has one of the largest populations of millionaires per capita, many of whom gained their wealth from American Indian arts and crafts. Gallup is notorious for its population of "inebriates" and its large market of American Indian arts and crafts and was once dubbed "Drunk Town USA" by ABC's *20/20* (1997). American Indians are subject to mistreatment and racial injustice within the town, even though the municipality profits economically off them and their labor. Gallup is not alone in its maltreatment of Native Americans.

There is a large and visible unsheltered relative population in Farmington. Though the unsheltered relatives are often vilified by white and non-Indian townspeople, there is little to no discussion of treating alcoholism as a disease. Some of the unsheltered population struggle with alcoholism. The misconception that Navajos and other Native Americans are all alcoholics is predominant, when only a small segment of the population are alcoholics. Additionally, whites and non-Indians alike have problems with alcoholism, but the portrayal is that alcohol consumption in border towns is solely an "Indian problem" (New Mexico Advisory Committee to the U.S. Commission on Civil Rights 2005).

One factor in the high rates of alcohol consumption in border towns is that most reservations are dry, prohibiting alcohol sales and alcohol possession. This hearkens back to early federal Indian policies that prohibited alcohol sales to American Indians and in Indian Country. In the reservation era, shortly after the Indian Wars, these policies continued, and alcohol sales were banned (Prucha 1984). Most reservations still prohibit alcohol sales, leaving border towns and off-reservation liquor stores the only place to buy alcohol. Clearly, this provides an economic boon to border towns, which want Native American business but do not want any responsibility for providing treatment for the disease of alcoholism. This issue is important because in my findings unsheltered relatives are the main targets of Indian rolling. Additionally, in the cases I analyzed, most of the Navajos and Native people that were victims of the most violent assaults and murders were consuming alcohol prior to being attacked; intoxication made them appear as easy and convenient targets for perpetrators of hate crimes, who often were also consuming alcohol themselves. Navajos were targeted, stalked, and "rolled" because the perpetrators knew they could get away with the crimes.

Alarmingly, I've found during this research that denial about racism and racial violence is widespread in border towns. City leadership and many border town citizens deny there is any type of discrimination or racism, making them complicit in the racism and racial violence (chapter 4).

The modern era has shown that the racism from border towns can be spread online. For example, during the COVID-19 pandemic Dan Franzen, a white male, made threats of violence toward members of the Navajo Nation on Facebook: "Danger Danger if you see these Navajo any Where call the police or shoot to kill these Navajo are 100% infected with the Cornavirus and needs to be stopped leathel Force is Athoized. Page Arizona do not need this spreading stop these people in any way or from. The Navajo police are not taking responsibility."

The Page Police Department took this threat seriously. Franzen was arrested and charged with

"suspicion of an attempt to incite a terrorist attack, which is a class three felony. . . . The Page Police Department recognizes the alarming nature of this incident and shares the justified concern this behavior has caused the Navajo community and others," department officials wrote in a statement. "The police department wishes to remind community members that unlawful hate speech, especially that which singles out protected classes (race, religion, gender, etc.), will be aggressively investigated and violations will be prosecuted to the fullest extent possible" (C. Curtis, azcentral.com, April 7, 2020)

The way the Page Police Department handled this threat and hate speech was commendable. Also, it was unique that the threat was considered terrorism. Page residents expressed a mixed reaction on social media. Some were supportive and horrified by the threats, while other Facebook users agreed with Franzen's hate speech but stopped short of making threats themselves. Obviously, many reservation border town residents continue to espouse white supremacy and Indian-hating sentiment, which in turn fuel the hate crimes committed against Native Americans discussed in the next chapters.

two

"Diné da Bidziil"

Theorizing Hate Crimes

When documenting and analyzing hate crimes, I am informed by a combination of Indigenous theories and concepts, such as Indian hating, anti-Indianism, colonization, settler colonization, and hate crimes. Few Native American studies scholars examine race, which is why I've broadened the theoretical scope of this book to include frameworks commonly used in ethnic studies, women's and gender studies, and Black and African American studies. The theories I present about American Indians, race, and hate crimes fit like pieces of a puzzle. As an American Indian studies scholar, I consider it critical to take a multidisciplinary approach to this research because the struggles across disciplines are the same; we all seek justice.

Indigenous Theories and Methods

Critical and moral questions need to be carefully formulated and deliberately asked by researchers when research is conducted on Indigenous peoples, especially when Native scholars study Native peoples. Any research design involving Indigenous people should involve Indigenous people so they can create, own, and judge research about themselves (L. T. Smith 1999; G. Smith

2005). Indigenous research seeks to improve conditions of Indigenous peoples and is not merely research for the sake of advancing one's academic status. Additionally, research involving Indigenous peoples should be led by Indigenous scholars, who have a vested interest in the research. As an Indigenous researcher I take these recommendations seriously.

Indigenous theories incorporate storytelling and the importance of "writing from the margins" (L. T. Smith 1999). Thus, marginalized people tell their own stories and establish their authority over research that affects them and their histories. For Native scholars like me, the tradition of storytelling comes naturally and often surfaces without force or effort, as you may have noticed throughout my previous chapters. Native researchers must harness this tradition as a strength in their research and employ it while combining the methods of other disciplines to engage in the process of decolonization by conducting research that focuses on the community's needs (L. T. Smith 1999). I take on this responsibility as a Native scholar and frequently apply a decolonized process that informs this research.

Indian Hating and Anti-Indianism

There is no doubt that the United States is still undergoing cultural and social change because of its ugly roots and underbelly of systemic racism. The most noticeable movements confronting systemic racism arose from African American leaders, organizations, and communities. The historical racial barriers put in place to disenfranchise and oppress African Americans are without a doubt like those used to oppress other people of color. The system of racial oppression in the United States is the same for all, since the common denominator for racial injustice in the United States is white supremacy and white terrorism. Simply put, people of color share this struggle, and each group must do what it can to dismantle it.

Native Americans do have a different history than other groups, however. And because of the Native experience with colonialism, the racist attitudes that whites developed and institutionalized are much different from those other people of color endure. Aboriginal land loss, genocidal warfare, and policies of forced assimilation are all experiences exclusive to Native

Americans. The white institutions of power that employed these genocidal tools created and re-created a specific type of racism directed exclusively toward Native Americans. It is my contention that this type of racism is the root of race-biased hate crimes and evidence of persisting efforts to commit genocide against American Indians and colonize Indian lands.

In the process of documenting hate, I use the phrase *Indian hating*, borrowed from American writer Herman Melville and historian Richard Drinnon. Melville authored an essay, "The Metaphysics of Indian Hating," that describes the type of racism Native Americans are subjected to. Drinnon (1980) expands on these concepts in *Facing West* and describes how the colonization of the western United States was justified by Indian-hating ideology. I also build on Cook-Lynn's (2001) concept and definition of "anti-Indianism." Cook-Lynn is the first American Indian scholar to write about and theorize hate crimes as anti-Indianism and Indian hating, and I draw from and expand on her scholarship throughout this study. I prefer to define the type of racism that is linked to colonialism and exclusive to Indians as Indian hating. Both terms are crucial when studying hate crimes against Native Americans.

Native Americans face a visceral type of racism when they are targeted and attacked, especially in reservation border towns. *Indian hating* explains the context of this visceral hate more fully: it's the kind of hate that leads to genocide. I strongly believe that Indian hating was at the center of white westward expansion, Indian removal, broken treaties, and genocidal war, and now it is at the center of racial violence and hate crimes. Indian hating is alive and well.

Cook-Lynn (2001) explains that "anti-Indianism, like anti-Semitism, displaces and excludes; thus its distinguishing purposes have been to socially isolate, to expunge or expel, to fear and menace, to defame, and to repulse indigenous people." She explains that anti-Indianism has its origins in American Christianity and, unlike anti-Semitism, has had free rein within American literature and culture. Her treatise examines anti-Indianism in literature and policy and as a reason for genocide. She argues, "What America wants in its race relations with American Indians is to steal and occupy land, to kill and otherwise destroy the land's inhabitants, and yet society provides an ethical example throughout the world of democratic and 'good' society developed for the purpose of profiting off that activity" (Cook-Lynn 2001, 53).

She further argues, much like Drinnon (1980) and Pearce (1988), in *Savagery and Civilization*, that "the hating of indigenous people have gone hand in hand in the making of America" (Cook-Lynn 2001). Cook-Lynn examines hate crimes committed in South Dakota, linking hate of Indians, namely Sioux in South Dakota, to the "ultimate expression of Anti-Indianism." Cook-Lynn likens hate crime to genocide.

Most hate crimes inflicted on Native Americans occur in reservation border towns. Within border towns, race relations are polarized because whites and American Indians make up the predominant populations there, and there are few other people of color. In these towns, there is little to no interaction with the mainstream culture of large cities. Therefore, racial tensions and attitudes that have existed since colonization are ever-present in these isolated border towns. Indian hating, without a doubt, is at the core of the colonization and settlement of most border towns and of the persisting racial violence there. Based on my data, I can state with certainty that, especially in reservation border towns, white residents consider Indian hating normal, and indeed so normal that it is deeply embedded in social, political, and justice systems. Indian hating is an integral part of colonialism, and together they thrive and perpetuate each other.

Hate crimes committed against Native Americans are reflective of ongoing Indian-hating ideology meant to segregate, instill fear, and terrorize. The segregation aspect is meant to keep Native Americans on the reservation (Perry 2008), figuratively and literally, even though border towns are on traditional Native homeland. Hate crimes committed against Native Americans serve as a message for members of the whole Native nation that they need to "go back to the reservation." This common form of hate speech cannot exist without a belief in white racial superiority. Ironically, within the current racial climate, "go home!" has been hurled at Native Americans, even though Native peoples are the original inhabitants of this country (C. Mathias, *Huffington Post*, December 23, 2019). The entire idea that Indians should go somewhere else is at once perplexing and revealing of the truth that America was founded in anti-Indian ideology, that "America's tongue is cloaked in ignorance and racism" (Cook-Lynn 2001). Indian hating is still alive, and Indian hating and white supremacy are central to the colonization of the United States.

Racism against Native Americans

The construct of race is often difficult to discern from legal status for Native Americans. In general, few scholars discuss race when identifying Natives as peoples of color. For the most part, Natives are not included in discussions of race because of the overemphasis on tribal sovereign rights of Indian nations to determine who is an American Indian via tribal enrollment. This over-emphasis diminishes real concerns that "Indians of color" (Killsback 2020) face when confronting discrimination, racism, and hate crimes based on their physical appearances. However, race and racism has also undeniably impacted the treatment of Native nations and peoples and influenced the creation of laws and policy (Williams 2005).

In the academy, the discussion of race within American Indian and Native American studies has been a controversial and sensitive topic because American Indian identity and citizenship is based on the sovereign rights of each Native nation. It is up to each Native nation to create their own citizenship requirements. American Indian identity and citizenship are not based on race. Historically, the academy has been a space for debate when it comes to American Indian and Indigenous issues, but the conversation about race, racism, and related topics like hate crimes tend to be reserved for ethnic studies programs and criminology. American Indian and Indigenous studies programs do not necessarily prioritize the studies of race, racism, and hate crimes experienced by American Indians. Much scholarship in American Indian studies has understandably focused on sovereignty of Native nations, their relationship to the federal government, and the protection and asser-tion of their rights. Race and racism have undeniably impacted the treat-ment of Native nations and peoples and influenced the creation of laws and policy (Williams 2005), but few studies and fewer scholars explore race and racism as experienced by Natives on a comparable level as they do in other ethnic studies disciplines, such as African American studies. It is time for the scholarship in American Indian and Indigenous studies to catch up with that of peer disciplines.

For my study in race, racism, and hate crimes against Native Americans, I chose to focus on a specific area, considering the diverse landscape of Indian Country. I found that an analysis of hate crimes in the Four Corners must include an intense examination and discussion of racism, privilege, and the motivating factors behind the persistence of hate crimes. The ongoing racial violence against Navajos in Farmington has been explained partially in the literature (Perry 2008; Barker 1992; NNHRC 2009; New Mexico Advisory Committee to the U.S. Commission on Civil Rights 1974, 2005; Donaldson 2006; Dinebeiina Nahiilna Be Agaditahe 2006; Barker 1992), but no study thoroughly analyzes racism and white privilege as the root cause of racial violence manifested in the form of hate crime.

Defining Racism

Many scholars have theorized and defined racism (Foucault 1982; van Dijk 1993). For my purposes I draw upon French Tunisian writer Albert Memmi's definition, also used by critical race studies law professor Rob Williams (2005), which explains racism in a colonial context and specifically parallels the experience of Native Americans with racism. Memmi described four elements of the "racist attitude": real or imagined differences, assigning values to those differences, making these differences absolutes by generalizing, and finally, justifying privilege (Williams 2005).

Throughout U.S. history, white colonists constructed and perpetuated the idea that the white race was superior to all other races. Racism, then, is the impetus behind the colonization and racial violence against Native Americans: "Racism is the generalized and final assignment of values to real or imaginary differences, to the accusers benefit and at his victim's expense, in order to justify the former's own privileges or aggression" (Memmi 1991).

The alleged difference between two races, particularly the colonizer and the colonized, is institutionalized and normalized in colonial systems, casting the oppressor as always superior in all ways to the oppressed. This normalization of racism explains the situation of oppressed groups and ethnic minorities and reinforces the racist assumption that the colonizer is superior. It is the source of the Indigenous debasement used to justify the conquest and subsequent violence committed against Indigenous peoples throughout the world (Memmi 1991). Within this context, racism is the major motivating factor in hate crime perpetrated against Native Americans. It is a legacy of colonialism.

Native Americans as People of Color

Robert Williams (2012), a critical race scholar, discusses race in terms of how it impacted federal Indian law, the legal system, and the justification for stripping the land from Native Americans. Williams unveils how the U.S. legal system dealt with Indians by labeling them as "savage" in a centuries-old European construct. The juxtaposition of savage and civilized began with the Greeks, who deemed anyone not Greek as savage. This attitude persisted as Europeans continued to justify the colonization of the Americas through violence, and it is the basis of the racist treatment Native peoples in the modern United States. This is a compelling argument, but Williams does not address how skin color and physical features factor into racism and views of savagery.

Racism is a shallow means of judging entire groups of people based on physical characteristics like skin tone, hair texture, and facial features. Without a doubt, all humans have unique physical features. The racist creates racism by claiming that a certain subset of features are inferiority. There is no doubt that racism against Indians based on their physical features exists. Yet there is little discussion of how physical appearance affected how whites came to treat Native peoples with racial disdain, undeniably targeting the skin tone and physical appearance of Native peoples when committing violence and genocide against them. But discussions about this type of racism have been ignored or marginalized in American Indian and Native American studies. Additionally, the field avoids discussion of colorism among Native communities in the United States. Colorism is defined as "prejudicial or preferential treatment of same-race people based solely on their color" (Walker 1983). Colorism is a product of racism that exists in Indian Country even in the absence of whites. It is part of the system of racism.

Native Americans have an additional challenge when confronting race, racism, and hate crimes: racial identity. Whites target Native Americans who "look Indian," even though Native American identity goes beyond the bounds of who looks "typically" Native American. Native nations base their membership on their own criteria, which varies from nation to nation. Some tribes have very low blood quantum requirements, and some base their membership on dependency alone, which creates a situation where there are a significant population of white-presenting Native Americans who are enrolled members of Native nations. However, in all the cases I have analyzed, bias-motivated hate crimes are perpetrated against Native Americans who are darker in skin color or who look phenotypically Native American. Simply put, Native Americans who present as white do not face the same type of hate.

Racism against Native peoples is multifaceted, but in general, ethnocentrism and white supremacy have undeniably been the foundations of the colonization, genocide, and violence inflicted upon Native peoples. Hate crimes committed against Native peoples are different from hate crimes committed against other people of color. The hate crimes perpetrated against Native Americans are rooted in colonization, political relationships, skin color, and the "savage" Native construct.

Racist Stereotypes

Native American stereotypes are rooted in a multitude of racist, inaccurate historical depictions. They have been stereotyped in varied forms since 1492, beginning with journal entries and art, and continuing on through the centuries to film and social media. By the time the English colonized Jamestown, the image of the Indian as the scarcely clothed noble or bloodthirsty savage of the Americas was entrenched in the minds of colonists. This portrayal, as well as the depiction of Native people as either naive innocents or savage heathens, paved the way for colonization and its associated genocide and land theft (Berkhoffer 1978; Cook-Lynn 2001; Stannard 1992).

Pearce (2000) asserts that Native peoples were always depicted as barriers in the way of civilization, and this ideology has become a core belief in American thought and culture. Related to the noble savage stereotype is the "vanishing Indian" stereotype, which promotes the assumption that Native people were a fragile race that would simply vanish amid the presence of the superior whites. President George Washington expressed this idea in his 1780 Indian policy: "the gradual extension of our settlements will as certainly cause the savage, as the wolf, to retire; both being beasts of prey, though they differ in shape" (George Washington Papers 1783). The idea of the vanishing Indian remains central to white American culture. American Indian people and their culture, however, have proved that they and their cultures are anything but fragile. They are resilient, surviving the most horrendous attacks from colonialism, assimilation, and the persistent forces of white supremacy and racism.

Another myth is the belief that the Indian was the common enemy of white people and that Indians had a long history of committing violence against innocent whites. This began in the 1700s with rumored "Indian scares." Historically, the United States encouraged settlement through newspaper and magazine advertisements, which targeted and influenced white settlers to move west and capitalize off the gold rush and prospecting in the western frontier. Berkhoffer (1978) and Slotkin (1973) refer to the printing press as giving currency to the myths and fantasies of savage Indians. News reporters covering the Indian Wars described an often one-sided account of conflict or inflated minor incidents, casting Indians as irrational brutes. These accounts propagated the concept of Manifest Destiny, the imperialist belief that the United States was destined by God to expand westward despite the land being aboriginal territory, resulting in the forcible removal and genocide of Native Americans. The so-called Indian fighters, whites who made reputations by killing Indian men, women, and children, became the national heroes as early as 1600.

Meanwhile, the "frontier men" were lauded as the "pilgrims of the plains," celebrated as saviors or tamers of the savage West. Throughout the 1800s and well into the 1900s, the image of the Indian as killer of white settlers and the popularity of the captivity narratives of the era spurred on the Indian-hating ideology of the new America. This myth remains prevalent; to see it one needs to simply turn on the television or watch a Western film. The racist stereotypes and images have persisted in the minds of the American public today. Simply saying "Indian" in the English language conjures strong mental images of a horse-mounted noble savage.

Scientific scholars have theorized the Asiatic origins of American Indians. Vine Deloria Jr. (1997) maintained that this racist theory alleviated white guilt because it enabled whites to argue that there was scientific proof American Indians were not indigenous to Native America. The assumption, therefore, is that whites can easily justify taking Indian lands when Indians are also considered immigrants to this continent. Stereotypes, especially those reinforced by racist core assumptions, are dangerous because they can influence how people perceive and treat American Indians and shape policy and the opinions of lawmakers. Unchallenged, these perceptions created and perpetuated America's racist culture, which resulted in the breaking of so many Indian treaties, the outbreak of so many Indian wars, and the existence of so many problems related to white racism. These racist stereotypes are persistent in the hate speech hurled at Native Americans and present within the interview narratives and within the data from Internet forums.

Anti-sovereignty

American Indian political and legal scholars argue that Native Americans are not the same as other minority groups (Deloria 1988; Wilkins 2018), while downplaying the fact that American Indians face many similar injustices as other groups. While it is true that American Indians' defined political status in the United States is different from that of other people of color, it is important to affirm that American Indians are still confronted with similar hate and racism despite their unique political status. American Indians also face another form of racism that other people of color do not face: they are maltreated and targeted *because* they are sovereign.

There is growing literature regarding anti-Indianism as it relates to sovereignty and assertion of rights (Grossman 2005). Anti-sovereignty groups have been created by white Americans in the guise of "citizens' groups." In other areas, anti-Indian groups have been created in response to fishing rights and hunting rights. The term "rich Indian racism" refers to the anti-Indian backlash to successful Indian gaming enterprises (Akee et al. 2015; Flaherty 2013; Corntassel and Witmer 2008), coinciding with many Americans' misconception that Native peoples have "special," unfair rights and privileges. This misconception is also often part of a white supremacist narrative that American Indian rights take away from the rights of other Americans. This backlash is fueled by negative media portrayals, which in turn influences public policy and federal Indian laws (Bennett 2018; Mankiller 2005; Corntassel and Witmer 2008).

Although there are not any identified anti-Indian groups in the Southwest, the racist stereotypes these groups perpetuate about American Indians in other regions of the country are similar. Grossman (2005) identified anti-Indian organizations in the Northern Plains, Northwest, Great Lakes, and Canada. These groups call themselves citizens' rights groups and perpetuate the false narrative that American Indian nations' sovereignty is "un-American" and dangerous to the rights of white Americans.

Hate crimes and police violence rose along with Natives' exertion of rights during the #NoDAPL movement on the Standing Rock nation. The sovereign status and rights of Native nations and their citizens are points of envy and bitterness and motivation for hate crime. During the COVID-19 pandemic, American Indian nations exerted their sovereignty by enforcing their regulatory jurisdiction over their lands to slow down the spread of the virus. Nations such as the Makah, Northern Cheyenne, and Crow, among many others, restricted travel of non-tribal members on their reservations. Some nations had checkpoints monitoring their borders and stopped outsiders from entering their vulnerable communities.

The Northern Cheyenne Nation issued an ordinance to close Highway 212, a main road through its lands. This came under intense criticism from surrounding white communities. I documented violent hate speech on Facebook that included threats by truck drivers with photos of firearms and some threatening they would go through the reservation regardless of any road closure. Natives' exertion of rights has been viewed as a threat to white supremacy and resulted in an uptick in hate crimes against Native peoples. Other examples of anti-sovereignty-motivated hate speech and hate crimes include racist attitudes toward American Indian nations in their pursuits for treaty rights, gaming rights, water rights, jurisdictional rights, and a plethora of rights that Indian nations retain as sovereign entities (Perry 2008).

Colonization and Settler Colonization

Unquestionably one of the most obvious forms of racism against Indians has been the historical injustices committed by colonial powers through the violent and systematic colonization of Indian lands. Colonialism has adapted to oppress American Indians in various ways, but its racist roots are evident. Farmington and surrounding areas are considered aboriginal Navajo territory, consistent with Navajo oral history and clan locations. The poor economic situation many Navajo people face today is a result of continuing colonial practices of discrimination. For example, businesses continue to deny Navajos employment, and banks continue to deny them loans. The initial goal of colonization is to profit from land, resources, and cheap labor (Fanon 1961). This practice is ongoing in Farmington, where the ensuing colonization and settlements thrive off the dispossession of Navajo and Native populations, even as Farmington residents and officials adamantly deny the dispossession of land. Town residents stubbornly continue to reject that racism is alive and well in Farmington and that there is a historic record of the theft of Farmington (Farmington Topix forum, October 8–14, 2008). The denial is a phenomenon of colonization by which succeeding generations of the colonizers continue to profit off the dispossession (Memmi 1991). In this context, colonization remains central to the culture of succeeding generations of the colonizers of Totah. Colonization creates the culture of racism and hate against the Indigenous people, the Navajo.

These theories and concepts build a solid foundation for my discussions on racism and in bias-motivated hate crimes against Native Americans. They provide the language necessary for engaging and interrogating hate crimes and a way to understand hate crimes against Native Americans and the differences from those perpetrated against other groups. These concepts provide an understanding of how the border town environment fosters continuing hate crimes against Native peoples. With this understanding we can work to dismantle years of oppression and examine hate crimes against Native Americans in the twentieth century and in the present day.

three

"Farmington Is on Indian Land"

Occupied Totah and Colonization

I think the most wonderful place the Navajo have is Many Farms, and Farmington too. I think if I ever got married I would live in Farmington. That is the place I pick out when I was twelve years old. I think my father will be with me all my life and that he will find a girl for me around that area. I realize later that I am wrong. Instead, my father gets killed there, and I have to think about that place all of my life. There will be war again someday. There won't be peace all the way. The white people were going to take the land away from us, but we fought for it and kept part of our own land. . . . nowadays the men and the boys should be thinking about how they could survive like I survived. It must be in your thinking and in your life to be brave and to be safe.

—Bighorse the Warrior

Within this chapter, I examine the history and argue that modern-day racial attitudes and race-biased hate crimes against Native peoples are rooted in the bitter history of colonization in the Four Corners. Navajo history in the Four Corners area is largely unexplored. Even as a lifelong resident of this area, I did not learn about the historical conflict with white settlers that gripped this region until much later in life. I grew up hearing stories from my grandfather Joe Redhorse Benally about our ancestors living in the area on traditional Navajo homeland. Few histories have been authored by Navajos, but our oral history is alive, extensive, and reliable. I analyze sources such as oral histories, newspapers, reports, and historical monographs, with secondary sources from both non-Navajo and Navajo perspectives. Yet I strongly believe that Native histories must be retold from a Native perspective and with a Native lens and that Native historians have begun privileging Native oral narratives and decolonizing history.

The history of white settlers and the Diné in the Four Corners region is fraught with racial violence and racial tension. The historical record shows three trends that correlate to racism and hate crimes: Indian hating, colonization, and a fight for land and boundaries. What is also important, and what I focus on in this chapter, is the relationship between the Navajos and each of the colonizers they encountered: the Spanish, Mexicans, and Americans. Each relationship was marked with hostility, violence, and the taking of resources. Spanish and Mexican colonizers sought to take slaves, riches, and land, while American colonizers primarily desired land and resources.

The Navajo lived in the region encompassing the Four Corners for thousands of years and considered the Farmington area to be traditional Diné territory. According to my grandfather, Navajos lived throughout San Juan County, all the way to Durango, Colorado. The territory was cherished as bountiful farmland. Farmington was known in the Navajo language as Totah, which translates as where three rivers, Animas, La Plata, and San Juan, meet. White historians often falsely maintain that the Navajo are relative newcomers to the Southwest, that Navajos have only been in the Southwest for five hundred years (Acrey 1988a; Bailey and Bailey 1982). This assertion by white historians is an attempt at justify the theft of land and dispossession of the People by creating the narrative that the Navajos are "newcomers" and "settlers" themselves. This dangerous narrative feeds into the racism that has created race-biased hate crimes. On the contrary, according to traditional Navajo oral history, the Diné are not foreign newcomers. The territory between the four sacred mountains is Diné Keyah (Navajo land).

Dinétah: Pre-contact

One of the oldest Navajo settlements is found at Dinétah, east of Farmington. Gobernador Knob, within Dinétah, is the birthplace of the primary Navajo deity, Changing Woman, who created the four main clans of the Navajo people. The area spans east of Farmington and north into Colorado and is sacred to Navajos. In a traditional Navajo story, Changing Woman took the People west for a period. After the Navajo clans returned, they came to Gobernador Knob. Even archaeological evidence supports the claim that Navajos have been in the region for hundreds of years (Iverson 2002). Nearly thirty-five archaeological sites relate to the Navajo hero twins. The first conical-shaped hogan and plentiful rock art have been found in this area. Many sacred and archaeological sites are also found near the Farmington area, including Dinétah and sacred areas near present-day Navajo Lake. Navajos lived in this region for years and shared parts of the San Juan Valley with Utes and other tribes. There were occasional skirmishes and disagreements over territory, but such conflicts were minimal compared to the struggles the People would face with European colonizers.

Spanish and Mexican Colonizers

The Navajos first came into contact with Spanish conquistadors in the 1500s. The Navajos' relationship with the Spanish and Mexicans was different from that of the Pueblos. For example, the Navajos benefited from the livestock and goods that the Spanish brought with them (Iverson 2002). It was difficult for the Spanish to determine the Navajo population size and to learn much about the people because Navajos lived for the most part further north and in scattered communities: "The Navajos were far more able to pick and choose, to take advantage of non-directed cultural exchange, even amidst the complications, and, at times, the horrors brought by the Spanish presence" (Iverson 2002, 23).

The Spanish were dismissive of the Native people they came across and were only interested in them for the land they occupied and the labor they could provide. The Spanish had just come off the heels of colonizing the West Indies and utilizing the 1493 Doctrine of Discovery, legalizing their conquest and colonization of the "New World." The Doctrine of Discovery allowed Christian colonizers to conquer non-Christian people, simply because of the racist concept that non-Christian peoples did not have the rights that Christians had. The racist characterizations that justified conquest and genocide grew from these initial encounters between the Spanish and the Indigenous populations of the West Indies. The Spanish dealt with the

Native populations in the Southwest the same way they had dealt with those in the West Indies, with force: "The Spanish felt no need to consult with people they considered to be barbarians; the king gave to his colonist not only Indian land but the right to the labor of those Indians unfortunate enough to occupy specific parcels" (Iverson 2002, 24, 25; Spicer 1962). In the Spanish view, Native peoples were savages, and because they were not Christian, they were justifiably conquerable.

Native nations of the Southwest, most notably the Pueblos, resisted Spanish invasion. During the Pueblo uprising of 1650, Navajos allied with numerous Pueblos against the Spanish (Iverson 2002). Following this conflict, the Spanish became relentless against the Navajos and grew tired of their dismissal of Spanish authority and control. In 1675 and 1678, they waged military campaigns against the Navajos, targeting their villages: "These initiatives resulted in the massive destruction of Navajo fields of corn, the capture of men, women, and children, and the killing of other Diné" (Iverson 2002, 27). The Spanish kidnapped Navajos for the slave trade, and Navajos retaliated by raiding Spanish settlements (Iverson 2002).

The Spanish continued their campaigns against the Navajo in the early 1700s, wreaking havoc across Dinétah with slash-and-burn tactics: "The Spaniards destroyed many of their fields, killed an undetermined number of Diné, and took still others captive" (Iverson 2002, 27). Throughout the 1700s and into the 1800s, Spanish military campaigns doubled as a great threat to Navajo life and Dinétah's greatest environmental foe. In 1805 at Canyon de Chelly, the Navajos experienced the horrendous tragedy of Massacre Cave, when Spanish soldiers killed more than one hundred Navajos, most of them women and children. Nonetheless, the Navajos continued to resist. Spanish correspondence during and after the massacre reveals the Spanish government's persisting frustration in their efforts to exert control over the Navajos. Navajos responded and continued to raid Spanish settlements for supplies and to retaliate against the slave trade (Acrey 1988b). The Navajos were not going to leave without a fight.

During the colonization of Native America, the Spanish brutalized all the Indigenous populations they came into contact with, repeatedly proving their reputation as the "Black Legend of Spain." Spanish violence against the Navajos was no different (Spicer 1962). When Mexico won its freedom from Spain in 1821, the Mexican government dealt with the Navajos in the same manner as the Spanish had, by use of force and violence. Despite the change in colonizers, the slave trade of Navajos persisted into the 1860s, accompanied by high rates of Navajo kidnapping (Denetdale 2007; Iverson 2002; McNitt 1990; Acrey 1988a). Astoundingly, it is estimated that there were between 1,500 and 3,000 Navajo slaves in Spanish and Mexican households in 1862 (Denetdale 2007).

In 1854 the United States purchased areas in the Southwest, including New Mexico. General Stephen Kearney marched into Santa Fe in 1846 and declared to the New Mexican citizens that they would not be harmed and that the United States would protect the citizens against all of their enemies, including the Navajos. The Navajos' hostile relationships with their Spanish and Mexican colonizers continued then with the Americans (Iverson 2002, 34). The same Indian-hating ideology that the Spanish and Mexicans espoused continued with the Americans. After all, America adopted the Doctrine of Discovery and its racist principles when Chief Justice John Marshall ruled that Indians had no property rights in *Johnson v. M'Intosh* (1823). America, Mexico, and Spain shared the same racist views against Indians in principle and in practice.

American Colonizers and Navajo Territory

White historians are careful to characterize Farmington and the San Juan Valley as only and exclusively *winter* grazing land of the Navajos (Bailey and Bailey 1982), creating a narrative that Navajos were not continuously living in the Farmington and surrounding areas. For example, historians Garrick Bailey and Roberta Glenn Bailey contend that families were "wintering" in the San Juan Valley, but that is based solely on conjecture (Hughes in Bailey and Bailey 1982). It is crucial to assert here the fact that Navajos lived in this area year-round, not exclusively in the cold winter months. Gus Bighorse was born in 1846. Navajos have a distinct oral history record of occupying the Farmington area for generations before the Long Walk in 1864.

Gus Bighorse (1990, 10) recollected, "we often go to Farmington in the summer. There is lots of corn. It grows about 6 feet tall. There are lots of watermelon, pumpkins too, and cantaloupe and apples and peaches. My father has clan relatives that live there. Whenever it is time to go, they pack our horses with lots of goodies."

Miguel Garcia, a trader between Utes and wealthy Navajo families in this area, noted a large number of Navajos were living in the La Plata, San Juan, and Animas Valleys in 1844 (Bailey and Bailey 1982). Furthermore, American troops attempted to contact the Navajos after New Mexico territory passed to the United States: "They found the valley was everywhere filled with Indians, watering their numerous herds of horses, sheep and other animals. From this cause the pasturage was greatly exhausted near the river" (Bailey and Bailey 1982).

Navajo cornfields extended throughout the San Juan Valley, affirming the continued presence of the Navajo people (Bailey and Bailey 1982). Some Navajo families also fled to the San Juan Valley after conflict in Canyon de Chelly. A map drawn by Lieutenant John G. Parke confirms that Navajo farms were spread throughout the valley and on both sides of the San Juan River near Farmington. Early settler Jacob Robinson confirmed and wrote that the San Juan area was "occupied at all seasons of the year by old men and worn out warriors, women and children; and is a kind of storehouse of all their surplus articles of trade, as well as of the corn which is raised in the neighborhood, it is also the head-quarters of their manufacture of blankets, clothes, baskets, etc." (in Bailey and Bailey 1982, 64).

These written accounts corroborate the oral narratives of my grandfather and of Gus Bighorse, as well as almost every Navajo elder who now resides near the area. The Navajo had continuous occupation of the San Juan Valley and the area that later became Farmington. The arrival of the whites obviously created problems for the Navajos.

In 1853 five Mexican Americans were killed near Abiquiu, and seven trappers were killed near Farmington. Three thousand sheep were also stolen (Bailey and Bailey 1982). The Navajos who lived in the San Juan Valley were blamed for these incidents. U.S. Army Lieutenant Robert Ransom was commanded to negotiate the situation. Ransom and his cavalry marched along the San Juan River and met with a group of four hundred Navajos and several headmen and war chiefs, including respected headmen Cayetano and Archuleta. But the meeting became contentious and almost erupted into a battle when American soldiers captured and held a Navajo head-man at gunpoint. The whites released the Navajo chief in exchange for a dozen sheep, and the confrontation ended without bloodshed (Bailey and Bailey 1982). This altercation deepened the paranoia of already frightened and inexperienced American soldiers toward the Navajo people. Governor David Meriwether described the San Juan Valley Navajos and their leaders, asserting they were "guilty of most of the mischief attributed to the Nava-jos. This chief and his band together with a few other Navajos live near our settlements and on the border of the Utah's with whom they associate and are a bad set of fellows in my opinion" (66). It is highly likely that nearly all whites in the area were racists and viewed the Navajos with disdain even before this incident. After 1853 the whites likely became more fearful and hateful toward the Navajos.

In this contentious period, Indian Agent Henry L. Dodge was concerned that a Navajo and Ute alliance would materialize against the whites. Dodge's concerns may have been unfounded, but they were sensible considering the simple-minded racist thinking that American Indians would unite based on race the same way that whites unite. The Navajo-Ute alliance did not occur. According to Bailey and Bailey (1982), the Navajos' relationship with the Utes soured because the Utes raided Navajo camps. Bailey and Bailey (1982, 68) contend that before the Long Walk most Navajo families fled the San Juan area due to Ute raids, but a small group of families remained until they were forcibly removed during the Long Walk in 1864. They do not mention how many remained, but it was enough of a Navajo population for a trader named Cayetano to come to the San Juan and set up business. From 1859, Cayetano's family remained along the La Plata River. The Navajos and Utes share a colonial history of the area, and today they experience the same rac-ism. In short, one can say they have always been united against colonialism.

The Long Walk

The most catastrophic events in Navajo history were the Long Walk and the subsequent imprisonment at Bosque Redondo in 1864. It remains a topic of pain and sorrowful remembrance among the People. Navajos had a long history of war and conflict with colonial powers: first the Spanish, second the Mexicans, and third the New Mexicans. After the New Mexico territory came under American control, New Mexico settlers requested U.S. Army General Stephen Kearney to protect them against Navajo raiding. Kearney encouraged the New Mexican settlers to march into Navajo territory and take Navajo land and property to "reclaim" it on behalf of New Mexico (Iverson 2002, 38). The New Mexicans were supported by the powerful Americans.

Navajo leader Narbona argued that the Americans should not interfere in the conflict:

> Americans! You have a strange cause of war against the Navajos. We have waged war against the New Mexicans for several years. . . . We have just cause for all of this. You have lately commenced a war against the same people. You are powerful. You have great guns and many brave soldiers. You have therefore conquered them, the very thing we have been attempting to do for so many years. You now turn on us for attempting to do what you have done yourselves. . . . This is our war. We have more right to complain of you for interfering in our war, then you have to quarrel with us for continuing a war we had begun long before you got here. (Iverson 2002, 39)

The Americans became the third colonial power from whom the Navajo people had to protect their land. The Americans were anxious to continue with expansion, and Colonel John Macrae Washington was not interested in peaceful negotiations. He wanted the Navajos to stop raiding the New Mexicans, but he was unconcerned with the reasons behind the Navajo raiding, which was retaliation for the slave trade (Acrey 1988a).

From early Spanish invasion and into the late 1800s, the Navajos were incessantly hunted and harassed by slave traders. Navajos had raided Spanish and then New Mexican settlements in retaliation. As mentioned, slave raiders were particularly interested in Navajo women and children, primarily for sexual and domestic purposes. Women were sex-trafficked and used for their knowledge of farming and home building, and children were enslaved because it was easier to assimilate children into colonial society (Acrey 1988b; McNitt 1990). Historian Frank McNitt (1990) cites the slave raids as the primary reason for the continued hostilities between the Spanish, Mexicans, and Navajos. At the core of all this conflict, what McNitt may have missed, is the dehumanization of the Indigenous people of the land, a crucial element of Indian hating. The colonial powers employed the same methods of dehumanizing Black slaves as they did when taking Native land, and throughout the Indian Wars and Navajo slave raids. This level of hate is complex in that the whites did not exterminate what they hated but found a way to benefit and capitalize from it.

The American military undertook numerous expeditions against the Navajos in the years before the Long Walk. The Navajos negotiated three treaties with the United States 1849, the treaty of Ojo del Oso, the Newby Treaty, and the Washington Treaty, and all three were ratified in 1850 (Acery 1988; Iverson 2002). All three treaties promised peace, but were all broken, primarily by the continuing slave trade.

During the same year of the three treaties, in August 1849, Colonel Washington led one of the most infamous expeditions into Navajo territory, remembered among the Navajos as yet another violent invasion of Dinétah. The white troops and volunteers forced their way into Navajo lands, looted Navajo crops, and destroyed what remained. This invasion amid treaty negotiations was devastating, and because Navajo families relied heavily on their crops to last them through the winter, they faced another wave of genocidal war from the whites. Would-be New Mexican slave raiders also joined the expedition as volunteers to scout out hiding areas in Navajo territory for later slave abductions (Acrey 1988a). The whites viewed Navajo land as a resource to be taken at will and the Navajo people as without any rights to be respected. This is the racist legacy of the Doctrine of Discovery and Manifest Destiny in Dinétah.

In 1849 Colonel Washington met with several hundred Navajos and Navajo leaders and accused them of murder and robbery. The Navajo leaders expressed that only a handful of warriors raided white settlements. Nonetheless, Washington had his interpreter read treaty provisions to the Navajos, emphasizing peace. The Navajo leaders responded by demanding that slaves be returned home as promised in the previous Newby Treaty and requested the American soldiers stop the inhumane scorch-and-burn policy (Acrey 1988a). The Navajos demanded peace, not revenge.

Narbona, a prominent Navajo leader, was killed after the treaty negotiations were over, during an altercation with a New Mexican volunteer. The

New Mexican claimed that a Navajo was in possession of his stolen horse. The accused Navajo refused to return the horse, and Colonel Washington ordered his soldiers to retrieve it. The Navajos fled, and the American soldiers and volunteers opened fire on them. Narbona was killed during the fray, which is remembered as a massacre, and his body was defiled and mutilated. The great chief's head was severed and given to a medical doctor to study (McNitt 1990). The mutilation of Indians—men, women, and children—was a common practice by the U.S. Army in the Indian Wars. Such inhumane and blatantly savage behavior only adds to the vile culture of Indian hating.

From then, Navajo leaders who advocated for peace were rightly angry and distrustful of any further treaty negotiations with the whites. Manuelito, another prominent Navajo headman, refused to attend the meeting at Canyon de Chelly. Lesser headmen that did not necessarily speak for the Navajo people eventually signed the Washington Treaty in 1849, and it was ratified in 1850 (Acrey 1988a). From then, the Navajos remained in a precarious situation with the whites, who had earned their reputation as unpredictable and therefore untrustworthy.

The Navajos continued raiding New Mexicans due to the relentless slave trade of Navajo women and children. Indian Agent James S. Calhoun conceded that much of the "Indian problem" would cease if the slave trade ceased. In one policy change, Agent Calhoun issued a notice that only licensed traders could operate stores in Navajo land, curbing the slave trade. However, the new policy did not stop the slave trade but instead forced it underground because it remained so profitable to whites and Mexicans. The slave trade continued and flourished; Navajo boys and girls were priced at two hundred dollars each. Given the demand and supply, it's highly probable that there was a Navajo slave in every Mexican family (Acrey 1988a) well into the time of the Long Walk (1863–64).

In the years after the signing of the Washington Treaty of 1850, conflict between Navajos and New Mexicans persisted. In 1851 a Navajo delegation traveled to Santa Fe to demand for the return of Navajo children captured by slave traders. One leader pleaded:

> My people are crying in the same way. Three of our chiefs now sitting before you mourn for their children, who have been taken from their homes by the

Mexicans. More than 200 of our children have been carried off and we know not where they are. The Mexicans have lost but a few children in comparison with what they have stolen from us. . . . From the time of Colonel Newby we have been trying to get our children back. . . . Eleven times we have given up our captives, only once have they given us ours. My people are crying for the children they have lost. It is American justice that we must give up everything and receive nothing? (Acrey 1988a)

In most historical narratives, the Navajos are often unfairly portrayed as the aggressors in the conflict that occurred with the Spanish and Americans. But comparatively, the number of slaves the Navajos captured was much smaller than the number of Navajos who were captured and traded by the Spanish and Mexicans (Acrey 1988a; McNitt 1990). In addition, Navajo tradition dictated that captives become members of families and be absorbed into the tribe as adoptees. This was the common practice among American Indians long before the arrival of whites. Slave raiding, however, was purely a colonial concept, motivated and justified by racial differences. Under this system, slaves were never to be considered as potential family members and were never granted the rights and privileges of being adopted into the family and community of their captors. The Navajo leaders knew this, which is why they were so adamant that their relatives be returned.

After the ratification of the Washington Treaty, the Americans and the Navajos coexisted for a few years of peace, although the Navajo captives had not yet been returned. In 1855 the Navajos signed the Treaty of Laguna Negra, which was supposed to establish reservation boundaries for the Navajos, but it was never ratified by the U.S. Congress. Navajo headman Manuelito opposed the treaty boundaries from the beginning, arguing that the Navajos were giving up too much of Dinétah (Acrey 1988a). Tense relations continued between the Navajos and white settlers, culminating in two events: when Manuelito's cattle were slaughtered by New Mexicans and when a Navajo killed Jim, a Black slave at Fort Defiance. Jim was enslaved by Major William Brooks, but after Jim died, Brooks was more concerned about the monetary loss of a slave rather than the loss of life (Iverson 2009; Kiser 2017). These incidents were all that the Americans needed to once again declare war on the Navajos.

The Americans attempted to broker peace with the Bonneville Treaty of 1858. The treaty provisions were much stricter and commanded the return of white captives taken by the Navajo (Acrey 1988a). The treaty limited Navajo grazing of their aboriginal territory. After the treaty Navajos continued raiding, and the civilian New Mexico governor eventually called for war and "total extermination" of the Navajos. This tension peaked in 1860, and Navajos prepared for war. Nearly a thousand Navajo warriors attacked Fort Defiance and were almost successful in capturing the fort. After the siege, U.S. troops and white volunteers led by Colonel Edward Canby prepared to attack the Navajo villages. The New Mexican volunteers enlisted once again to capitalize on the situation and raided for slaves and "murdered scores of people and took women and children captive" (Acrey 1988a, 30).

The campaign against the Navajo was largely unsuccessful, as, Canby realized, the Navajos could easily hide and disappear within the vast Navajo territory. However, the Navajo leaders wanted peace after years of fighting off the white settlers (Acrey 1988a). The Canby Treaty of 1861 was more favorable to the Navajos than the previous Bonneville Treaty. The Navajo territory boundaries were larger, and the Americans promised protection against the slave traders. However, this provision resulted in more aggressive raids against the Navajos as the white slave traders realized the Americans were patrolling the nation's borders, making it more difficult to capture Navajos (Acrey 1988a).

After years of back-and-forth raiding between the Navajos and the Americans, the Navajos were forcibly rounded up and removed to Bosque Redondo. The American government officials had previously considered the concept of a large Navajo reservation, but it was not until after the Civil War that the military followed through with this plan. The driving motives behind Navajo removal were the vast lands, resources, and, Agent Calhoun mistakenly hoped, gold of Dinétah; the whites wanted it all (Acrey 1988a).

Navajos were informed that they had to report to either Fort Wingate or Fort Defiance to surrender for removal. Once they arrived they were coerced to traverse on foot one of several routes, after which they were imprisoned. It is estimated that nearly eight thousand Navajos were imprisoned at Bosque Redondo. However, many Navajos, such as my grandmother's family, did not go to Hweeldi (Navajo for Bosque Redondo). My aunt Patty Chee (Lake

Valley Navajo School, 1991) interviewed elders in the eastern agency including my grandparents. Annabelle Redhorse Benally recalled: "I was told by my late father that our ancestors of the Naaneshet'szhi [Charcoal Streaked, otherwise known as Zuni] clan never went to Hweeldi. They hid in the canyon of Tse'kooh hah zhoozh near the land of the Beehai (Jicarilla Apache) people. My maternal grandmother and my maternal grandfather did not go to Hweeldi. They were left behind and hid until other people came back."

The Navajo people who resisted removal managed to hide and evade seizure but lived in constant fear of either being captured or killed by the Americans, slave traders, or enemy tribes. In fact, General James Henry Carleton had encouraged Zuni raids (Acrey 1988a). The Diné who hid held ceremonies and prayed for peace and the safe return of their relatives. Not only were their lives threatened, but so were their culture and spiritual beliefs, as recalled by Bighorse (1990, 45):

> The medicine man named Many-Whiskers and another called Old-Arrow go to the top of Navajo Mountain to pray to the Holy people. They pray that these captured Navajo will come back to their homeland safely, soon be free. At this time there are lots of medicine men. They pray every time before they eat—the whole family, all the time praying for the safe return. . . . And they pray for the warriors that are protecting them and for the white people who are holding all these people captive, pray to soften the white soldiers hearts to let these people go free.

The soldiers burned cornfields and peach trees and contaminated wells throughout Navajo land. If Navajo people questioned the soldiers, they were shot and killed. Gus Bighorse described the brutality of the white soldiers, emphasizing that "some of the families hide, and some are found by the cavalry and killed right there" (Bighorse 1990, 15). He also told of a heartbreaking incident in which Navajo families jumped off cliffs and killed themselves rather than face being caught by soldiers (28). The Navajo people had never encountered such violence, even from their worst Native enemies. The whites inflicted the most gruesome acts of genocide, no different than the Black Legend nearly four hundred years earlier in Hispaniola. During the Long Walk to Bosque Redondo, pregnant women and their babies were shot and killed. Women were kidnapped and raped by the soldiers. They tried to protect each other by walking in groups and with family members. Murder along the walk became commonplace, as described by one witness: "On the journey the Navajos went through all kinds of hardships, like tiredness and having injuries. And, when those things happened the people would hear gun shots in the rear. But they couldn't do anything about it. They just felt sorry for the ones being shot" (30). The soldiers did not let the families bury the bodies when they were killed or died of exhaustion, as another witnessed: "There is absolutely no mercy. . . . They are heartbroken because their families die along the way. Right outside Fort Defiance when the trip just starts, they sleep there and leave lots of bodies there. That's the way it is for the rest of the trip" (34).

Once the people arrived at Fort Sumner, the conditions were no better. Countless people died of sickness and starvation at Bosque Redondo. They were treated like animals; in every sense they were slaves of the U.S. government (Bighorse 1990). Navajo families were forced to build the soldiers' quarters while living in holes dug into the ground, covered loosely with tree branches or hides, providing little protection from the elements and enemies. Another painful fact about this time in Diné history, and one rarely discussed in written and oral accounts, is that women engaged in prostitution for rations to feed their families. This coerced form of sex work is forever branded in America's history of the West; it remains as part of Native America's unhealed pain.

At the end of the Long Walk, it became apparent even to the Americans that the Bosque Redondo experiment was an utter and miserable failure. The whites underestimated the Navajo population, and by 1866 there were nearly eight thousand Navajos at Bosque Redondo, much more than the fort could hold. The fort rations and supplies were insufficient to feed all the people, and they continued to starve. Numerous Navajos escaped the prison and made it back to their homelands. More wanted to leave. In early 1868 President Ulysses Grant created a peace commission to deal with the "Indian problem." The commission planned a trip to Bosque Redondo to negotiate a treaty with the Navajos. New Mexicans were opposed to the idea of Navajos returning to their homeland because Dinétah had not yet been explored for its mineral wealth (Acrey 1988a). Editors of the *Santa Fe Weekly New Mexican* emphasized the sentiment of their citizens who "felt that whites now needed the area for their own use" (Acrey 1988a, 71). Clearly, the same Indian-hating sentiment that had spurred on colonization was accepted as the norm in the views of New Mexican citizens. In fact, some folks in the Southwest still hold the idea that Indian hating is a natural response to Indian people.

The Diné conducted numerous ceremonies and prayers while imprisoned at the fort. They called upon the spiritual powers that would ensure successful negotiations so they would be allowed to return home to live within the bounds of their four sacred mountains (Bighorse 1990). On June 1, 1868, the spiritual powers blessed the Diné and Navajo headmen, including Barboncito and Manuelito, who signed the final treaty that permitted the Navajo people to return to their homeland. More than eight thousand Navajos journeyed home seventeen days later (Denetdale 2007). Sadly, some were so exhausted and in such poor health that they did not make it, but their families buried them in their beloved homeland. Manuelito informed the people that the war was over and told the warriors to lay their weapons down and "go make a living." But he also said, "just in case, have your weapons ready all the time," understanding that the whites were proven liars, unpredictable, and quick to violence (Bighorse 1990, 58). His words remain part of modern Diné philosophy.

The Return to Diné Bikeyah: 1864

When the Navajos returned from incarceration at Bosque Redondo, a significant number of Navajo families returned to the San Juan Valley, where they had lived before the Long Walk. These Navajos continued to graze and water their animals in the same areas their ancestors had for generations. Unfortunately, they returned from Bosque Redondo very late in the planting season and had to struggle through a difficult winter after their incarceration. They also returned to find unwelcome newcomers in the San Juan: white settlers had squatted on their ancestral lands and stolen their farms, waterways, and structures (Bailey and Bailey 1982).

Navajo and Ute Relations

Whites flooded the area during the Colorado gold rush and began mining indiscriminately in the mountains north of Durango. The Coloradans
forced the Utes further south into the San Juan Valley, creating more conflict between the tribes. In the 1870s white prospectors were eager to squat
on Navajo land and camped throughout the area without restriction or
respect for Indian rights (Bailey and Bailey 1982). Navajo and Ute relations
were often contentious, yet at the same time some bands and Ute families
were friendly to Navajos, trading among each other. Some Ute bands had
occupied the San Juan Valley during the Navajo incarceration at Bosque
Redondo, and traditionally much of the valley was shared between the two
nations. But some Utes were involved in the capture of Navajos during the
Long Walk period, and they had targeted Navajos for the slave trade for generations (Acrey 1988a). These Utes did not necessarily represent the entire
Ute Nation, but their actions created resentment among the Navajos, especially those families who lost members to the trade.

Navajos who had previously farmed the area returned and made conces-
sions of peace offering parcels of land to the Utes. But reports from Indian
Agents and surveyors reported that the San Juan Valley was unoccupied.
Presumably, both the Navajos and the Utes were wary of agents and surveyors. Agent Hatch reported a Navajo sheep camp along the Animas River,
but others made conflicting reports shortly before the land was taken by the
United States and opened for white settlement. Indian agents and surveyors
agreed that the San Juan Valley was prime farmland, and they wanted it for
their own (Bailey and Bailey 1982).

Despite the Ute occupation of traditional Navajo land, some Navajo
families continued to farm along the La Plata River next to Ute camps. As
Indigenous people, they were able to share the land peacefully, and the area
became known as "Indian Farms": "(on) the San Juan the Navajos are indus-
trious farmers, corn being the main product. . . . The corn tassels were of
the height of a rider's head upon horseback" (Ruffner in Bailey and Bailey
1982). Ute and Navajo relations remained strained throughout this period,
primarily because of the dispute over lands and resentment over the slave
trade. In 1878 Fort Lewis was established nearby in Colorado, and the Utes

were removed from Navajo lands and confined to a reservation (75). With the establishment of Fort Lewis, Navajo conflict with the Utes ended, and the two groups remained amicable. Today there is a peace between the two nations, and both have worked to combat hate crimes in modern times.

Navajo Territory and White Settlers

Portions of the San Juan Valley was allocated to the Jicarilla Apache Indians in a presidential executive order in 1874, but in 1876 the United States took it back and opened it to white settlement (Bailey and Bailey 1982, 75). When the Navajos returned from the Long Walk, they found white settlers squatting and eagerly eyeing their prized San Juan Valley and rich farmland. Because the San Juan Valley had been opened up as public domain, settlers were allowed to stake land claims. White settlers flooded into the area. Obviously, this resulted in another conflict between the Navajos and the white settlers over land and resources. White American settlers also expanded their herds and their livestock and overgrazed the once pristine and lush area (76). By 1876 settlers had stolen areas along both the La Plata and the Animas Rivers. There was hardly any available land left near the rivers; "public" lands became private lands, while the Navajos were cut out of any dealings (Bailey and Bailey 1982).

In 1875 William Sutherland of Colorado filed the first land claim in the area, for 160 acres northwest of present-day Farmington. His was the first white settler home built in Farmington near the San Juan and Animas Rivers. On November 13, 1876, the first homestead was filed (Daily Times 2009). By 1878 at least three hundred white families resided in the San Juan Basin, which spans Colorado and New Mexico. Farmington was the largest settler town, with at least sixty families residing within the town itself. Smaller communities sprang up, such as Bloomfield, Aztec, Jewett, Fruitland, and Olio. The city of Farmington was established after this period. In 1881 around 1,000 to 1,200 whites were living in the area in and around Farmington (Bailey and Bailey 1982, 76). And by 1890 there were at least 1,889 whites living in San Juan County (Bailey and Bailey 1982). This settler colonialism obviously had a direct impact on the lives and livelihoods of the Navajos.

The Navajos had used the San Juan River and farmed the Farmington region for generations. They could not fathom the seemingly endless numbers of whites infesting their homelands. The whites, on the other hand, viewed the Indians as a nuisance, less than human peoples without any rights or claims to the land. Some, however, knew that the Indians were in fact the rightful owners of the land. This settler account from Jose Valdez explains first encounters: "Shortly after we arrived the Indians began to bother the people to get out, that this was their land. In order to get on friendly terms with the Indians, the new settlers butchered a beef and divided it with the Indians and that seemed to pacify them for a while" (in Furman 1977). Settler William McRae did not dispute the Navajo land claims, either: "We, the early settlers, found the Navajos in possession of the valley. They camped along the river bottoms with their sheep in summer, and moved back to the hills in the winter. We had no trouble with the owners of the sheep herds, but had considerable bother with roaming bands of young bucks, who were dubbed 'coyotes.' They would steal anything they could load on a pony that they could make any use of" (66).

Farmington residents grew increasingly upset that Navajos continued to water and graze animals on the north side of the San Juan River, something they had done long before the arrival of white settlers. In 1880 Farmington residents passed a resolution to "remove Navajo herds from all off-reservation areas north of the San Juan and along the Animas." Four days later, an armed group of twelve Anglo-Americans drove the Navajo herds and herders from their winter camps in this area (Bailey and Bailey 1982, 85). Settlers also met after this to discuss driving out the rest of the Navajos in the San Juan area, though this never came to fruition. Such policies reveal the same Indian-hating ideology as expressed in violent conflicts, all motivated by the taking of Navajo land and resources.

Rumors of Indian scares spread easily throughout white settlements during this period. However, none of the rumored scares have been corroborated, as they were merely fantasy, part of the age-old colonial narrative of "savage" Indians. In November of 1880, rumors of a Navajo uprising escalated among the white settlers, who made a report to Fort Lewis, the nearest American fort, from which soldiers often quelled uprisings, that "between 500 and 700 Navajo warriors had gathered below the Hogback and that they were preparing for war" (Bailey and Bailey 1982, 85; Furman 1977, 107, 59). White settlers organized, and though only a few blatantly stated that they "were in favor of killing any Navajos who did not immediately remove their herds from the valley," most agreed with that sentiment (Bailey and Bailey 1982, 85). The goal then, as it has always been with white settlers, was to maintain boundaries and eventually to push for the removal of Navajos out of their traditional territory.

Other settler accounts discuss other less volatile encounters and misunderstandings between Indians and whites. The settlers were quick to refer to anything as "Indian troubles" and scares, knowing the Indians would be met with full force no matter how large or small the complaint. For example, white settlers resorted to violence about minor land and water disputes that likely could have been resolved peaceably: "A somewhat noted character, Cositano by name, had a bunch of sheep and goats which he brought to water each day at the river on Mr. horn's place, but Mr. Horn so seriously objected to this, that in order to settle the matter for all future generations, thought to scare Cositano away with a gun. He pulled his gun on Costi, but not quicker done, than the wiry little Navajo grappled with him in the scuffle, took the gun away from Horn, and struck him a lick or two with his quirt" (Furman 1977, 64).

Locke describes that the Navajo Cositano was the victor in this fight and even returned the gun to Horn. But Horn, with a hurt ego from being defeated by an Indian, took the matter to the soldiers, knowing they would employ as much military force as possible: "To show how little a thing it takes to create an Indian scare, I would say that on the strength of this occurrence, Mr. Horn with a flaming petition in his possession, setting forth in glowing terms, the bloody encounter and recounting many other bloody occurrences of like nature, proceeded to the fort to engage the minions of Uncle Sam, to at once annihilate the remaining few of our noble red men" (Furman 1977, 64). Settler McRae also writes of the circulation of the petition to have the Navajos moved from public domain land and back to the reservation (66). This method of using higher authorities to attempt to inflict the most violent responses to Indians had become common practice and remains part of the arsenal of discriminatory behavior against Indians, rarely against whites.

Throughout 1868–80, the Navajos and white settlers continued their conflicts over land and resources. Although Navajo families and communities had maintained a consistent presence and use of the San Juan and La Plata

Rivers, these areas were not designated as reservation lands. Indian agents noticed that the Navajos had limited access to water, reporting, "with the exception of one or two little springs, the Navajos have no water except at the San Juan River" (Atkins in Bailey and Bailey 1982, 81). White settlers farmed along the south San Juan River, but when they came into the San Juan area, they "attempted to drive Navajo from their fields and deny their herds access to the river" (Bailey and Bailey 1982).

By 1880, after Navajo lobbying efforts, the reservation had been expanded by executive order, and the white farmers on the south San Juan River were forced to vacate the land. The ensuing series of executive orders ignited more conflict between Navajos and whites. The reservation was extended to the east, based on advice from the commissioner of Indian Affairs. The white settlers protested, and conflict arose again, primarily instigated by Mormon settlers who were opposed to the expansion. The Mormons held meetings to try to remove the Navajos from the area (Bailey and Bailey 1982) and resorted to threats of violence.

In 1878 in Colorado, the Meeker Massacre took place when a fight erupted between Utes and whites on the White River Ute Agency. Nathan Meeker, an Indian agent, had implemented policies that affected Ute culture and prohibited ceremonial practices. A group of Utes attacked the agency, killing twenty-one whites; thirty Utes died in the clash (Bailey and Bailey 1982). This incident was used as an excuse to ignore the Ute Treaty of 1868 and aboriginal territory, and as a result most of western Colorado was opened up for white settlement.

Before the reservation period, Navajos and Utes had sporadic amicable relations, primarily deterred by the increase in the slave trade (Bailey and Bailey 1982, 63). Narbona, a leader among the Navajo, spent winters among the Utes (Bailey and Bailey 1982), showing that Navajo-Ute relations were complicated, sometimes friendly and other times contentious. But they were both Indian nations, and in the eyes of whites, both were threats.

White settlers in San Juan County became nervous as a result of the Meeker Massacre and thought that the Navajos were plotting an uprising to wage war on the whites in Farmington. Farmington settler William Locke described "Indian scares" as being a large part of life in pioneer times.

During the summer of 1879 we had an occasional Indian scare, but nothing of a serious nature. This was the season of the Meeker Massacre, and many predicted that it would result in a general uprising of the Indians. In 1881 on the 24th of January, we had a genuine scare. Some drunken rowdies tantalized an Indian until he got angry, then shot him, after stealing his lariat. The shooting was done just in front of what is now the Farmington Times office. The Indians rallied on the 28th of January, and about fifty of them, painted and equipped for war, surrounded the town, while about three hundred more were stationed in the bend of the river near the mouth of the La Plata, ready to come if the fight came on. (Furman 1977)

In another incident, a "cowboy" shot and wounded a Navajo in downtown Farmington. Thirty-six Navajos entered Farmington and demanded justice. The Navajos asked for troops to come into Farmington because there was no law enforcement in the area. A few months later, troops arrived from Fort Lewis to handle the situation, but the "cowboys" involved in the shooting had already fled. During this period, the Navajos were not well equipped with arms, as it was illegal for anyone to sell guns to Navajos and for Navajos to possess them. Settlers were frightened of Indian violence, but the majority of the time their fear was unfounded because they outnumbered and outgunned the Natives and were more often the aggressors themselves, either directly or by calling upon the U.S. military to comfort their paranoia (Bailey and Bailey 1982). The whites lived in constant fear and were quick to resort to violence.

In another alleged "Indian" incident during this period, a Navajo was accused of burning down a house belonging to the Porter Mining Company in 1881. The settlers wrote letters to Fort Lewis that exaggerated the incident and requested that a military post be built near the San Juan River. The settlers successfully petitioned the United States to relocate the Navajos to the reservation. Camp Roy was thus established in 1882 on the La Plata River. During this time there were Navajos living on south side of the San Juan River (Bailey and Bailey 1982, 88). The Navajos who had occupied off-reservation areas were told to vacate immediately. Numerous families suffered loss because a single white settler lost property to a likely accidental fire.

Being the original inhabitants of a large area of land, the Navajos of this time likely thought of reservation life and the concept of imaginary boundaries with contempt. Nonetheless, Navajos frequently were found "off the reservation" when they were merely doing as they and their ancestors had done since time immemorial, traveling their homelands. When caught by white officials, they insisted that they were unaware of the new reservation boundaries—understandable, considering that the Navajos had occupied, grazed, and farmed a much larger area for generations. Agent Denis Matthew Riordan advocated on behalf of the Navajos and wrote to the commissioner of Indian Affairs about the situation, arguing that the Navajos had occupied the area "since time immemorial" and should be able to graze their animals on public land, as white settlers did (Bailey and Bailey 1982, 90).

Confusing the situation even more, the Executive Order of 1880, which had previously extended the reservation boundaries to include the south side of the San Juan River, was rescinded. An executive order in 1884 restored the land to public domain: "It is hereby ordered that the Executive order dated January 6, 1880, adding certain lands to the Navajo Reservation, in New Mexico and Arizona Territories, be, and the same is hereby, amended to as to exempt from its operation and exclude from said reservation all those portions of townships 29 north, ranges 14, 15, and 16 west of the New Mexico principal meridian, south of the San Juan River, in the Territory of New Mexico" (Bailey and Bailey 1982).

Disputes raged between Navajos and white settlers during the 1870s and through the early twentieth century. One of the most serious conflicts occurred in 1889. A Navajo man, Chischilli, was hunting deer with his family in San Juan County. Accounts of this altercation vary, but John Cox, a white settler, stole a blanket from Chischilli's camp. Chischilli pursued Cox and his companions and requested that the blanket be returned. One of Chischilli's companions accidentally discharged a rifle, and Cox's group killed Chischilli. Other accounts report that Chischilli fired first. Whatever happened, troops were once again sent to the San Juan Valley to subdue the "upset Navajos." Again, white settlers claimed they were the victims and that they were afraid of Navajo retaliation, even though Cox had murdered Chischilli. John Cox was arrested after a long period, but his case was dismissed, and justice was not served in his murder of Chischilli (Bailey and Bailey 1982).

One serious armed conflict between whites and Navajos occurred in April of 1893 at Hogback, on the eastern border of the Navajo reservation. Mr. Welch, a white employee of Hogback Trading Post argued with a Navajo, and the Navajo man shot him. A rumor circulated that one thousand Navajos were gathering near Hogback, preparing to attack (Bailey and Bailey 1982, 187), and troops were sent from Fort Wingate to quell the situation. The Navajo who killed Welch was arrested and handed over by the Navajos (188). It appears that most of the panic among the settlers was only paranoia. When Major Refferty arrived on the scene everything was peaceful: "I do not believe that at any time the Indians intended any attack upon the settlers unless they themselves were attacked" (188). The whites were once again reassured by their potential to inflict worse violence against Indians.

The Last "Indian War"

The Shiprock Agency was opened in 1903 because the Navajos in the northern regions were considered too far from Fort Defiance. The last reported incident involving Navajos and American troops occurred near Beautiful Mountain, thirty-five miles southwest of Shiprock Agency. Superintendent William T. Shelton banned plural marriage among the Navajos. A Navajo man was accused of having three wives, despite the new law, and Agent Shelton demanded that the family be brought in to the Shiprock Agency. The agents were unable to find the husband, so the three wives were taken into custody. Bijoshi, the reported elderly leader of this family, was incensed about the imprisonment of his daughters-in-law and led a group of Navajo men to the Shiprock Agency to free them. Shelton wanted to make an example of the group and issued warrants for their arrest, charging them with "riot, horse-stealing, deadly assault, stealing a government revolver, and flourishing arms in a settlement." Bijoshi and family then camped up in Beautiful Mountain to avoid arrest, and Shelton formed "a citizens posse in Farmington and Aztec" (McNitt 1990, 349), pursuing the Indians.

Several months of negotiations and discussions followed, but the Bijoshi party would not turn themselves in. The standoff also drew much attention in national and local newspapers, which significantly misconstrued the events. Franc Newcomb, the wife of an Indian trader, recalled the events:

> No wonder every newspaper in the country carried a front-page article broadcasting such comments as "the Navajos were never subdued by the whites?" and "the only uncivilized tribe of Indians in the United States goes on the warpath!" Few people who read the newspapers knew who the Navajos were or where they were located but they could imagine painted Indians on horseback, waving tomahawks and chasing white women and children. I wonder if they ever knew how far from actuality this was. It was really not much of a rebellion as we have come to think of Indian revolts and uprisings, as the only Navajos concerned were one elderly Navajo patriarch, his four sons and their seven or eight wives. . . . The affair was noteworthy in American history because it was the last time in this nation that a large force of soldiers were sent out against any Indian tribe. (in Newcomb 1966, 28)

Volunteers were sent from Farmington and Aztec to join the army troops in case the standoff turned violent. Superintendent Shelton called in troops from Fort Robinson, Nebraska. The standoff was obviously blown out of proportion but was mediated peacefully by Chee Dodge, respected Navajo leader, and Father Anselm Weber, a priest from Fort Defiance. The siege on Bijoshi and family ended peacefully with a trial in Santa Fe. They served one month in jail (Newcomb 1966). This encounter is yet another example of the paranoia and fear generated by newspapers and hearsay. Indian scares were still in the white settler imagination and perpetrated in the news media throughout the country and the San Juan Basin.

In testimony, Bijoshi explains his version of events that led up to the standoff: "One day I went to the Black Mountains. Some of my relatives had given me a pony. While I was gone a policeman from San Juan arrested some of my children and took them to San Juan. . . . When I found my family was gone I went out and rode toward San Juan. The rest of these men followed toward San Juan. We did not intend when we started to have war or have a fight" (in Iverson 2002, 124–25). He also explained that when he found his family they were starving. Bijoshi recalled that Agent Shelton had also taken small children into custody. Bijoshi felt his actions were in the best interest of his family (Iverson 2002). The incident demonstrates that the whites believed they knew what was best for American Indians and that they would take the most dramatic and forceful actions necessary to promote their self-perceived supremacy.

The last Navajo uprising wasn't really an uprising at all but a defensive maneuver on the part of Bijoshi and his family. The Navajo people, especially during this period, believed that the army could slaughter them all for the smallest of infractions. The Long Walk was still fresh in the memory of Navajo people, who held the whites to their violent actions and unpredictable behavior. Years after the Long Walk, Gus Bighorse (1990) warned,

> There will be war again someday. There won't be peace all the way. The white people were going to take the land away from us, but we fought for it and kept part of our own land. Or maybe not war. Maybe someday the white people will give you something you like that will be getting rid of you. This is an old Navajo word they always say, *baahadzid*, danger. It means you think it's harmless, but you have to be careful. Something will sting you, like a scorpion or an ant. But don't try to bother with it. Don't try to touch it. It's just the same as an enemy. It kills people. . . . Nowadays the men and the boys should be thinking about how they could survive like I survived. It must be in your thinking and in your life to be brave and to be safe.

Bighorse's advice remains relevant to modern Indian-white relations.

The history of the Navajos' relationships with each of their colonizers, particularly white Americans, makes clear where racial violence against Navajos began. After the Navajos returned from Hweeldi, white settlers undertook a determined effort to dispossess the Navajos of prime farmland, justifying these actions by Indian hating and Navajo uprisings fabricated by Farmington residents and perpetuated in newspapers.

During the period of the Indian Wars, Navajos and other American Indians were racially characterized as bloodthirsty savages, drunks, redskins, murderers, marauders, and thieves (Slotkin 1973). These racist stereotypes about Navajos took hold and ignited further conflict in Farmington. Additionally, the battle over boundaries and borders reflects the American settler position that Navajos did not have rights to the land. These attitudes remain evident, as residents and officials of Farmington and San Juan County still deny the aboriginal claim to these areas (*Daily Times*; Farmington Topix forum, October 14, 2008). Furthermore, the settlers did not want Navajos in Farmington and constantly pushed to remove Navajos from the Farmington area and back inside the Navajo reservation boundaries. This view remains prevalent in hate speech, which reflects an ongoing effort to keep Navajos within the boundaries of their reservation.

The conflict between the Diné and each colonizing entity was driven by a bitter fight for land and resources and fueled by Indian hating. The Navajo steadfastly held onto their traditional homeland in the face of mass genocide, slave trade, and violent war. Although this history is important to remember, it is still painful for the people to recollect and talk about. Reviewing the history of white and Navajo contact makes apparent that the current racial violence in Farmington is part of a much larger cycle of violence that has been ongoing for more than five hundred years. In the following chapters I further explore how this history is the root of the current bias-motivated hate crime against Navajos and Native peoples in the Four Corners.

four

"Our Indian Brothers Will Not Be Forgotten"

The Chokecherry Massacre and Navajo Activism

Among Navajo people, the most known incident of hate crime in Farmington, New Mexico, is remembered colloquially as the Chokecherry Massacre. The "massacre," a string of three murders in 1974, made Farmington infamous, and it was dubbed during this time period the "Selma, Alabama, of the Southwest." The heinous acts of torture and murder at the hands of whites drew national attention to Farmington. This period is remembered among the Navajos as a dark and tumultuous one, when the townspeople of Farmington commonly carried guns and Navajos feared for their lives. Today, the Chokecherry Massacre and related events are rarely discussed in the community, as they have been buried in the memories of those who lived through it. Most younger Navajos do not know about the murders and the resulting community efforts to seek justice through organizing and activism in 1974. The massacre and the community response should be known to all residents in the area for generations to come because knowledge and action based on that knowledge lead to justice and change.

This chapter recounts the historical events following the murders and highlights the Navajo and white communities' responses. I do not examine the murders in detail out of respect for the victims and families. Indeed, the murders have been written about with much zeal elsewhere (Barker 1992; Buchanan 2006a, 2006b; Banish, *Daily Times*, April 2004). Instead, I analyze the outcomes of these level 5 hate crimes and explore the climate of Indian hating that allowed them to occur.

In 1992 Rodney Barker published *The Broken Circle*, a salacious journalistic account of the torture and murder of the three Navajo men by white teenagers, and proudly decided to promote it in Farmington. Many Navajos perceived his presence as a shameless attempt to capitalize on a community tragedy, and his book was negatively received by many. The book detailed the murders in gruesome and shocking detail, demonstrating a severe lack of respect for the victims and their families. Barker went so far as to speculate that supernatural dealings and Navajo "witchcraft" were part of the events. In the end, he was accused of profiting off the pain of the victims, and he was told as much when he spoke at Farmington High School, when an outraged Navajo student emotionally confronted him and accused him of digging up the past and capitalizing off tragedy. *The Broken Circle* was peppered with gory details and speculated "supernatural revenge," but the journalistic account included a sharp firsthand interpretation of the riots and rare interviews that captured the events and aftermath of the Chokecherry Massacre. Barker, a white man, had the privilege to easily obtain interviews from the white residents of Farmington, documenting the raw and racist opinions of the white residents who would not have been so forthcoming with a Native journalist. He did contribute some things worthy of note, despite his careless treatment of the Navajo victims and their families.

The first time I heard of the Chokecherry Massacre was in 1992. I was fourteen years old and had spent most of my life in the Four Corners. Even at this age, I knew the racism that was pervasive, primarily in hard glares, snide remarks, and police profiling. But I hadn't yet heard of anything as shocking, gruesome, and traumatic to the Navajo community as the massacres. When I reflect to when I first heard about the Chokecherry Massacre, one word sums up my reaction: horror. I ask traditional Navajos to heed my reflection as a warning and take caution in reading this chapter.

The Chokecherry Murders

According to Navajo tradition and custom, it is disrespectful and taboo for living Navajo people to talk aloud of the deceased, especially the murdered.

As a Navajo person who follows this tradition, I do not use the full names of the victims, and I provide only a cursory summary of the savage brutality they endured in the desert outside Farmington. These crimes were heinous. They were not only hate crimes but torture, white terrorism, and Indian hating.

In April of 1974, the bodies of three Navajo men, Mr. Benally, Mr. Harvey, and Mr. Ignacio, were found in Chokecherry Canyon, a wilderness area north of Farmington, New Mexico. They had been brutally tortured, burned, stripped naked, and sexually defiled, and their heads had been crushed with rocks. Strong evidence suggested that Harvey was bound and tied to the back of a vehicle and dragged for miles before he was beaten to death (New Mexico Advisory Committee to the U.S. Commission on Civil Rights 1975). These murders were the most gruesome in Farmington's recent history.

The police concluded that Benally and Harvey were murdered by the same perpetrators at different times. Several days later, the mutilated body of Ignacio, a Navajo, was discovered, and the medical investigator determined that he had been dead for two weeks (New Mexico Advisory Committee to the U.S. Commission on Civil Rights 1975). When Benally and Harvey were identified, the police classified them as "inebriants" because a witness claimed that one of them was seen at a Farmington bar. It was rumored that all three victims were known to abuse alcohol. The assumption was that these men lived an unstable lifestyle, a judgment commonly placed on Indians in the area. Without a doubt, the unsheltered population of Farmington is predominantly Navajo and Native American. They are not homeless but migrate back and forth between the border towns and the Navajo Nation, often staying with different friends and family or camping in secluded areas. During the 1970s, unsheltered relatives frequented the west side of Farmington and often slept on the streets, which made them easy targets of racial assaults. The three victims of the massacre were likely members of this population.

Nearly ten days after the bodies were discovered, two white Farmington teenagers were identified as suspects and arrested. Matthew Clark, age fifteen, and Howard Bender, age sixteen, both attended Farmington High School. Another sixteen-year-old suspect, Delray Ballinger, was later detained in connection with one of the murders. Both Clark and Bender were charged with three counts of murder, and Ballinger was charged with one count of murder. They were held in Albuquerque, and Bender and

Ballinger underwent psychiatric testing to determine whether they would be tried as adults (*Daily Times*, June 6, 1974). Clark, the youngest of the suspects, could not be tried as an adult because he was fifteen years old.

The three perpetrators all had a history of violence against Navajos. They engaged in the common nefarious pastime referred to as "Indian rolling," assaulting drunk Navajos and Native people and stealing their money and other property. Teenagers in Farmington rolled drunk Navajos for amusement. This may not be the first time Indian rolling escalated to murder, but it is the first time Indian rolling garnered national media attention. All three perpetrators admitted they had a history of rolling Indians but denied that these crimes resulted in the death of any Navajos or Native peoples. During police interrogations, Ballinger admitted to "rolling" more than ten Navajos with at least six other youths (Barker 1992), proving that the practice was not isolated but in fact common among white boys.

Barker (1992) interviewed at least a dozen Farmington residents that had been involved in Indian rolling. One forthcoming white individual described the activity as sport:

> That was what we did on Friday and Saturday nights: Drive around looking for drunk Indians to roll. "Subs," we called em, as in subhumans. . . . They weren't hard to find, they were everywhere. Lyin' in the alleys shit-faced. . . . Lets kick some Indian ass. Maybe it don't make a whole lot of sense to other people, but it might if they grew up in Farmington or Gallup or Winslow, where this kind of thing went on all the time. And it wasn't just a few who did it. My big brother did it before me, my little one after. I remember going through my older brother's desk and finding a bunch of belt buckles . . . called em his trophy buckles. . . . It wasn't like it was even committing a crime. We did it for the kick, man. I mean, they were just Indians. (170)

This testimony reveals how Indian rolling represents the vilest of white terrorism. The perpetrator acknowledges that the violent crimes he and others perpetuated would likely go unpunished because they weren't considered criminal. It was so common that it was hailed as a family and community tradition in which white boys could even collect trophies for their violence. This perpetrator admitted that white teenagers frequently asked Navajos to purchase alcohol for them. He also described targeting Navajos walking along deserted highways, picking them up, and leaving them in Chokecherry Canyon. It was not uncommon for the violence to intensify.

The perpetrators described Indian rolling as influenced by a combination of peer pressure and what was considered normal behavior in Farmington. One proudly said, "Like Indians had a way of proving their manhood— going out and killing a buffalo or enemy or whatever. Well in Farmington, New Mexico, you weren't a man until you rolled an Indian" (Barker 1992, 173). Clearly, Indian rolling and Indian hating were traditions in Farmington that were engrained as a rite of passage in a white terrorist network.

Barker (1992) discussed the escalating violence of Indian rolling, speculating that it reached a height between 1973 and 1974, possibly because of economic envy and retaliation for a popular white student who had been killed in a car accident involving an intoxicated Navajo teenager. However, I think that these reasons are generous conjectures at best because they lack any discussion of the obvious: the dehumanization and hating of Indian people that led to the murders. All the narratives and testimony provided by whites show patterns of overt racism, a precursor to race-biased hate crimes against Navajos and Native Americans. There is no doubt that Indian rolling was an act of white superiority created by white grandfathers, employed by white fathers, and sustained by white youths. When Indians were killed during these acts of terrorism, it was widely accepted that no crime was committed. This system has all the elements of a terrorist organization, in this case one with historical roots. For the perpetrators, who may not even have known this history, their most heinous acts of violence began with their least threatening views and most accepted belief: that Navajos were simply "subhuman." This is the legacy of Indian hating.

Indian hating has been part of the settlement of the West. We have seen how throughout the colonization of the Americas, particularly in the Southwest and Four Corners, Indian hating has justified the taking of land and killing of Native peoples. The attitudes prevalent in reservation border towns differ from those in areas without large Native populations. The structure of border towns is built on systematic racism, and unlike in other regions where Native populations have been forgotten, the memory of historical conflict is recent, the crimes ongoing. Others have explained hate crimes as actions whereby whites seek to maintain a boundary, even reinforcing it with violence via hate crimes (Perry 2008). This can be true, but I further argue that Indian hating goes beyond boundary seeking because Indian hating remains even when Native peoples are confined to reservations.

Groups of young white men have been at the forefront of violence against Native peoples historically, and they remain so in the twenty-first century. Levin and McDevitt (2002) explain this as hate crimes commonly being motivated by young men in groups. "Indian rolling" becomes a mark of "manhood" for white youths continuing their forefathers' tradition of racism, Indian hating, violence, and hate crimes toward Native peoples.

The City of Farmington's Reaction

The police officers involved with the investigation into the Chokecherry murders utilized both city and county personnel. The city of Farmington praised their quick investigation and arrest of the three suspects. The assistant district attorney, Byron Caton, stated that the motive of the killings would probably never be known, that they were "senseless killings" without any provocation (*Daily Times*, May 1, 1974). An editorial in the *Daily Times* argued that the killings deeply concerned the white population of Farmington and that the Indians should not be skeptical of the justice system. The editorial claimed that the age of the perpetrators warranted precaution on the part of the media, prosecutors, and investigating officers. The editorial began what would become a long pattern of denial about racism in Farmington:

> A few persons can be expected to seize on the current case in an attempt to turn it into a racial issue. Without denying that some anti-Indian—as well as some anti-white—prejudice exists in the Four Corners area, we nonetheless feel that Farmington and San Juan County in general have proved their ability to get along with one another and to work for the benefit of all our people. . . . The overwhelming majority of Indians and non-Indians in our area reject the stereotyping of an entire group on the basis of individual behavior. With this in mind, we are confident the perpetrator or perpetrators will be brought to full justice. (Editor, *Daily Times*, May 1, 1974)

The mayor of Farmington, Marlo Webb, extended his sympathy and outrage to the family members and the Navajo Tribe. In a letter to Navajo Chairman Peter MacDonald and reprinted in the *Navajo Times*, Webb wrote, "It is incomprehensible that such an action could take place in this community that prides itself as being ever ready to open its heart and arms to those in need of a helping hand. Farmington and its citizens over the years have enjoyed an especially close relationship and friendship with the members of the Navajo Nation" (Marlo Webb, *Navajo Times*, May 9, 1974). The mayor then pledged support of the city administration in improving the city's relationship with the Navajo people: "These violent actions reemphasize the need for our mutual involvement and continuing efforts directed towards eliminating any barriers that exist between our people and solving any problems that might be keeping the Navajo people from fulfilling their rightful place as citizens of this community and of this great nation" (Marlo Webb, *Navajo Times*, May 9, 1974).

The Farmington Chamber of Commerce condemned the murders in a statement as well. In response to the murders, the mayor created a Navajo Relations Committee consisting of thirteen men; only three were Navajo. The committee consisted of white Farmington businessmen and one Black employee. Mayor Webb stated that the committee would investigate grievances from the Navajo people and make recommendations to the city. The committee also met with the newly appointed Navajo Tribal Commission on Civil Rights to arrive at "peaceful" means to resolve conflicts (*Navajo Times*, May 23, 1974). The city chose to focus on "peace keeping" and denial of racial issues in each response. This process placed the Navajo people in the same position as the whites, who were ultimately the ones who produced and harbored the racist murderers. Farmington, like most predominantly white communities, still uses this standard response to racism and hate crimes.

The Navajo Nation and Navajo People Act

The Navajos demanded justice and responded with activism. A press conference was held at the Farmington Inter-tribal Indian Center, and nearly two hundred people crammed into the small space. Most of the crowd was

Navajo. A statement by the center and the San Juan Human Rights Commission urged the city to address the harassment of Navajos by white teenagers. The statement also recommended that communication improve between the city and the Navajo people and that services such as law enforcement and social services be improved as well. The statement addressed the fact that racism was an ongoing issue in Farmington and that the murders represented a climax to that problem: "It should be made clear that calling for the death penalty for the perpetrators of the murders the basic problems of the area will not be resolved. A few young persons should not be made scapegoat sacrifices for the whole community. This is not a call for vengeance but for justice, fairness and a decent life for all" (*Navajo Times*, May 9, 1974).

During the press conference, attendees made suggestions to improve the climate of racism in Farmington by hiring "minority" teachers and implementing cultural studies programs in the schools. Wilson Skeet, the vice chairman of the Navajo Nation, stressed patience with the justice system. He had met with Mayor Webb and was assured that the maximum penalties would be given to the perpetrators and justice would be served. Skeet maintained that everyone must work together. Navajo activists such as Wilbert Tsosie also urged nonviolence. But Navajo student John Redhouse of the University of New Mexico Kiva Club stated that if justice was not served on the perpetrators, then they would "take the law into their own hands and apply it accordingly" (Mike Andrews, *Navajo Times*, May 9, 1974).

Navajo Chairman Peter MacDonald also issued a statement regarding the heinous murders: "From my discussions with authorities in San Juan County, I have been assured that justice will be done, and the perpetrators of this terrible act will receive the punishment they merit. Of course, no punishment can bring back those people whom we have lost. We do hope however that those who are responsible for this outrage will make sure this will never happen again" (Peter MacDonald, *Navajo Times*, May 9, 1974). In the following weeks, MacDonald established a five-person commission to investigate conditions in Farmington and surrounding communities. Navajo government officials and staff were appointed to this commission, which was tasked with hearing grievances of Navajo people, then reporting those grievances to either city officials or tribal officials. The newly appointed commission recommended that the U.S. Civil Rights Commission intervene regarding the issues in Farmington. Additionally, the Shiprock Chapter recommended that the Navajo Nation take a strong and aggressive stance against the violence in Farmington (*Navajo Times*, May 23, 1974).

The city leadership and many Farmington residents argued that the murders were isolated incidents perpetrated by misguided teenagers. But most Navajo people, justifiably outraged by the brutal Chokecherry murders, believed they were a culmination of Indian-hating sentiment that had persisted in Farmington for years (*Daily Times*, June 2, 1974). Unlike Peter MacDonald, many Navajos were skeptical of the justice system. Navajo activists organized and rallied. The following summer months were filled with protests and marches through downtown Farmington.

In May, shortly after the murders and in direct response to their brutality, the Coalition for Navajo Liberation (CNL) was formed. CNL leadership was composed of young, educated Navajos: Fred Johnson, Wilbert Tsosie, and John Redhouse. I interviewed Navajo leader Duane "Chili" Yazzie (Shiprock, July 25, 2012), who recounted the formation of CNL and the subsequent Navajo activism:

> I considered myself an activist even going back to the late sixties . . . when AIM [American Indian Movement] first came to town. One would tend to think that there had been other murders that occurred that didn't get the public notice that the three did. But we had a tribal council member at the time, Fred Johnson, was an activist. Between Fred and certain local other individuals—I think notably, Lucy Keeswood, Wilbert Tsosie and John Redhouse from Albuquerque. They began strategizing on what type of response we should make to what was happening in Farmington. The big plan was developed where we would do peaceful marches in Farmington. We would march and then demonstrate the mistreatment, and at the same time we would boycott. So, we did these marches . . . consecutively. At the high point of the marches, there were well over . . . two thousand people.
>
> And I was there for most of the marches—Fred would send us out to different gathering points around the region. He would have us go out there and bring caravans in. And this was happening from all points. That was great. Drums were beating, people would be yelling. . . . One young Navajo activist,

I think, said it precisely, named Norman Brown—he called those marches . . . a time of greatness for us, it was a moment of greatness. And it was. I think the frustration, the anger, that's been just held within over the generations. Perhaps even, a display of the result of the historical trauma. So, the marches were predominantly young people and traditional. Which means that the more BIA educated group and the tribal administration—the politicians—they weren't there. They had nothing to do with it. It was mostly young people and traditional grandmas and grandpas. It was a beautiful scene. From that staging point we would march either up Broadway and back down Main or we would march up to city hall. With all the signs, and of course all these people would line the streets, Native supporters, non-Native supporters and then the people who did not like what we were doing. So there would be clashes between different people. So the organizers would have us walking as security between the main body of marchers and the spectators. So we would walk spaced along the march route to try to maintain some order. So that's where I was and they put these red armbands on us. Most armbands had "AIM CNL" on them. CNL was born out of that whole effort with different Navajo activist groups. Then from Albuquerque, I think predominantly a group called Red Dawn—and they were a university group based out of UNM. And then the NAACP, AIM and the different groups that came together—was born the Coalition for Navajo Liberation, CNL.

The first of the marches took place on May 4, 1974, and was organized by the bereaved family of the victims, Navajo activists John Redhouse and Larry Anderson, and the Farmington Inter-tribal Indian Organization. Rena Benally, the widow of Benally, led the march with her son (*Daily Times*, May 5, 1974). Benally later recalled how the townspeople jeered and taunted her during the march (Barker 1992). Viewers described the march as a somber event that peacefully commemorated the slain Navajo men. There were more than 150 marchers, including several white priests and reverends. Speakers included Larry Anderson, the son of Ignacio. One marcher, Harris Arthur, said that there was a great need to investigate racism in Farmington and that it was "running rampant in this town": "What happened here today ought to start people thinking about this present attitude that brought about these incidents. I'm not just talking about the murders but the intimidations toward the Navajo. . . . I'd like to come to Farmington without having my kids followed about like they're going to steal something" (*Daily Times*, May 5, 1974).

CNL organized five marches during five consecutive weekends in Farmington. The elderly and younger Navajos were frustrated. From their perspective, there was not enough support on the part of the Navajo Nation. Additionally, during the second march, CNL read a list of requests that included bringing the U.S. Commission on Civil Rights to conduct hearings in Farmington and hiring Navajos for City of Farmington job positions (*Daily Times*, May 19, 1974).

However, Mayor Webb was not receptive to these requests, essentially backtracking his intent in his letter the Navajo Nation chairman. He also denied that Farmington had a racist attitude toward Navajos, citing the various economic development projects that Farmington whites had been involved in, such as the Navajo Irrigation Project. Webb argued that "Farmington is not a racist town," and he and the city councilmen requested that the marches cease until "such a time as solutions are arrived at" (*Navajo Times*, September 5, 1974).

During the May 18, 1974, march, Fred Johnson spoke of the mistreatment of Navajo people by the city of Farmington. Johnson and others claimed the bars and other businesses took advantage of Navajos, relying on their patronage even as they discriminated against them. Johnson also accused the *Daily Times* newspaper of being racist, a biased mouthpiece for the city's businesses. During the five weeks of the marches, protesters threatened to boycott the town and encouraged Navajos to shop in neighboring Cortez and Durango. Protesters stated that the protesting and marching would stop when Farmington ceased its racism. Protesters were labeled by townspeople as "hotheads" and "radicals," but Navajo protester Lorenzo Levaldo insisted, "We are not the outsiders. We are not tough instigators of violence. We have families here" (*Daily Times*, June 2, 1974).

Navajo activists were not surprised when Judge Frank Zinn declined to sentence sixteen-year-olds Howard Bender and Delray Ballinger as adults. The three, including Matthew Clark, were sentenced to attend a boys' school in Springer, New Mexico (Ogilvie, *Daily Times*, June 9, 1974). Three separate psychiatrists evaluated each. Clark, at fifteen years of age, was automatically given a juvenile sentence. However, both the public and prosecutor presumed

Bender and Ballinger would be prime candidates for adult sentences (Barker 1992). But two psychiatrists determined that Bender and Ballinger could be rehabilitated, even though their crimes were extremely violent and horrific in nature. When Bender, Clark, and Ballinger were tried as juveniles and sentenced to time in a youth home, the Navajo community felt that justice had not been served. One Navajo woman remarked at a public forum that the three perpetrators should have been given the death sentence. Even some members of the white Farmington community admitted that perpetrators were given slaps on the wrist (Barker 1992).

The Outcome

Fourteen years after the murders, Rodney Barker interviewed Walter Winslow, the lead psychiatrist who assembled the team that analyzed the perpetrators. When Winslow was first asked to evaluate the perpetrators in 1974, he admitted that he may not have been the best psychiatrist for the case because he was not from Farmington and not familiar with the culture. Originally from Vancouver, Winslow was based in Albuquerque, worked at the Bernalillo City Mental Health Center, and was chair of psychiatry at the University of New Mexico. However, he had only been to Farmington one time, to lecture, and had passed through three times on his way to ski in Colorado. He was hardly an expert on the cultural dynamic and racial dynamics of Farmington or any reservation border town.

Winslow was assigned to analyze Howard Bender, the sixteen-year-old reported ringleader of the murders. His interviews with Bender were not as in-depth as they might have been if he were analyzing Bender outside of the court order. In the interviews, Bender "represented the killings as an activity that everyone did that had simply gotten out of hand" (Barker 1992, 178). Winslow also told Barker that he was not privy to Bender's "deepest feelings." Winslow ended up making many inferences regarding his diagnoses, and while he suspected that Bender may have been schizophrenic, he did not include that assessment in his final report (180).

Several criteria had to be met for juveniles to be tried as adults in New Mexico during this time period. Bender and Ballinger did not meet those criteria. In his interviews with Barker, Winslow maintained that the murders were not hate crimes. Instead, Winslow contended that the atmosphere and public perception of Navajos in Farmington encouraged brutalization of Navajos and allowed the crimes to occur. He claimed that the three perpetrators did not have an "obsessive hatred" toward Navajos and that race was not the motivating factor in the crimes. Instead, he cited the community's negative attitudes toward Navajos, according to which the assault of Navajos by Indian rolling was considered acceptable. In this "environment of entitlement," he said, the community disapproved of drunken Navajos and allowed crimes against them to flourish (Barker 1992). However, Winslow's analyses of the perpetrators were not thorough, and he admitted the limitations and inferences in the interview with Barker. Evidently, Winslow was uncovering the attitudes of Indian hating that were prominent in Farmington.

The Indian hating and racism against Navajos and Native Americans in the Four Corners cannot be denied; the crimes fit any modern legal and sociological definition of hate crime. The victims were targeted because they were unsheltered and Navajo. Race was the main factor in the murders, and it is negligent to claim otherwise. I categorize these as level 5 hate crimes, the most violent. Winslow focused his assessment on the fact that the victims were targeted primarily because they were intoxicated and unsheltered, but in reality a combination of factors bred these hate crimes. First, the victims were both unsheltered and Navajo. Second, it is unlikely that they would have been targeted if they were white, but the fact that they were intoxicated made them more vulnerable. Third, the group dynamic was a large factor in the crimes. Winslow also admitted that the boys would not have acted alone.

Racial violence scholarship in the 1970s was sparse, but the most similar comparison is that to the lynching of African Americans. Much like Indian rolling, lynching was conducted by groups of white men. With lynching, victims were Black people or other members of marginalized groups who had committed some perceived transgression. Unlike with lynching however, these murderers were teenagers. Finally, at the center of the Chokecherry Massacre was the white supremacy that made Indian rolling accepted in Farmington, the same way that lynching terrorized Blacks and other marginalized groups in the southern United States.

The Navajo and Native American community were devastated by the rulings (Cella, *Daily Times*, June 1974). Many Native Americans argued that if three Navajo youths had murdered and tortured white teens, they would have not been treated with such leniency. The systemic, institutional racism in Farmington meant that the Navajo and Native American population were inadequately represented in the criminal justice system, and in the Navajo and Native view, the rulings in this case were the epitome of how the justice system targets and fails Native people.

The first five CNL marches organized were peaceful, but violence erupted during the annual Sheriff's Posse Parade. CNL had applied and was denied a permit for their sixth consecutive march, allegedly because the San Juan County Sheriff's Posse had been granted a permit instead. The sheriff's posse invited the cavalry from Fort Bliss to lead the parade, further igniting tensions because of the violent history between Navajos and the U.S. cavalry. Navajo protesters blocked the passageway of several of the cavalrymen. According to a Navajo source, a policeman was unable to get them to move and yelled "Charge!" When a Navajo protester was poked with a flagpole bearing the U.S. flag, he grabbed the pole, and chaos ensued (*Navajo Times*, June 13, 1974). Riot teams were dispatched from neighboring towns and tear gas was used to dispel the crowd of more than one hundred protesters. Thirty-one Navajos and American Indians were arrested, and one police officer was hospitalized. Initially, further parade permits were blocked by court order (Cella, *Daily Times*, June 9, 1974). However, the court upheld the rights of CNL and Navajo protesters to obtain later parade permits and conduct marches (*Daily Times*, July 14, 1974).

According to John Redhouse, the Navajos were outraged by the presence of the cavalrymen and repeatedly requested that the grand marshal remove them from the parade. The presence of the cavalry added insult to injury: they were dressed in nineteenth-century uniforms, a painful reminder of the Long Walk and other campaigns waged against the Navajo (*Navajo Times*, June 27, 1974). Redhouse (2006) recalled the events:

> Someone then yelled "charge" and several of the mounted cavalrymen charged
> toward us. Then more policemen came at us from the front and back and

began to physically attack us. I was shoved from behind by a police officer who then wrapped his handcuffs around his hand and physically threatened me. After that, we again requested to see the Grand Marshall. Several moments later the tear gas was brought out and thrown indiscriminately at the crowd of onlookers along the sidewalk. The crowd then began running in all directions.

I ran west to the intersection of Main and Behrend and across Behrend. I was then pointed out by a police officer and several men from the riot squad came running at me waving their riot sticks. I then turned and almost immediately at least two unidentified white males grabbed me and began to push me toward the plate glass window of Russell Foutz's Indian Room. I then pivoted and one or both of them hit and shattered the window. They then pushed me up against a pickup. A National Guardsman then camped a riot stick up against my neck and someone behind me put handcuffs on me. They then pushed me to a police car and threw me in. Once in the car, the police officer that was driving then turned around to us and said, "you fuckers asked for it now! I don't care who we call in, we'll kill all of you fucking Indians!" We then got to the police station and were taken into the booking section. The police officer then pointed his finger at us and said, "you're in real trouble now!" We were then taken into the holdover cell.

The Navajo protesters maintained that they did not start the violence that erupted (*Navajo Times*, June 27, 1974). Redhouse was charged with inciting a riot, but charges were later dropped. This incident culminated in the City of Farmington filing suit against him. He was later convicted of obstruction. CNL member Wilbert Tsosie and his sister Dorothy were also arrested and accused of assaulting a police officer. Dorothy Tsosie was driving the car that hit a police officer when tear gas was used to dispel the crowd. In the hearings of Dorothy Tsosie and Wilbert Tsosie, the defendants claimed that they had not intentionally hurt the police officers, and witnesses stated that an officer attacked Ms. Tsosie's car with a nightstick. Tear gas may also have confused the already-chaotic situation (*Navajo Times*, June 13, 1974; *Navajo Times*, June 27, 1974).

Rodney Barker's (1992) account corroborates Navajo witnesses' claims of police instigation before ensuing chaos and violence. Barker described how police officers ignited tear gas into the crowd of civilians and arrested Navajos who were not even participating in the protest. One Navajo arrested was in line at a food stand. Barker was arrested with other members of CNL.

After the chaos of the Sheriff's Posse Parade, Navajo and Farmington government officials met at city hall and called for the end of the marching. The tribal council did not agree with a Farmington boycott, unlike members of CNL and other concerned Navajos. The mayor also continued his denial of responsibility or accountability. He stated, "I wish we could assure you there will be no more slayings, but it is beyond my control." But it was within his control. As mayor, Webb had an obligation to address the institutional racism in Farmington and lead by example. Mayor Webb also encouraged the meeting participants to "sell" to the Navajos the idea that Farmington was not as bad as it was made out to be. He claimed that the city wanted to solve the problems, but he wanted to prevent CNL from holding any further marches (Ogilvie, *Daily Times*, June 10, 1974).

Farmington citizens believed that the marches were negatively impacting their businesses in downtown Farmington. In a meeting with Farmington business owners, former mayor William Nygren expressed hope for an end to the marching. Nygren and others claimed that CNL had attempted to desecrate the U.S. flag and blamed the group for instigating racial violence. The Farmington merchants focused on their lost revenue, ignoring the grievances of Navajos who had been treated with racial prejudice (*Daily Times*, July 12, 1974).

The Navajo Civil Rights Commission, newly formed and appointed by the Navajo Nation, heard testimony at the Farmington Indian Center. The testimony included complaints against liquor stores, mistreatment by store merchants, employer prejudice, police brutality, and the murders of the three Navajo men. Rena Benally, widow of one of the victims, testified that she did not think the sentencing of the perpetrators was fair and that the children's code that allowed the perpetrators to be sentenced as juveniles should be rewritten. "And what I really want to know," she said, "is what happened out there (at the murder scene). What was the motive for that killing?" Other testimony cited police brutality. One witness accused a police officer of pulling his gun on him and while asking, "what do you think of your red power now?" (Cella, *Daily Times*, June 14, 1974). Despite the public hearings, CNL criticized the Navajo Commission on Civil Rights for not assuming an active role in mediating the issues with Farmington.

At the urging of local groups such as CNL and the National Indian Youth Council, the New Mexico Advisory Committee to the U.S. Civil Rights Commission visited Farmington to evaluate the need for a hearing and further investigation. After meeting with Navajo and Native people, CNL, and City of Farmington leadership, the advisory committee deemed investigation necessary and returned to Farmington in September of 1974 to gather formal testimony from Navajo leadership, both government and grassroots organizations, community members, and townspeople (*Daily Times*, May 16, 1974).

The mayor's Navajo Relations Committee also held hearings to listen to grievances from Navajos. However, the mayor's actions appear to have been intended to pacify CNL and other critics of the City of Farmington. Critics pointed out that the mayor did not appoint any members of CNL, or indeed many ethnic and Navajo representatives at all, to the newly formed committee, although the city agreed to meet with CNL members to keep them informed. In a June 18 meeting, after the three juveniles were sentenced to Springer Boys' School, Mayor Webb's Navajo Relations Committee met. CNL leader Fred Johnson told the committee that CNL would file lawsuits against the liquor establishments and the city for employment practices. Johnson argued that trading posts were another area that needed investigating due to their predatory practices and discrimination. Participant testimony reiterated accusations of racist and biased news coverage by the *Daily Times* (Redhouse, *Daily Times*, July 1, 1974).

Mayor Webb accused CNL of seeking violent confrontations and referred to the outside influence of AIM. He labeled coalition leaders Johnson, Tsosie, and Redhouse as radicals and troublemakers. During a private meeting with CNL, Webb took a phone call and was baffled when the members of CNL got up and left. Wilbert Tsosie later recalled the meeting and cited Webb's disregard for them and the mayor's rude behavior. The relationship between Webb and CNL further disintegrated when Webb disbanded the Farmington Civil Rights group after a confrontation between Johnson and a city leader. Webb commented that the Navajo people should support elected leadership and committees to resolve problems (Ogilvie, *Daily Times*, June 10, 1974). Webb claimed he was fearful of Navajo retaliation and began carrying a gun. CNL referred to Webb as the "Custer of Farmington" and were open in their disgust for the mayor and his lack of action and continued denial of non-Indian racism in Farmington (Barker 1992).

Farmington's Indian Hating and the *Daily Times*

The editorial section of the *Daily Times* became a battleground. Letter writers, both white and Native American, argued back and forth for months during the summer of 1974. Using an intense literature review and a selective content analysis model, I analyzed the *Daily Times* and newspaper articles and editorials from neighboring communities during this period. I found that these periodicals adequately and accurately disclosed the depths of the systematic racism and racist attitudes toward Native people. Several themes emerge within the editorial section, including whites blaming "outside agitators" and "radicals" for conflict (such as AIM and CNL), overt and covert instances of Indian hating and racism, accusing Navajos of receiving "special privileges" in the forms of government handouts, white denial of racism, references to racist remarks about history to prove a point, and the use of racist stereotypes such as Navajos' being lazy, drunks, and thieves.

Daily Times reporters and editors frequently characterized Navajo activism as militant and out of control. Other border town newspapers also shared this viewpoint. In an editorial from the *Gallup Independent* reprinted in the *Daily Times*, the editor maintained that the Indian activists were trying to "create a racial division out of three seemingly senseless killings." According to the editorial, Navajo Nation Chairman Peter MacDonald claimed that there was no motive to the murders. The editors of the border town newspapers and especially the *Daily Times* frequently used the editorial page to chastise Navajo activists, labeling them as opportunists and accusing them of turning tragedy to benefit their cause.

Articles printed after the murders focused not on the perpetrators or even the victims but on Navajo and Native American activism and marches. The editorial section of the *Daily Times* was inundated with letters claiming that the town should gather up the members of CNL and ship them to another location. Letter writers blamed the unrest on "self-appointed leaders" of the Navajo (Elizabeth Ramsey, *Daily Times*, June 12, 1974). One called members of CNL "dissidents" and claimed that they were "stirring up trouble." He argued that the Navajo people should "silence the radicals in your communities and force them to shut up and get on the side of law and order, by the weight of numbers and common sense" (Richard Evans, *Daily Times*, June 12, 1974). Farmington townspeople also argued that the activists and CNL were not representative of "their Navajos." They characterized "their Navajos" as being misguided by CNL and peaceful or not party to the recent unrest.

The citizens of Farmington and San Juan County also took an aggressive Indian-hating stance against the Navajo outrage regarding the murders. This attitude is most visible in the editorial letters, where citizens of Farmington and surrounding communities exposed their vast ignorance. Letter writers denied racism and discrimination in Farmington and were very offended by accusations against the town and townspeople. Citizens argued that Navajos were not treated unfairly and demanded documented proof of these alleged injustices. One writer also argued that Farmington merchants had every right to suspect individuals, including Navajos, of shoplifting (Richard Evans, *Daily Times*, May 8, 1974).

Many of the letter writers used racist stereotypes to prove their arguments. They contended that Navajos were used to government handouts and wanted "special privileges" (Anne Wojtuleqicz, *Daily Times*, March 19, 1974). One writer pointed to Indian Health Service health care and falsely claimed that Navajos also did not pay state or sales tax. Racism and stereotypes shaped how the whites in Farmington and San Juan County viewed Navajo people and the Navajo Nation. One letter stated:

> For two hundred years the Spanish tried to help the Indians improve their living conditions, for the last two hundred the white man has tried to help them. Have they changed? Or improved as we see it? Not a great deal, and apparently not according to their own thinking, either. . . . We read frequently in the newspaper Congress granting huge sums of money to help them improve conditions. . . . History has proven that no man, nation or people ever became anything more than an indolent, degenerate people as long as they depended on others to support them. (Elizabeth Ramsey, *Daily Times*, June 12, 1974)

Another letter writer argued that the Navajo claim to Farmington was invalid, that the land was not stolen but had been obtained legally. This writer insisted that Navajos were Siberians and immigrants just like everyone else. He also argued that whites were not the originators of land wars and that Indian tribes warred with each other prior to European colonization (Richard Evans, *Daily Times*, June 18, 1974). Such ignorant rants and arguments are still common even today, even for the most trivial of disputes (Farmington Topix forum, October 8, 2008).

Farmington citizens claimed that violence was rampant among both races. One writer criticized Chairman Peter MacDonald's statement that such brutal violence would not happen among the Navajo people. The writer argued that Navajos were also violent and that race should not be considered an issue in the murders (Nancy Webber, *Daily Times*, May 7, 1974). Several letter writers argued that Navajos had no reason to be outraged about the murders because they were no different than the instances of Navajos being responsible for white deaths in DUI accidents. The mother of a white student killed in a DUI crash, with a Navajo teen at fault, argued that the family members of the Navajo murder victims should move past the incident and let the courts handle the crimes (Sandy Akins, *Daily Times*, May 1974).

Navajo letter writers responded to many of the allegations and misconceptions in the *Daily Times*, adamant that many Navajos experienced discrimination in Farmington daily, and that Farmington was a very racist community. The Navajo respondents tried to dispel negative stereotypes and address the racist allegations on the editorial page (P. Atcitty, *Daily Times*, May 26, 1974). The letters continued for months and incited further racial divide in Farmington. The editorial page became a zone for conflict, demonstrating the seriousness of the Indian-hating sentiment and racist relationship between whites and Navajos. The non-Indian letters show a pattern of stereotypes, racism, and white privilege. Although many of these letter writers sought to defend Farmington against its characterization as a racist town, the letters showed that racism and Indian hating were embedded in Farmington, and embedded deep.

The Chokecherry Massacre ignited national media interest. The situation also drew attention from the state and federal governments. The riot and parade appeared in the national newspapers on television. Farmington was dubbed the "Selma, Alabama, of the Southwest," and the most racist town in America. Farmington citizens decried this characterization and instead pointed blame at outside agitators such as AIM and Navajo activists (Phyllis Eeds, *Daily Times*, June 1974; Percy Tillman, *Daily Times*, 1974). Sadly, during this time, the horrific murders of the three Navajo men became lost amid the hostility toward Native American activism.

The *Farmington Report*

The Investigation

From August 28 to 30, 1974, the New Mexico Advisory Committee to the U.S. Commission on Civil Rights held hearings in Farmington to investigate violations of civil rights of Navajo and Native people. The committee gathered individual testimonies from Navajo tribal leaders, CNL leaders, and Farmington representatives to assess the white community's attitudes toward Navajos and Native Americans. The committee also identified topics of concern within the testimonies and found discrimination in the following areas: administration of justice, health care, employment, alcohol, and community responsiveness toward Navajos.

Much of the testimony was riveting, describing allegations of police brutality in Farmington and discrimination and racism in the town. A trading post employee claimed that Navajos were taken advantage of and cheated in trading posts. Others spoke of discrimination and harassment in Farmington businesses: "We are looked upon as dogs. We want to be able to walk the streets of Farmington and receive service—like anyone else" (*Navajo Times*, September 5, 1974). Other testimony encouraged the creation of an alcohol detoxification center to address the alcohol abuse problem.

Not surprisingly, Mayor Webb maintained the status quo of white supremacy and denied any pervasive racism in Farmington. During his testimony, he said Farmington was wrongly blamed for the murders and that "there may be prejudiced Anglos, just as there are prejudiced Navajos" (Barker 1992). He thought the results of the hearings were predetermined and that the New Mexico Advisory Committee on Civil Rights would be swayed by the testimony, though he himself was not moved at all. Instead, he insisted that the testimony was unfounded, and that the committee should require proof of racism and mistreatment. He accused the advisory committee of being biased and influenced by preconceived notions, insisting that Farmington's relationship with Navajos was not based on prejudice or mistreatment (Barker 1992).

The Report

The findings and recommendations of the committee were compiled into *The Farmington Report: A Conflict of Cultures* (1975) and included a detailed and fair history of the investigation. The report focused on administration of justice, community attitudes and responses, alcohol abuse and alcoholism, health and health-care access, economics, economic development, and employment and detailed some of the interviews and testimony collected both individually and during the three days of hearings. It also addressed the Navajo critique of institutional racism within the justice system, especially in relation to the murder trials of the three accused. The report found that under the juvenile code the two sixteen-year-old perpetrators would be bound to adult court only if a psychiatrist had deemed them unable to be rehabilitated. There was no discussion of Winslow's inconsistent evaluation or critique of his inexperience with Native populations and reservation border towns.

Findings and Recommendations on Discrimination

The committee found that Farmington city leaders failed to adequately understand their relationship with Navajos. It recommended that the city create human relations community representative positions for all ethnic groups, as well as a center promoting Navajo culture. The report recommended that Farmington public schools be required to implement a cultural awareness curriculum. Further, according to the report, there was no "mechanism available in Farmington to investigate and process complaints alleging discrimination," so the committee recommended that Farmington create an anti-discrimination ordinance that allotted resources to investigating allegations and issuing sanctions. The human relations committee, whose role should be clearly defined in the ordinance, would be given the authority to investigate complaints. The committee also found that the city had failed to investigate or act on the allegations made during the public hearing and recommended that Farmington create a human resources department under the mayor that would be responsible for "conducting and creating an assessment of present and future needs" in collaboration with other agencies (New Mexico Advisory Committee to the U.S. Commission on Civil Rights 1975).

Despite testimony that called Webb the "Custer of Farmington," the report did not critique Mayor Marlo Webb in any way. Still, its recommendations would not be taken seriously or implemented under his leadership. Webb's denial of racism in Farmington was a main factor of the problem. His inaction and racist attitude, which set the tone for the city, allowed white supremacy and racism to fester in Farmington, fostering an environment in which Navajos were being physically assaulted.

Most importantly, under the recommendations for improving discrimination, the New Mexico Advisory Committee to the U.S. Commission on Civil Rights failed to address the most important issue at hand: the lives of Navajos and Native people in Farmington were under threat. The committee failed to recommend any protections for Navajos and Native people who were unsheltered or vulnerable to attack by white teens or a change in the laws that prevented juveniles from being tried as adults. Yes, the recommendations were reasonable, but they also ignored the most urgent problem. Without any serious intervention, Navajos and Native people were not safe in Farmington.

Findings and Recommendations on Policing

Only three out of seventy-four police officers in Farmington were Navajo. The report recommended that the chief of police create an affirmative action plan in order to increase Native Americans and minorities on the police force and carefully screen applicants for cultural bias against Navajos. "Upgrading" budget and staff of the current, ineffective community relations committee, the report argued, would improve communication between the community and the police. The report recommended that the chief of police develop long-term goals to improve the relationship between the police and Navajos. Finally, the committee advised that the Navajos and minority populations should have input into a cultural awareness training program, which the current system had not implemented.

Again, these recommendations would have been useful had they been implemented. In the years after the report, the Farmington police were consistently accused of racist and discriminatory practices. Although the police force was diversified a bit, it failed to include adequate training or to improve with respect to racially profiling Navajos and Native Americans. The issue of policing is discussed further in the next chapters.

Findings and Recommendations on Substance Abuse

The committee found that there were no substance abuse treatment facilities in the Farmington area or on the Navajo Nation, despite the large number of alcohol-related arrests and incidents. Recommendations in this area included creating a joint task force appointed by the governor and the Navajo Nation to study the extent of the alcohol problem. Testimony claimed that Navajos had been denied care at San Juan Regional in Farmington, so the commission recommended that San Juan Regional Hospital create a policy for treating Navajos and American Indians and investigate the claims of refusal of treatment (New Mexico Advisory Committee to the U.S. Commission on Civil Rights 1975). This was one of the only recommendations that was implemented to some degree: a detox and treatment facility was later opened in Farmington. However, the accusations of discrimination regarding San Juan Regional Hospital remained.

Disappointingly, the report made no correlation between the issue of alcohol abuse and Indian rolling assaults against Navajos. All the Chokecherry Massacre victims had been intoxicated and some were considered by modern standards "unsheltered." Recommendations should have included a plan to build a shelter to house this population and protect them from white assaults and terrorism.

Findings and Recommendations on Employment

Most Navajos who worked in Farmington were employed in labor jobs. The committee recommended that the Equal Employment Opportunity Commission investigate private employers to uncover any discrimination and create an employee development department (New Mexico Advisory Committee to the U.S. Commission on Civil Rights 1975). The report concluded that Navajos were "in almost every phase of life . . . basically unequal" because of the discrimination and enormous economic disadvantage. Further, "the relationship is one of dominance and very little cooperation on the part of the predominantly Anglo community of Farmington towards Navajos instead of mutual understanding." The committee recommended discussions between city leaders and Navajo officials to address economic development, as well as the creation of a consumer protection department to address grievances against businesses.

Many of the recommendations in *The Farmington Report: A Conflict of Cultures* (1975) were fair, and if they had been fully implemented, they might have improved race relations and civil rights in Farmington. However, few of these recommendations were ever executed. Though the report mentioned the murders in its introduction, it did not recommend any interventions at Farmington High School to prevent Indian rolling or more patrolling of the west side of Farmington to protect unsheltered Navajos and Native people from racist violence. Like a sordid family secret, this time period is only whispered about. Unlike other instances of racial violence, such as the lynching of Emmett Till, which became a catalyst for a movement, the Chokecherry Massacre largely disappeared, relegated to folklore and rumor. Instead, Farmington wanted to quickly repair its image. Farmington's answer to the Chokecherry murders and its aftermath was to forget it ever happened.

After the *Farmington Report* (1975) Navajo activists continued efforts to improve conditions at the Fairchild Factory in Shiprock and advocate against natural resource development. Navajos' response to Navajo activism was mixed. Some agreed with CNL's methods, but others thought their assertiveness was counterproductive. In the following years, several members of CNL ran for Navajo public office. Fred Johnson was elected to the Navajo Tribal Council but died in a plane crash in 1975. CNL member Duane "Chili" Yazzie also served as Shiprock Chapter president and tribal council member and was later instrumental in creating the Navajo Nation Human Rights Commission.

Unfortunately, Rodney Barker chose to focus on salacious myths of "witch-craft" and supernatural Navajo justice in his 1992 account of the Chokecherry Massacre. Howard Bender was struck and killed by a car while jogging in Texas two years after his release from the Springer Boys' School. When Barker interviewed both Delray Ballinger and Matthew Clark, they admitted they were aware of an alleged curse or so-called Navajo witchery. Neither returned to Farmington after being released from Springer Boys' School. Ballinger and Clark offered no remorse, only excuses and embarrassment for the murders they committed (Barker 1992). They refused to participate in the *Daily Times*'s series on the Chokecherry Massacre in 2004.

Navajo and non-Native retort to *The Broken Circle* was varied. Many Farmington residents did not want Barker to shed light on the 1974 murders. Some Navajos argued that Barker was profiting off the pain of the families, but Navajo activist Wilbert Tsosie and widow Rena Benally were Barker's primary informants. In 2010 independent film producers obtained funding to turn *The Broken Circle* into a film. Twenty members of the three victims' families gathered for a meeting with producers, upset at the prospect of a film and disturbed that Barker's book had both documented the murder of their relatives and portrayed them inaccurately. They were justifiably concerned that a film would propagate the same inaccuracies (A. Landry, *Daily Times*, May 29, 2010). As of this writing, no news of the film has surfaced; presumably the project fizzled out after the families voiced objections.

In the years after the Chokecherry Massacre, race relations may appear to have improved in Farmington. Absent were national headlines announcing the murder of Navajos and likening Farmington to the Deep South. But racial intolerance continued to be the norm in Farmington. During the 1993 hantavirus outbreak, Navajos were cruelly discriminated against, and the news media labeled the illness a Navajo disease (Alvord and Van Pelt 1999). Although public service announcements encouraged businesses not to discriminate against Navajos, some restaurants refused to serve Navajos, and colleges and universities issued statements that they were concerned with Navajo students returning from summer break and spreading the disease (Valenti 1995).

The Navajo Nation's reaction to the Chokecherry Massacre, the Navajo Civil Rights Committee, became inactive in later years, as did the City of

Farmington's civil rights committee. In 2005 the New Mexico Commission on Civil Rights returned to Farmington to assess civil rights issues and
found that the city had never created a forum to hear complaints. To the
city, improving race relations was not a top priority. In the years after the
Chokecherry Massacre, city leadership made some effort to communicate
and work more with local Navajo chapters and Navajo officials. But in 1998
and through 2007, Navajo murders in Farmington would once again make
national headlines.

"Our Fight Has Just Begun," sign at Navajo protest march, 1974. Bob Fitch Photography Archive, Department of Special Collections, Stanford University Libraries.

Navajo matriarchs lead the Navajo protest march through Main Street in Farmington. Bob Fitch Photography Archive, Department of Special Collections, Stanford University Libraries.

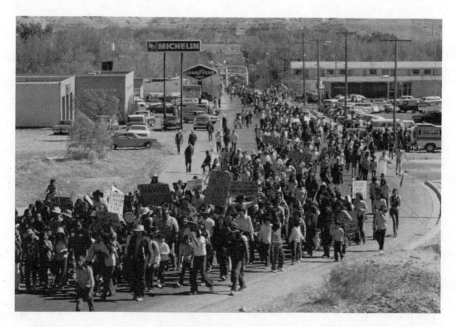

Navajo protest march travels along Broadway in Farmington. Bob Fitch Photography Archive, Department of Special Collections, Stanford University Libraries.

Children lead Navajo protest march with "March for Liberation" banner. Bob Fitch Photography Archive, Department of Special Collections, Stanford University Libraries.

Navajo protest march. Bob Fitch Photography Archive, Department of Special Collections, Stanford University Libraries.

Navajo matriarch attends the Navajo protest march. Bob Fitch Photography Archive, Department of Special Collections, Stanford University Libraries.

Children lead Navajo protest march. Bob Fitch Photography Archive, Department of Special Collections, Stanford University Libraries.

Police officers with helmets and batons stand by. Bob Fitch Photography Archive, Department of Special Collections, Stanford University Libraries.

Coalition for Navajo Liberation member Larry Anderson speaks in front of crowd at the protest march. Bob Fitch Photography Archive, Department of Special Collections, Stanford University Libraries.

Fred Johnson speaks with police regarding permit. Bob Fitch Photography Archive, Department of Special Collections, Stanford University Libraries.

Coalition for Navajo Liberation members prior to police violence. Farmington Museum, Daily Times Collection, 2010.20.80.

Violence ensued after the Sherriff's Posse Parade. Farmington Museum, Daily Times Collection, 2010.20.78.

Protester clashes with police after the Sheriff's Posse Parade. Farmington Museum, Daily Times Collection, 1982.14.2d.

On September 2, 2016, Manuel Heart (*center*), chairman of the Ute Mountain Ute Tribe, at a memorial march near Farmington, for victims of racial violence. Craig Robinson/*The New York Times*/Redux.

five

"They See Navajos as Animals"

Indian Rolling in Farmington

Racial violence has been ongoing in the United States for hundreds of years, but the term *hate crime* did not develop until the 1980s, when journalists and sociologists popularized it to describe hate-based incidents of violence. Since the 1920s, the FBI had been investigating the Ku Klux Klan's lynchings of African Americans and other crimes against marginalized groups and people of color. Lynching and hate crimes are both classified as "racial violence" (fbi.gov). During the turmoil of the Chokecherry Massacre, the crimes were not discussed within the framework of hate crime because that terminology had not yet been conceptualized. Navajos and civil rights investigators realized there was a racial context to the killings, but labeling them hate crime has remained controversial, as evidenced in Rodney Barker's (1992) interviews with the lead psychiatrist who evaluated the perpetrators, Walter Winslow.

As we have seen, hate crime against Native Americans is an extension of Indian hating, white supremacy, and white terrorism. This chapter examines these concepts in the context of level 4 and level 5 hate crimes, particularly Indian rolling, perpetrated in Farmington and the Four Corners since 1974.

Based on my findings, the two main demographics of Indian rolling victims are Native American males who are considered unsheltered relatives, meaning that they may be residing on the streets. Furthermore, I draw two significant conclusions: first, the perpetrators were young white males, and second, the crimes were likely condoned, meaning the white Farmington community chose to ignore them because of its racist systems and attitudes toward Navajos, Native Americans in general, and unsheltered relatives.

Hate Crimes after 1974

To the American public, it appeared that hate crimes and racial violence abated in Farmington after the Chokecherry Massacre in 1974. However, racism in Farmington remained just as prevalent as before, though it was often described as being more subtle or concealed (New Mexico Advisory Committee to the U.S. Commission on Civil Rights 2005). Writers and citizens continued to discuss the topic of racism and racial violence against Navajos sporadically in the *Daily Times*. Barker's 1992 recount of the Chokecherry murders also reopened old wounds. Twenty years after the Chokecherry murders, Navajos in the area continued to experience violence, including brutal assaults and murders, perpetrated by whites. Natives always mistrusted Farmington's attitude toward Navajos, but the persisting violence placed that culture under public scrutiny at the national level once again.

The Prevalence of Indian Rolling

Violence against Navajos and Native people remained rampant in the Four Corners after 1974 but was largely ignored by those outside the region. In my estimation, the invisibility of this violence is not because hate crime and Indian rolling was not occurring but because these types of hate crime were not being reported or analyzed as racial violence. The Native American newspaper *Akwesasne Notes* mentions several suspicious murders in the Four Corners after 1974, but they do not appear to be related to Indian rolling. Three violent assaults demonstrate violence perpetrated by whites against Native Americans occurred between 1978 and 1995. For instance, in 1978 Duane "Chili" Yazzie was shot by a white hitchhiker. The perpetrator served less than five years. In 1988 Navajo teenager M. Wilson was stabbed and killed in a "satanic" killing by a white teen and Hispanic youth. In 1995 two young Ute women were shot and robbed by white youths, targeted for their per capita payment from their nation (Bennett 2018). Newspapers reported several Navajo and Native American homicides perpetrated by white youths, but it remains unclear whether these were Indian rolling. It was not until the 1990s that distinct cases of Indian rolling reemerged in Farmington (Donaldson 2006).

The accounts in this chapter provide a chronological history and basis for analyzing the hate crimes committed in Farmington and the Four Corners region after 1974. Data from this time period was often challenging to obtain, but news sources proved to be valuable and provided the most data. In some cases, I relied on my memory of certain incidents and verified these accounts using newspaper archives. Throughout the years, I have heard accounts from friends and family members who were assaulted or knew of someone assaulted in Farmington. The vast majority of these have gone unreported, for reasons discussed further in the next chapter.

After the Chokecherry Massacre

One night in 1992 Hjay Wright, eighteen years old, and Terry Lynn Pearson, twenty-one, assaulted two Navajo men. When they were caught by police, they admitted to assaulting a third person. They beat their victims with a nightstick and metal bar, inflicting severe head injuries. Wright and Pearson were charged with three counts of aggravated battery, and both pled guilty to the charges. Pearson was the son of a magistrate judge, and two judges recused themselves from the sentencing.

I categorize the beatings perpetrated by Wright and Pearson as level 4 hate crimes. The violence ignited justifiable outrage by the Navajo community, especially when, a few months later, another Navajo man was beaten in a separate incident by different perpetrators. On July 22, 1992, three white men beat R. Ross, a Navajo, with a baseball bat. Although fortunately Ross survived the assault, the Indian rolling would continue.

Following these violent attacks, numerous Navajo leaders began to organize to confront yet again the long-standing racism in Farmington. Dr. Larry Emerson, a former activist and writer during the 1974 Chokecherry Massacre, who at the time was on the New Mexico Commission on Indian

Affairs, stated in an interview in the *Daily Times*, "There is real hard evidence that the city of Farmington has done nothing to address the problem." "The result is children grow up with hate and anger, rather than working on their own problems. They project that anger on the Navajo people. Because of racial superiority, they see Navajos as animals and inflict harm and pain. To them it's like kicking a dog" (Brenda Norrell, *Daily Times*, July 27, 1992). Shiprock councilwoman Genevieve Jackson stated that "the people of the City of Farmington can no longer deny they have a problem. They have to acknowledge it." She further maintained, "The city officials of Farmington kept stating that the first incidences were isolated cases involving two troubled teen-agers. But we've always stated that these acts demonstrate a pattern of racism. . . . We would like to know what is the City of Farmington going to do about it?" (Brenda Norrell, *Daily Times*, July 27, 1992). Just like before, the Navajo Nation rallied against the racism and violence.

The Navajo Nation's Intergovernmental Relations Committee called for economic sanctions. "A boycott of business establishments was recommended but no legal action was taken," explained Council Delegate Genevieve Jackson. Indian rolling "seems to be a rite of passage for some Anglo teenagers. It makes you wonder what kind of values are being taught in the home." She also suggested interventions in the schools, if children were not being taught racial tolerance at home. The subject of Indian rolling was scheduled to be added to the Navajo Nation Council session.

Shortly after the assaults by Wright and Pearson, Rodney Barker's book *The Broken Circle* was published. During a book talk at San Juan College on June 4, 1992, Navajo audience members reflected that racism was still present in Farmington. Many Navajo audience members declared that nothing had changed since the Chokecherry Massacre and maintained that they faced daily discrimination. Again, excuses made by Farmington leaders were the norm. The Farmington police chief denied any pattern of wrongdoing by whites, and the violence continued later that summer.

On August 30, 1992, one Navajo and two Hispanic youths claimed they were attacked by a "crowd of bat wielding youths" at a gas station on the outskirts of Farmington. W. Kenneth recounted the events: "I went inside and when I came back out, I heard these guys calling me: 'There's a drunk Indian.' I didn't pay any attention to them. I just went and got halfway to my truck and some guy came up and hit me—people were coming from everywhere, hitting on me." Kenneth sustained injuries to his face, shoulder, and ribs, and his nose was broken; "I could feel it crack every now and then. I'm still coughing up blood." His two Hispanic friends came to his aid when they saw him attacked, and they also sustained numerous injuries, including a fractured skull and knocked-out teeth. Two perpetrators were charged with aggravated battery: white Farmington High School students Troy Pope, eighteen, and Pat Hall, seventeen (Brenda Norrell, *Daily Times*, September 11, 1992).

After the case, the *Daily Times* reported that the detectives who investigated the assault had accused the victims of not being forthcoming and cooperating with them. One detective also claimed that the assault was not racially motivated. The victims were chastised for not reporting it sooner and not showing up to make police statements on time (Roger Burr, *Daily Times*, September 11, 1992). Essentially, the detectives made it very difficult for the victims to report and pursue justice. Victims' distrust of police is a significant factor in reluctance to report hate crimes, an element of systemic racism I discuss in detail in the next chapter. In some instances, the police are accused of race-based assaults themselves, which is why they are viewed with suspicion (Bennett 2018).

The hate crimes against Navajos did not end. In 1994 sixteen-year-old Hussein Oshman killed J. Woody, a Navajo man, with a shopping cart in a Walmart parking lot. Oshman "towed a shopping cart behind his motorcycle" and flung it at Woody, who was intoxicated and asleep. Oshman claimed that he "made two passes at Woody and on the third try felt the shopping cart hit the victim" (Roger Burr, *Daily Times*, July 23, 1994). Unlike in other instances of Indian rolling, Oshman acted alone. Oshman pled guilty and was sentenced as a juvenile to two years at the boys' school in Springer (Roger Burr, *Daily Times*, July 23, 1994). Again, Farmington and the Four Corners region gained national attention. The story was featured on a CNN special focused on race relations in Farmington (*Native Americans: The Invisible People*, 1994). Farmington's legacy of Indian hating remained alive and unchecked.

On the early morning of September 3, 1997, R. Castiano, a Navajo man, was assaulted by four white youths in Farmington. Castiano and a woman companion were lying in a field in Farmington when Castiano was attacked by Blake Redding, Jordan Thompson, Theodore Richter, and Jesten Stanley (Sheri Holiman, *Daily Times*, September 19, 1997). After leaving a party in Farmington, the four white boys happened upon Castiano and his companion. Redding told the court that when they attacked Castiano, "three-quarters of it was because he was Indian." During his police interview Thompson "seemed to find the incident humorous because he laughed several times." Theodore Richter was sentenced to nine months in jail (Marley Shebala, *Navajo Times*, November 10, 1999).

In 1998 D. Armstrong, a Navajo man, was murdered by two white boys in Aztec, New Mexico, fifteen miles east of Farmington. Jason Fisher and Stephen Sanchez offered Armstrong a ride and asked him to buy them beer. The boys claimed that they were going to rob Armstrong but decided to brutally beat him as well. The boys then robbed him, taking his wallet and boots. Armstrong's body was later found in a ditch. Fisher and Sanchez were charged and convicted of murder, and both were sentenced to sixteen and a half years in prison plus funeral expenses (Nathan J. Tohtsoni, *Daily Times*, December 18, 1999; Mark Lewis, *Daily Times*, September 10, 1999). Farmington in the 1990s proved to be particularly rife with Indian rolling, Indian hating, and Indian killing, proof that the town's legacy of hate had not changed since the first Europeans invaded Totah. Each crime is evidence of a deep-seated racist culture that resurfaces in violent behavior from unruly and unpredictable young white males. Because the racism was never confronted, this trend continued into the 2000s.

Krazy Kowboy Killers

In June of 2000, white Farmington residents Robert Fry and Leslie Engh murdered B. Lee, a Navajo mother of five. After a night out at the Turn Around Bar with friends in Farmington, Lee was stranded and left to find her own ride home. On her way home, she encountered Fry and Engh while at a convenience store payphone. They offered Lee a ride to Kirtland, outside of Farmington, but Fry detoured to a remote area outside of Kirtland and attempted to rape Lee. She fought him off, but Fry stabbed her and bludgeoned her with a sledgehammer. Days later, an oil field worker discovered her slain naked body. The police investigation led to Fry and Engh. As with other hate crimes, it was reported that law enforcement debated whether the crime was motivated by race, if Fry and Engh had targeted Lee specifically because she was Navajo. What is known for certain is that Fry and Engh called themselves "the krazy kowboy killers," referencing the KKK acronym (Buchanan 2006b). Fry reportedly denied that he committed hate crimes even though he and Engh targeted Navajos when searching for prey.

After Fry and Engh were arrested for Lee's murder, both confessed to murdering D. Tsosie, a Navajo man. In 1998 Fry and Engh testified that they offered Tsosie a ride home, then drove to a secluded area, strangled him, beat him with a shovel, and sexually mutilated his body. Fry and Engh also confessed to murdering two white men in Farmington. Fry became the prime suspect in the disappearance of several other missing Navajos during his incarceration but has not confessed to any additional murders. Nonetheless, he was convicted and sentenced for the murder of D. Tsosie and two additional murders unrelated to Indian rolling, and he was eventually convicted and sentenced to death for the murder of B. Lee. Fry is the undeniable product of the racist and violent culture sustained in the town of Farmington. Without a doubt the two were racists, and mainstream media labeled Fry a serial killer. He represents the legacy of Indian hating and the long history of racial violence against Navajos.

Investigators reportedly followed a lead on the 1997 disappearance of Pernell Tewangoitewa that possibly connected to Fry and Engh. During the time of Tewangoitewa's disappearance, Fry was a bouncer at Gators Bar and Grill, where Tewangoitewa was last seen alive, and some reports claimed Fry was the last person to see him. As a result of this connection, the FBI reopened and reinvestigated Tewangoitewa's case, but the investigation was inconclusive. Investigators did speculate that Fry and Engh may have played a part in Tewengoitewa's death, but they could not prosecute Fry (Buchanan 2006b). In an interview, Fry discussed the four murders he was convicted of committing. He offered no apology to the victims' families. Instead, he discussed his newfound religious fervor as he awaited the death penalty.

In 2009 New Mexico repealed capital punishment, and in 2019 Fry's death sentence was vacated. The court found that his crimes were "disproportionate in contrast to similar murder cases" (Joshua Kellogg, *Farmington Daily*

Times, June 29, 2019). Fry escaped the death penalty but was sentenced for a total of 120 years for all the murders he committed. Fry, a racist serial murderer, will never be eligible for parole.

While justice was served for the murder of B. Lee, the family continues to heal. "It's not easy to come to terms with the fact that she is gone," her brother Phillip Joe told KRQE News 13. "To think about what she endured and the time that the assault was taking place was, I can't picture somebody doing that to her" (Larry Barker, KRQE, March 2, 2013). For most Navajo families, achieving justice through the appropriate legal means is merely a beginning to a long, arduous healing journey. The violent death of a family member is traumatizing, and this trauma compounds on years of violence perpetuated by whites that has gone unrecognized and many times unresolved and unpunished. The racial violence perpetuated by whites must be confronted; the Navajo people have already endured it for too long.

F. C. Martinez

In 2001 sixteen-year-old F. C. Martinez, a transgender Navajo youth, was killed in the neighboring Four Corners town of Cortez, Colorado. Cortez is approximately thirty miles north of Shiprock, and eighty miles northwest of Farmington on the Navajo Nation. Shaun Murphy, an eighteen-year-old white Farmington resident, bludgeoned Martinez to death. Martinez and Murphy had been introduced at a party. Murphy and his friend gave Martinez a ride, then happened upon Martinez again later that night. The circumstances of their encounter remain unclear, but what is known for certain is that Murphy attacked Martinez. Martinez's body was found in a canyon south of Cortez known as "The Pits." Initial investigations proposed that Martinez was beaten and left to die alone in the wilderness, with wounds to their abdomen. Martinez's mother speculated about the horrible events of that night when visiting the crime scene years later. "This is where I think he [*sic*] tried to escape," she said, identifying a path. "There was a trail of his blood on the rocks. I think they chased him down and then beat him with rocks" (Begay, *Navajo Times*, 2002). Martinez was likely able to escape an initial beating but succumbed to injuries inflicted after subsequent beatings. Martinez was not discovered until five days after they met Murphy.

Murphy bragged to friends about the attack, which eventually led to his arrest, thanks to an anonymous Crime Stoppers tip. During the trial Martinez's mother issued an emotional statement to her child's murderer in court: "You took my son away from me in the most vicious way I can imagine. . . . You beat him with a rock and you felt it break his skull . . . and my son lay there for a week and all you said about it was that you had 'bug-smashed a fag.' I think you should be put to death for that" (Sprinkle 2011). Murphy was convicted of first-degree murder and sentenced to forty years in prison. LGBTQ advocates pushed for the murder to be considered a hate crime, but Colorado's hate crime laws did not include hate based on gender or sexual orientation at the time. Additionally, there was no federal law that could extend hate crime charges. The Matthew Shepard and James Byrd Jr. Act, which included gender and sexual orientation without the stipulation that the victim had to be involved in a federally protected activity, was not passed until 2009. Martinez was also targeted because they were Navajo, but Murphy was never charged for a hate crime based on race.

After serving nearly twenty years of his prison sentence, Shaun Murphy was released on parole in 2019. He currently lives in Greeley, Colorado. Cathy Renna, an East Coast–based LGBTQ advocate, said it was "traumatic" for the local LGBTQ community to know Murphy had been released. Renna described it as "one of the most horrific hate crime murders [she'd] ever seen." Murphy may have served his time, but his plea deal may not adequately do justice to "the brutality of what they did" (Bret Hauff, *The Journal*, September 5, 2019).

Martinez's story was later memorialized in the documentary *Two Spirit*. The film frames the murder as a primarily a transgender hate crime, but the Martinez murder was part of a pattern of ongoing violence against Navajos in the Four Corners region, particularly during the late 1990s and early 2000s. Few discussions have considered that Martinez was targeted because they were both Navajo and transgender. Martinez's mother was not convinced that Murphy acted alone. Martinez was six feet tall and over two hundred pounds, and Murphy was "much smaller," suggesting that others may have aided in the attack (Begay, *Navajo Times*, 2002). Shaun Murphy is yet another product of Farmington's history of Indian rolling, Indian hating, and violence.

To see that Farmington is not only a breeding ground for violent offenders but has committed to sustaining its racist culture, one need look only miles away to find a stark difference in how a community responds to violence. The city of Cortez, Colorado, is located a mere thirty miles from Farmington, New Mexico. After Martinez's violent death, the entire community united in the spirit of healing, thanks to the organization efforts of national LGBTQ and local advocates. The community held several forums and vigils in honor of Martinez, demonstrating that the city of Cortez was committed to creating and sustaining a safe and healthy place for its LGBTQ and Native American citizens, a response that was in stark contrast to the community response to hate crimes in Farmington. In chapter 9, I discuss why community responses are crucial to healing, justice, and dismantling racist systems.

Patterns of Indian Rolling

Close examination of those hate crimes that fit the definition of Indian rolling revealed a stark pattern. Between 1975 and 2010, after the 1974 Chokecherry Massacre, nine identified level 5 hate crimes were committed against Natives in the Farmington area. All the perpetrators of these crimes were white males, and seven were committed by more than one perpetrator. All the perpetrators were also younger than twenty-five and therefore considered youths in the public's perception. Many were teenagers and boys under the age of eighteen. Accordingly, six identified incidents of level 4 hate crime occurred after 1974. Donaldson (2006) also documented many of the cases listed here and analyzed the elements of Indian rolling. My findings concur with many of hers in that Indian rolling is mostly perpetrated by groups of white males and often involves alcohol. Donaldson contends that Indian-rolling perpetrators are not necessarily racist towards Navajos; I adamantly disagree. Indian rolling is a hate crime motivated by race.

These hate crimes span three major eras: 1974, 1992–2001, and 2006–2010. In 1974, the first era, three level 5 hate crimes were perpetuated by white males on Native American males. From 1992 to 2001, there were ten hate crimes: five level 5 and five level 4; four of these level 4 crimes occurred in one year alone, 1992. All but one hate crime in this era were perpetrated by white males against Native American males. B. Lee's case is the only prosecuted case where the victim was a Native American woman and the perpetrators were white males. In the final era, 2006–2010, there were two cases: a level 5 hate crime in 2006 and a level 4 hate crime in 2010. Like most other cases in this data set, the perpetrators were white males, and the victims were Native American men.

Clearly, the prime perpetrators of violent assaults against Indians, especially Indian rolling, were white boys alone or in groups. They were also all local, not visiting from another place, which suggests they were fully aware of the Native American and Navajo population near them. In other words, they were predators and knew they could inflict violence on vulnerable prey, Native Americans and Navajos. Significantly, most of these incidents involved alcohol; either the victim or the perpetrators or both parties were consuming alcohol before the crime. Most of the Native American and Navajo victims were labeled as inebriates by the police and media, even when their families insisted that their disappearances were uncommon, but the white perpetrators did not necessarily have to confront negative stereotypes about their alcohol consumption.

One of the most defining traits about these hate crimes is that all but one incident had more than two perpetrators acting as a group, meaning they were all committed to achieving a desired outcome to inflict harm. Time and again, not one person in the group stopped the crime (Levin and McDevitt 2002). The perpetrators of hate crime are not necessarily members of hate groups, but they were certainly part of a community system enabled by the climate of Indian hating. This unseen system is an ever-present aspect of the Indian hating we have seen throughout this history. These small groups of marauding white boys use white terrorism to wreak havoc for personal enjoyment and to gain a twisted sense of notoriety. Most of the perpetrators admitted that they were thrill-seeking while committing these crimes (Donaldson 2006).

All the victims were Navajo in these cases. In some cases, the victims were unsheltered relatives; in others they were simply in Farmington as visitors. They were of different age groups, and because they were all Navajo, the crimes, all committed by white perpetrators, were necessarily racially motivated. In courts of law, crimes involving race must meet certain criteria to be prosecuted as hate crimes. In the court of public opinion, however, this bar can be reached with the answer of one defining question: Would the perpetrators have inflicted the same violence if the victims were white? I think in every case in the data set above, the answer to this question would undeniably be no.

All these hate crimes occurred within Farmington and in the Four Corners. This region was analyzed because the most infamous incidents of Indian rolling have been committed in this area, and in my estimation, Farmington has the most documented Indian rolling incidents in the Southwest. This is by far the most significant characteristic because it proves that the area is a haven for Indian rolling, has a deep-seated culture of Indian hating, and breeds white male youth who find it acceptable behavior to commit heinous crimes for the sake of pleasure. Farmington's environment of raising racists who are a threat to Navajos and Native Americans must be dismantled.

six

"We Have to Live among You"

Thirty Years after the Chokecherry Massacre

I n 2002 Ramona Tewa spoke before the New Mexico Advisory Committee to the U.S. Commission on Civil Rights and disclosed the botched
investigation into Pernell Tewangoitewa's disappearance. The Tewangoitewa family had been frustrated by numerous repeated attempts to file
a missing person report, none of which were taken seriously by the Farmington police. The police insisted that Pernell was on a drunken bender and
would return home eventually. In June of 1997, shortly after Pernell Tewangoitewa disappeared, the burned frame of the car he was driving had been
found by an oil field worker in Chokecherry Canyon. Romana Tewa stated:
"In desperation I contacted the FBI and told them about the vehicle that
was found burned and the driver is still missing and why is there no investigation? They contacted the Farmington police department to take a report.
You see, there was not going to be an investigation, until I notified the FBI
about my missing brother and the burned vehicle" (J. Mills, "Botched New
Mexico Murder Case Draws Eye of U.S. Civil Rights Commission," *Indian
Country Today*, February 5, 2002).

Ramona Tewa also attempted to have the car her brother was driving
forensically examined by an outside agency, but she discovered that the
police had disposed of it and sent it to an auto salvage yard two years before

her inquiry. The advisory committee found Tewa's testimony disconcerting and called for further investigation.

On April 30, 2004, the U.S. Commission on Civil Rights returned to Farmington to follow up on the city's progress on improving race relations. The commission held a public forum at San Juan College, titled Confronting Discrimination in Reservation Border Town Communities. The commission invited a variety of Navajo community members, local officials, health-care providers, law enforcement, and business community members to partici-pate in the public forum and also took responses from anyone who wanted to testify. The commission sought input from the Navajo and Farmington communities about what progress, if any, had been made in the last thirty years and to address the problems and findings in the report from 1975. In 2005 the commission published a follow-up report, which included findings from the public forum.

The *Farmington Report*: Civil Rights for Native Americans, Thirty Years Later

The *Farmington Report* of 2005 referenced the 1974 Chokecherry murders and recited the violent history of Indian-white relations in Farmington. It bluntly states on the first page: "The brutality of these crimes provoked an angry outrage and the Native American Community started holding protest marches through downtown Farmington denouncing the pervasive racism and bigotry of the community. The dismissive attitude of the white commu-nity to the Indigenous community, long a way of life in Farmington, was abruptly ended. As tensions mounted, much of the white community in Farmington found itself not only ill prepared to deal with the ensuing crisis, but indeed confused, threatened, and frightened."

Although the initial tone of the *Farmington Report* (2005) is aggressive, the report shifts to a much less goal-oriented tone that does not adequately identify and confront the race problem. The report highlights superficial improvements that had been made in race relations since 1974 but does not address the root problems of perpetual racism and racial violence in Farm-ington. The report is also at times one-sided. For example, it stated that in

1974 the whites in Farmington were "frightened" because of the activism and outrage of Navajos. Meanwhile, the report did not acknowledge Navajos' legitimate fears about traveling to and doing business in Farmington, especially after the Chokecherry murders. From its onset the report fails to highlight a crucial unresolved issue: What steps had the city taken to protect Navajo and Native peoples who feared for their safety?

The report revisited six major topics that the 1975 report covered: police profiling and mistreatment, economic disadvantage, discrimination, health care, and substance abuse. I summarize the major findings and analyze the report in the following sections.

Findings and Recommendations on Policing

The commission found that a disproportionately large number of American Indians were still being arrested and incarcerated in 2005. The 1975 report had cited police mistreatment, but according to Chief Michael Burridge, reports of mistreatment were investigated. However, Chief Burridge was quick to dismiss racial profiling accusations:

> The arrest information we provided will show statistical information during the last five years regarding arrests for violent crimes as well as drugs and alcohol violations. Have we arrested more Native American men and women for alcohol-related offenses more than any other race? Yes. Yes, we have by quite a large majority. Does it show or mean that we're picking on, profiling on, or have a bias against the Native American race? Absolutely not. It shows that we have a societal problem with alcohol that is prevalent in our Native American community as well as other members of our society. (New Mexico Advisory Committee to the U.S. Commission on Civil Rights 2005, 16)

The police chief did not present concrete data to demonstrate that any improvements had been made or that any allegations were being thoroughly investigated. On the other hand, Navajo citizens disputed the Farmington police's claim that they did not racially profile. Navajos testified that police violated their rights and cited numerous instances of police profiling or mishandling of cases. For example, Ruth Russell, a Navajo woman, testified that she had reported harassment by white teens but that the police had not responded. Also, police had pulled her over and accused her and her mother of drinking alcohol, even though both abstain from alcohol. Ramona Tewa testified about the mishandling of the case of her missing brother, Pernell Tewangoitewa, despite numerous attempts to file a missing person report (New Mexico Advisory Committee to the U.S. Commission on Civil Rights 2005).

The commission found that there was still a lack of American Indian and minority police officers in San Juan County and in Farmington, even though numbers had increased since 1975. Furthermore, American Indians had no representation in the court system. Additionally, Navajos experienced a high unemployment rate, and few American Indians worked as professionals in the city. Navajos predominantly occupied low-paying blue-collar jobs in San Juan County. Senator Leonard Tsosie testified that policies in place to promote Navajo employment were misunderstood:

> In terms of subtleties, programs that were designed to increase Native employment are under attack. I talk about the federal Indian Preference Law and also the Navajo Preference Law. Companies now use constitutional arguments to say that these laws themselves discriminate and, therefore, should be abolished. And such actions make tribal governments hesitant to vigorously advocate on behalf of their people to try to promote Indian preference within towns or by private employers because it is always under constant attack. (New Mexico Advisory Committee to the U.S. Commission on Civil Rights 2005, 21)

Findings and Recommendations on Economics

Navajos and Natives testified that Navajos were taken advantage of by unscrupulous practices in businesses such as pawn shops, mobile home dealers, payday lending, title loan operators, and car dealers (New Mexico Advisory Committee to the U.S. Commission on Civil Rights 2005, 27). This remains consistent with the testimony from 1974, which pointed to the same problems. However, in regard to hiring more Navajos since 1974, Farmington had made some improvement. In 1974 only 4 percent of Farmington's employees were American Indians, with five individuals working in administration. In 2005, 18 percent of Farmington's employees were American Indian, with twenty-one individuals working in administration. The city employed two American Indian police officers in 1974, as opposed to twenty in 2005 (22).

Regarding consumer discrimination, "detailed evidence was presented concerning predatory lending practices, payday loans, usurious interest rates, deceptive sales practices, misrepresentation." However, the committee claimed to believe that most Farmington businesses were not taking advantage of Navajos and that Farmington business should help "weed out the offenders." They also encouraged development of Indian-owned businesses and urged the governor to "consider reform efforts" for payday loan companies (55).

Findings and Recommendations on Discrimination

In 2005 Navajos still cited numerous instances of discriminatory treatment and unscrupulous business practices in Farmington. But Farmington business representatives denied discrimination, instead focusing on stories of positive treatment of Navajos. Business representatives also claimed that they hired Navajos and valued Navajo patronage. Many cited a "change in attitudes" and improvement regarding businesses' treatment of Navajos (New Mexico Advisory Committee to the U.S. Commission on Civil Rights 2005, 24).

The Navajo and American Indian perspective was quite the opposite. Levon Henry, executive director of DNA People's Legal Services, testified that the legal aid office "continues to see these problems and they do not seem to be getting any better." He stated,

> Many people in the Four Corners region have been devastated by the unscru-
> pulous business practices of car dealers, mobile home dealers, pawnshops,
> and the new payday loan and title loan operations. Many of the unscrupulous
> dealers and business operators are willing to take full advantage of the elderly
> who they know full well don't understand the terms and conditions of the
> legal documents they are signing. While some community members may say
> that the blatant discrimination of Native Americans and low income persons
> is tempered by the passing years, it remains alive and well in another forum
> shown through the well-documented business practices of these unscrupulous

car dealers, unscrupulous mobile home dealers, and unscrupulous pawn
dealers. (New Mexico Advisory Committee to the U.S. Commission on Civil
Rights 2005, 27)

Henry admitted that a certain segment of the population made all the
businesses dealers appears unscrupulous. Many of them also "look forward
to tax season" to take advantage of Navajo customers. Several other Navajos
expressed similar sentiments to Henry's (New Mexico Advisory Committee
to the U.S. Commission on Civil Rights 2005). The committee recommended
that the city undertake recruitment efforts to appoint more American Indians to leadership "positions within the public and private sectors," particularly "into top-level managerial and policy posts."

Findings and Recommendations on Health Care

The report cited improvements made regarding Navajos' and Native Americans' health-care access. A behavioral health center (Totah Behavioral
Health) had been operating for two years. The 1975 report cited that Navajos
were refused service at Farmington hospitals, but the 2005 report claimed
some improvement: "Despite the presence of the San Juan County Regional
Medical Center and a more accommodating attitude in the Farmington
community, American Indians in general continue to have disproportionately high levels of certain illnesses and diseases" (New Mexico Advisory
Committee to the U.S. Commission on Civil Rights 2005, 13).

However, Navajos still report being refused treatment and given poor
treatment at San Juan Regional Hospital in Farmington (Sally, interview,
Farmington, July 19, 2012). The 2005 report cited high levels of illness and
alcoholism among American Indians in general but failed to mention the
economic gain Farmington received from alcohol sales and the problem of
retailers and bars selling to intoxicated patrons.

Findings and Recommendations on Education

The *Farmington Report* (2005) attempted to address issues of education and
housing needs that the 1974 report had neglected. American Indian students

comprised 29 percent of the population in the Farmington school district, while Central Consolidated School District, with schools both on and off the Navajo reservation, had an 88 percent American Indian student population. The commission found that American Indian students performed at a lower rate than non-Indian students but did not mention any of the factors involved when analyzing low test scores of ethnic minorities and American Indians. A Navajo parent with a child in the school district, acknowledged that she was generally satisfied with the Farmington schools, but stated that her daughter had had only one Navajo teacher. Central Consolidated Schools had been cited for violations of civil rights

> for failing to provide adequate educational support for students with limited-English proficiency. In 2003, OCR [the U.S. Department of Education's Office for Civil Rights] investigated a complaint against CCD, alleging the district discriminated against students on the basis of national origin and race and that the district failed to provide adequate educational services to students with limited-English proficiency. The district acknowledged its non-compliance and resolved the complaint with OCR agreeing to ensure all newly enrolled students are assessed for English proficiency, and also agreeing to ensure an appropriately qualified staff to provide ESL/ELD instruction. (New Mexico Advisory Committee to the U.S. Commission on Civil Rights 2005, 36)

Additionally, Navajo students performed lowest at Central Consolidated schools. Linda Besett, superintendent at Central Consolidated School No. 22, acknowledged the low performance, telling the committee that "seven of our 17 schools [in the district] are in corrective action. Those seven schools are on the reservation, but we also have schools on the reservation that are not corrective action schools. In fact, we have four schools that are not corrective action that are located on the reservation" (New Mexico Advisory Committee to the U.S. Commission on Civil Rights 2005, 37). Besett also provided data on dropout rates for grades seven through twelve, noting that they were a little higher than the overall rate in the state of 5.3 percent.

The low number of American Indian teachers was also mentioned in the *Farmington Report* (2005). Only 131 of 511 teachers were American Indian. Hoskie Benally, a Navajo community member who testified before the commission, pointed to conflict with the Central Consolidated School District.

(The Navajo community) has been in a long struggle with Central School District for about a year and a half now trying to make sure that our Navajo youth get the entitlement of their rights to bilingual education and cultural instruction. But we have been experiencing just the opposite in the school district. The whole thing began about a year and a half ago when the school board president made remarks and tried to blame and scapegoat bilingual education as the reason for low reading scores in the school district. (New Mexico Advisory Committee to the U.S. Commission on Civil Rights 2005, 40)

Duane "Chili" Yazzie also cited conflict between the school board members:

Then there are the do-gooders who apparently cannot or will not comprehend the notion that we as Navajo people understand our world, our needs, and our aspirations. I refer to the Central Consolidated School District leadership who, unfortunately, exhibit the unfounded notion that only they know what is best for us. I do not suggest that this constitutes racism, only that it smacks of blatant disregard for the wishes of the community that it purports to serve. (41)

Findings and Recommendations on Substance Abuse

About alcoholism, the commission recommended that the "tribal, state, and local government" work to address the alcoholism problem in Farmington. The commission also discussed Totah Behavioral Health Authority as a successful example of an alcohol treatment facility, recommending that the center's efforts be expanded and funded and that the state consider stricter controls of alcohol sales.

The report concluded with a final recommendation to create a community relations committee composed of different racial and ethnic groups to address "complaints of discrimination" in Farmington. The committee went on to praise the leadership in Farmington and suggested that city leaders continue to dialogue with Navajos. The committee applauded Farmington for its changes during the past thirty years and noted the city's efforts to embrace Navajo culture and diversity (New Mexico Advisory Committee to the U.S. Commission on Civil Rights 2005, 57).

Findings and Analysis

Overall, the *Farmington Report* (2005) is ineffective in addressing the race problem, especially when compared to the 1974 report. The 2005 commission immediately expressed general satisfaction with Farmington's progress in "accommodating" Navajos. The report compliments and applauds Farmington for its improvements over the years. While the report mentioned the city's failure to create a mechanism where citizens could make complaints, the commission seemed not to consider this failure a cause for concern. The commission's enthusiasm for Farmington's "improvements" is disconcerting considering the fact of Ramona Tewa's and others' testimony about missing and murdered Navajos.

The report does recommend several areas for improvement, but most are superficial and even if implemented would likely not generate any long-term healing or change. For example, one recommendation was to encourage American Indians to participate in school board elections for Central Consolidated School District, but there is little evidence that Indians did not already participate in school board elections, and their participation does not guarantee that their voices will be heard. Similarly, the commission recommended that American Indians be elected to the Farmington City Council. As of 2005, there had not been an American Indian on the city council.

The commissioners also recommended mediation efforts and collaboration between tribal and state education officials to resolve racial conflict. This otherwise reasonable recommendation places significant burden on tribal education officials for racism that proliferates unchecked in predominantly white schools. A better approach would be to address the lack of training that white education officials have for dealing with racial conflicts.

The committee did not adequately address allegations of racial profiling by police, stating, "while many individuals presented allegations of racial profiling and other law enforcement misconduct, the Committee cannot determine the extent of this problem, based on anecdotal information" (New Mexico Advisory Committee to the U.S. Commission on Civil Rights 2005,

54). The committee made no effort to examine these allegations further, even though it was a major problem voiced by Native Americans.

The commissioners admitted that "there are tensions in the community . . . needing attention" and that many Navajos expressed a fear of police. However, they made no recommendations concerning racial profiling, and by not addressing the testimony that pointed to racial discrimination, the commission diminished Native Americans' concerns. They did not concretely provide any recommendations for the most serious allegations of racism and hate crimes. The commissioners had an opportunity to address Native Americans' concerns, but the report is proof that they could not even do that.

In 2005 the City of Farmington had not followed up with one of the most important recommendations of the 1975 report: to create a forum or mechanism whereby complaints could be made. This was a significant flaw. The 2005 *Farmington Report* was also published *before* major hate crimes and a police shooting in 2006 (discussed in chapter 7), and there was no chance to update the report to include data or testimony on these significant events. Another disappointing flaw is that the 2005 report makes no mention of the murders of D. Tsosie in 1998 and B. Lee in 2000. In the 2005 report's data collection and drafting phase, several news sources highlighted that Ramona Tewa returned to the area to participate, but the report makes no recommendations to address justice for murdered and missing Navajos.

Compared to the 1975 report, the 2005 report offered scant recommendations, and those it did make were not as critical or specific. The recommendations from 2005 also revealed more about how embedded the race problem existed within the system. One statement in the recommendations section speaks to apathy and a general lack of interest or concern: "while clearly, racist attitudes persist among some of its citizens, there is new leadership in Farmington that is concerned about the future" (New Mexico Advisory Committee to the U.S. Commission on Civil Rights 2005, 52). This statement reveals that admitting the state of racism in Farmington to challenge the racist status quo was of no concern in the present and future.

Farmington may have improved in some areas, but the report failed to address persisting racist attitudes or to provide suggestions for improvement. Instead, the report cited alleged progress and the willingness of the city leadership to improve race relations. Unfortunately, the city leadership may have just been telling the commission what they wanted to hear; in an interview with CNN, Mayor Thomas Taylor admitted that he never even read the *Farmington Report* from 1975. The mayor denied that there was any racism involved in Indian rolling, claiming that "inebriates" were targeted because they were alcoholics, not because they were Navajos (*Native Americans: The Invisible People* 1994; Donaldson 2006). These racist attitudes are still prevalent and are discussed further in the next chapter.

The committee also stated that it found the *Daily Times* helpful in "providing a major contribution to changes in community attitudes and multicultural understanding. The publication's extensive coverage of news from the Navajo reservation, and attention to educational and race-relations issues in the region, has served to better inform and educate" (New Mexico Advisory Committee to the U.S. Commission on Civil Rights 2005, 52). However, in the 1990s and early 2000s, the *Daily Times* was accused of biased news coverage (Brenda Norrell, Censored News Blog) and instigating "race baiting," and the organization has had few if any Native American journalists.

The *Farmington Report* (2005) found that "progress" had been made since 1975. However, there were still "problems that continue to persist." The report claimed that "the climate of tolerance and respect between the two cultures is a marked improvement from the conditions the Committee observed 30 years ago in 1974" (ii). Mayor Bill Standley of Farmington discussed the improvements this way:

> Because the bigotry in Farmington was so egregious 30 years ago and there was no mechanism available to investigate complaints alleging discrimination or an official body to provide recommendations on human rights, the mayor was asked whether Farmington had established a citizen-based human relations commission. Mayor Standley said such a commission had not been established, though he added that there has been "dialogue on this . . . and (he) would be open-minded to (the idea if) that would improve input or communications or help the community and city to move forward." (9)

The Navajo president of Shiprock Chapter, Duane "Chili" Yazzie, also remarked on the improved conditions between the two races.

Thirty years ago, we marched on Farmington to make a stand against racism and discrimination that we were subjected to, which we silently accepted as normal for many years. We made our point then and now we look back and ponder the progress we have made. I stand before you today with my report card that reads Farmington, which was dubbed "The Selma, Alabama, of the Southwest," in 1974 coming from a grade of D to a B– in race relations. I point to the deliberate efforts made by the city's elected officials and civic leaders through the years to improve our relations. These sustained efforts are to be commended. On behalf of my people, I do very much appreciate these efforts. Yes, there continue to be periodic problems but, for the most part, the efforts of the public servants, including law enforcement, the courts, the business community, and the major employers in the regions, there has been considerable advancement. Even so, the influence of the most effective programs will not reach all the people. That is the case here. Where we—even though we as civic and business leaders try to strive to make a better world, some of the citizens will always be rednecks, Indian-haters, and bigots. By the same token, I admit that there are Indian people who will also always be racist. (10)

Erin Chavez, the county commissioner, agreed that there had been marked improvements but also mentioned that "we still have a ways to go yet." Senator Leonard Tsosie argued that the racism had become more subtle. Dr. Larry Emerson of Hogback, New Mexico, pointed to the historical relationship between Navajos and whites. He characterized that relationship as "the dominant's relationship to the subordinate . . . in terms of legal, cultural, land, economic, political dimensions of our relationship" (New Mexico Advisory Committee to the U.S. Commission on Civil Rights 2005, 11). Emerson also agreed that racism had taken on a more discreet form in Farmington.

Overall, the recommendations did not address the root of the persistent problems with racial violence and racism: that racism in Farmington is intergenerational. The commission's recommendations should have included concrete ways to address racism toward Navajos, such as creating workshops, trainings, and education on racism in Farmington schools and should have addressed the problems of missing Navajos and ongoing racial violence such as Indian rolling. Interventions at Farmington high schools should have been included in order to prevent students from perpetrating hate crime. As late as 2005, Indian rolling was still happening in Farmington.

The report also ignored some of the most important and urgent testimony. In a public testimony summary chapter, two pages briefly summarized the testimony of thirty-three Navajos and American Indians. The testimony addressed mistreatment by law enforcement, employment discrimination (not hiring Navajos; offering only low-paying, low-level jobs, withholding opportunities for advancement; not honoring Navajo preference laws), specifically at San Juan College and detox centers; public accommodation discrimination in restaurants or stores; unscrupulous business practices (in auto and mobile homes sales, unfair lending, payday loans); racial conflict in Central Consolidated schools; lack of culturally competent health care; and non-enforcement of alcohol sale laws. Also, disappointingly, no direct quotes from the testimony were included in this section.

Most importantly, Navajo testimony detailing harassment and threats was not mentioned in the final report: "The Committee heard from several persons who believe that harassment of Native Americans by white persons, especially youth, is a continuing practice in Farmington. This includes acts of ethnic intimidation; threats of physical violence, assaults, and other potential hate crimes" (New Mexico Advisory Committee to the U.S. Commission on Civil Rights 2005, 49). Further investigation is needed regarding these serious allegations of harassment and threats, and the narratives should have been included within the report and addressed in their entirety.

The public testimony summary chapter concluded with the words of Ramona Tewa, who had been instrumental in bringing the commission back to Farmington:

> The problems of racial profiling in this community are far too common and almost accepted by the silent, passive Native American Indian. The statement "drunk Indian" isn't acceptable and should no longer be tolerated.
>
> Although the national consensus is the Indian is viewed as poor and drunk, the complex and long history between Indians and whites are open wounds that have never healed. The contemporary Indian versus the traditional Indian, but both being displaced, it has become a social problem. We are faced with socio-cultural and socioeconomic breakdowns.

We have to live among you. We have to progress sufficiently to compete in the modern world. Therefore, we must shop, live, work; learn along with the rest of you, along with the rest of the world. . . . I refuse to be shut out of the American dream. If we can't accept and face the problems of racial discrimination against American Indians in our community, then how can we solve and remedy these problems? They then lead to fatal, unwanted circumstances. If we can't face these problems, then is there no solution to our demise? Can we not bridge a new system, a resolution between the American Indians and Anglos? Are we too stubborn and ignorant to change? (New Mexico Advisory Committee to the U.S. Commission on Civil Rights 2005, 50–51)

Tewa explained that racial conflict between whites and Navajos is ever-present. Tewa's testimony was the only one included in the summary chapter, but the commission did not address it or mention the fact that she had been instrumental in bringing the commission back to Farmington. In addition, her brother's disappearance and lack of police investigation were not in any of the recommendations.

Overall, in comparison, the investigation and analysis of the *Farmington Report* (1975) was much more thorough. The commission had allocated several months of preliminary investigation and several days of testimony in 1974 but only one day of testimony in 2005. If the commission had spent more time in Farmington, it might have uncovered additional information showing that Farmington has not made as much "marked improvement" as the commission claimed. Despite these lauded "improvements" in race relations, another Indian rolling occurred in Farmington just one year later, in 2006.

seven

"We Seek Justice"

Hate Crimes Continue in Farmington

E ven after the New Mexico Advisory Committee on the U.S. Commission on Civil Rights concluded its investigation and published the *Farmington Report* in 2005, hate crimes and racial violence continued in Farmington and the Four Corners. There was no serious effort on the part of city leadership and within the non-Indian community to combat hate crimes in Farmington. Navajos were left unprotected, and the violence, left unchecked, continued.

In 2006 W. Blackie was beaten and robbed by John Winer, Freddie Brooks, and C. L. Carney in an incident reminiscent of the horrible violence of the Chokecherry Massacre in 1974. Blackie had left a bar on foot and was seeking a ride home when the three white youths offered him a ride. The three later admitted "they were trolling for a victim." Blackie became suspicious when they drove to the area of Farmington known as "the Glade." This popular party spot was in Chokecherry Canyon, the same area of Farmington where the 1974 murders took place. Blackie "asked Winer to pull over so he could relieve himself. . . . Blackie stepped out then he was clocked hard and fast in the head with a club. He fell to the ground and tried to crawl away as the men stomped and kicked his prone body, shouting, 'Die n——r! Just die!'" (Buchanan 2006b).

Winer, Brooks, and Carney left Blackie in the desert to bleed to death. Fortunately, Blackie had a cell phone and dialed 911. The police were able to use GPS to find him out in the Chokecherry Canyon wilderness (Buchanan 2006b). Anonymous tips led police to the three perpetrators.

John Winer, Freddie Brooks, and C. L. Carney were charged with kidnapping, assault, and hate crime. John Winer, nineteen, was sentenced to seven years in prison and charged under New Mexico hate crime laws passed in 2003. Winer's sentencing was the first time white perpetrators of Indian rolling in Farmington had been charged with a hate crime. The additional hate crime charge added two years to his sentence, but this was monumental in that it was recognized as a hate crime and taken seriously by Farmington police and San Juan County. Unfortunately, the judge declined to sentence Carney and Brooks with hate crimes, claiming that hate crime could not be proved. Carney was sentenced to five years in prison, and Brooks was sentenced to three and a half years in prison.

Police Killing of C. John

Only days after W. Blackie was brutally beaten, a white Farmington police officer shot and killed a young, unarmed Navajo man, C. John, in a Walmart parking lot. The shooting occurred after reports were made of a domestic violence incident between John and his girlfriend. The police officer shot him four times, later claiming that John had grabbed his baton and had a violent record.

The Farmington Police Department maintained that the shooting was justified. The officer who shot John was exonerated of charges. In 2007 C. John's family filed a wrongful death claim and a civil lawsuit against the officer involved in the shooting. The Navajo Nation helped the family with costs for the trial. The case went to federal court, and the officer, Shawn Scott, was found not guilty, even though a Walmart security camera showed that after C. John fought with Scott and wrestled Scott's baton away from him, Scott returned to his police car and only then shot C. John three times. Scott had claimed John was advancing on him and that he had shot in self-defense.

The witnesses claimed John had no weapon (Brian Hassler, *Navajo Times*, July 6, 2006). The jury did not include any members of the Navajo Nation; it was composed solely of white and Hispanic jurors. Though in this instance the family did not get justice, the issue brought some media attention and an investigation into the police department (Marley Shebala, *Navajo Times*, June 11, 2009).

March on Farmington 2007

After C. John was killed, his family contacted Duane "Chili" Yazzie, president of Shiprock Chapter. Yazzie had been involved with the Navajo activist group Coalition for Navajo Liberation. He described his involvement as being "like a lieutenant" in the group, led by Fred Johnson. Yazzie and others, at the urging of John's family members, organized a march. The families and community had had enough of the racial violence and tension. Navajos and local tribal leaders from the surrounding Southern Ute Tribe and Ute Mountain Tribe joined in the march.

Unlike in 1974, the Navajo Nation president and Navajo Nation leaders were present at the march. This time the families of the victims had the full support of the Navajo Nation. In May of 2007, the marchers met on top of Harper Hill, west of Farmington, and prominent members of the Navajo Nation and the victim's family gave speeches. They marched to ease the unrest that had brought up memories from the Chokecherry Massacre and all the later murders and "to memorialize the people that have died because of racial violence here," said Duane Yazzie. Yazzie said, "This was an outlet for people who are frustrated and angry." Nearly 1,500 people, primarily Navajos, attended the march. It was a peaceful march, and no one was arrested. The march gave the families of victims a venue in which to display their anger and frustration with the incidents that were happening in Farmington and to say that enough is enough, that the violence must stop (Buchanan 2006a). This time, the Navajo Nation offered its full support to the victim's family and created a mechanism to secure human rights.

The Navajo Nation Responds to Hate

The Navajo Nation Human Rights Commission was established in 2006 by the Navajo Nation Council, which "directed the Commission to immediately assess border town race relations" (NNHRC 2009, xi). The NNHRC held twenty-five public hearings to gather testimony and compiled their findings into a report. They concluded that "racism and discrimination exist, and its prevalence is more often obscured" (xii). Four main themes regarding discrimination emerged from their hearings: relocation, sacred sites, unattended death, and environment. Other areas of concern were public accommodation and poor service at restaurants, border town business practices, lack of economic development, racial profiling, and sentencing disparities (NNHRC 2009). The NNHRC, upon assessing the gathered testimony, concluded that "the most vulnerable Navajo is generally older, possesses little or no education, physically challenged, on a fixed income, indigent and without adequate transportation." The commission also determined that many Navajos may not report racial discrimination because they fear retaliation, are unaware of rights and available resources, or have had a discouraging experience while filing a complaint with state agencies (NNHRC 2009).

The report did not include any first-person narrative to better show the magnitude of the issues. Most importantly, the NNHRC report did not discuss racial violence as a hate crime. In an interview I conducted with Duane "Chili" Yazzie, he mentioned that "they might have been attempting to be diplomatic" (Shiprock, July 22, 2012). However, it is imperative to use the term *hate crime* where appropriate to bring about justice and address the severity of the problem. Additionally, the NNHRC did not discuss the Chokecherry Massacre or any other level 4 and 5 hate crimes, nor did it discuss the patterns of racism and racial violence. It is essential to make these connections in order to obtain justice for future victims and to implement interventions.

In 2010 another brutal hate crime occurred. Two white youth and one mixed-race youth, all employees of a Farmington McDonald's, attacked V. Kee, a mentally disabled Navajo man. Kee was held against his will and branded with swastikas, and his hair was shaved in the pattern of a swastika. Paul Beebe was sentenced to eight and a half years and Jesse Sanford was sentenced to five years. William Hatch, a mixed-race white, Navajo, and Lakota man, was sentenced to eighteen months in prison. Both Beebe and Sanford sought to appeal the federal hate crime charges. Hatch pled guilty to all charges including federal hate crime charges. Beebe was a reportedly a white supremacist and had numerous white supremacist symbols and memorabilia in the apartment where he held Kee. This was the first time in an instance of Indian rolling that federal hate crime charges were filed. U.S. Attorney for New Mexico Kenneth J. Gonzales said, "The young victim in this case was assaulted, branded and scarred because he happens to be a Native American—that simply is inexcusable and criminal. Today's guilty pleas demonstrate the law enforcement community's resolve that anyone who victimizes a person because of the color of their skin or ethnic heritage is brought to justice." Assistant Attorney General for Civil Rights Thomas Perez stated, "The facts of this case shock the conscience—the defendants took advantage of a young man's mental disability and assaulted him because he is Native American. They defaced his body and branded him with some of the most obvious symbols of hate. . . . We must acknowledge the reality that across America we are sailing into a strong headwind of intolerance that rears its ugly head in many different ways, shapes and forms. . . . Hate-fueled violence is on the rise. To those who want to use violence to divide our communities . . . we are here today to deliver a clear and unmistakable message. We will throw the book at you" (Schmidt, *Navajo Times*, August 25, 2011).

The notable difference in this case was that the NNHRC was available to provide support for Kee and his family (NNHRC Press Release 2011). The Navajo Nation also assisted Kee in obtaining an attorney to file a civil suit against McDonald's. The complaint was for damages and claimed that McDonald's was negligent in hiring Beebe, Sanford, and Hatch with their known convictions and poor characters. McDonald's later settled the suit with Kee for an undisclosed amount.

Memorandum of Agreement with Farmington

To pave the way for improved race relations, the NNHRC sought memoranda of agreement (MOA) with border towns neighboring the Navajo Nation. The MOAs were nonbinding agreements on improving race relations in border towns. At first, the NNHRC's approach to the MOAs with border towns was "aggressive." The NNHRC provided a "laundry list" of grievances against the border towns and included a history of the border towns' relationship with Navajos. When it immediately became apparent that this approach would not work, the NNHRC switched to a diplomatic approach (Gorman, interview, Window Rock, November 29, 2012).

The NNHRC signed MOAs with several border towns, including Farmington. The MOA process with Farmington was controversial and took more than a year to negotiate. Mayor Tommy Roberts of Farmington stated "that he believes that the Preamble contained language that would likely create unnecessary divisiveness because it focused on the historical treatment of Native Americans and contained statements that could be interpreted as conciliation, contrition and apology. As a result, he suggested that the Preamble be revised to simply set forth the purpose of the MOA" (Farmington City Council Minutes, September 14, 2010).

The mayor suggested a section that spoke of Farmington's improvements in race relations to make it more "balanced." The city councillors brought forth concerns about the MOA still being "unbalanced," and Councillor Fischer asked what the sanction would be if a business was found to discriminate. It was explained that "the purpose of the MOA is to create a relationship of cooperation between the CRC and the NNHRC, but is not to create any substantive law since the Federal and State governments have adopted anti-discrimination laws. Discussion followed concerning the role and authorities of the CRC" (Farmington City Council Minutes, September 14, 2010). At this meeting, the MOA was tabled to give the NNHRC and Navajo Nation time to review Mayor Roberts's suggested changes.

After the MOA process was negotiated with the city, a revised MOA was signed on November 17, 2010. The MOA stated:

The civil, political, cultural and economic history between the United States, Navajos and other indigenous peoples is significant, complex and tragic. As a result of that history indigenous peoples as well as other minorities have needlessly suffered from discrimination. While the majority of the people in the CITY and on the Navajo Nation do not tolerate racism, we must never forget the tragedies inflicted on Navajos by a minority in the community and ensure that the Navajo people's stories are acknowledged and told in their words. Racism and discrimination must be eliminated now and forever at every level of government in the hearts and minds of all peoples.

Farmington officials also noted within the MOA the "positive strides" made since 1974. The MOA mentioned that city had established a mechanism for complaints to be heard, though it was not until *after* the New Mexico Advisory Committee to the U.S. Civil Rights Commission returned in 2005. The MOA included language from the *Farmington Report* (2005) that stated, "If true measures are to be taken to advance race relations in other border towns, they need to merely look at Farmington and learn from them." The MOA acknowledged that the Navajo Nation and Farmington are "neighbors and they rely on each other for many goods and services including the treasures of Navajo culture and the economic benefits that are realized by the collective communities."

In 2012 Navajo Nation Council criticized the NNHRC and their MOAs with the border towns. Some council members argued that MOAs were not working or improving race relations in border towns. The NNHRC defended their MOA process, maintaining its value as a mechanism to begin dialogue with border towns to create positive relationships (Gorman, interview, Window Rock, November 29, 2012).

The negotiation of the MOA with Farmington happened after the hate crime branding of V. Kee, during the time of the trial. Unfortunately, the mayor held a similar stance of denial as had many previous Farmington mayors. Rather than taking the opportunity to learn about the record of hate crimes and race relations in Farmington, city officials used the MOA as another opportunity to laud the "progress" the city had made.

Hate Speech Online

Following the Chokecherry Massacre, Farmington residents expressed their largely racist opinions on the *Daily Times* editorial page (chapter 4). Similar types of racist and hate-fueled rhetoric continue today but via a different medium: social media and Internet forums. On a page discussing Native

Americans, one Facebook user wrote, "Navajos in Farmington, NM=trash" (2008). This type of rhetoric is common on social media.

Previously, a popular venue for Farmington residents was the now-defunct local forum on the site Topix, a site formerly dedicated to news in small towns where users discussed a variety of issues. As of 2018 Topix removed commentary for newspapers from its website after being accused of fueling hate speech. The following posts are no longer available online but are part of the data I collected in 2012. Within Farmington's forum posts, it was apparent that racist attitudes had changed little from the period after the Long Walk, through the Chokecherry murders, and to 2018. During 2008–2013, members discussed issues related to race and discrimination involving Navajos in over 2,800 posts.

The Topix forum posts demonstrate similar themes that emerged within the editorial section of the *Farmington Times* during the Chokecherry Massacre. I studied the 2,800 posts using content analysis and categorized them according to themes. The major themes that emerged were characterizations of Navajos as dirty, stupid, drunks, living off government handouts, or having special privileges; historical racism; and denials of racism: "Farmington is a racist town, try being intoxicated on a Friday and being Indian, you have the stupid white kids driving by and saying racial comments. What do white parents teach their kids these days? Looks like very little" (Farmington Topix forum, October 10, 2008).

Numerous posts also described Navajos as dirty or filthy. One writer referred to Navajos as "Navawhores." Another wrote, "Half the Indians live within the city of Farmington now, your trying to escape the filth you have created on your so called reservation just drive through Shiprock your so used to it so you don't notice until you get out of your new truck and step on a beer or whiskey bottle" (Farmington Topix forum, October 2008). The stereotypes continue with lies about financial wealth, free monthly money from the Navajo Nation, and free education or money for schooling.

There is a gross misunderstanding about Navajo and American Indian preference laws. Most non-Indians view these policies and preferences as special treatment and special privileges, believing that they are the ones being discriminated against: "All remember the car accident in Albuquerque a few years back an entire family was killed because of one really stupid act. Now the driver was Navajo and the family was white, I would wonder what would be said if it was all reversed. I think I might open my own business and advertise for applicants in the newspaper and say white man preferred. How often do you see ads NA preferred and consideration given to NA. Wow, who is really being racist?" (Farmington Topix forum, October 15, 2008).

Another person criticized the Navajo government's spending: "I think the Navajo people and the march organizers last year who put this on stopped short by a few miles and should of hung out in Farmington a little longer, and maybe they should of taken the time to look for their relatives, friends and neighbors, look at all the money that was spent going to Hawaii, maybe some of that could of helped them off the streets. . . . Clean the trash up in your back yard and we will take [care] of ours" (Farmington Topix forum, October 2008).

Competition for employment was another point of contention: "Farmington is a racist town for as long as the Navajo's compete with the Bilagaana's [white people] for jobs in San Juan Co. Unlike the old days when we were hated for just being 'Injun', we now threaten the jobs held primarily by Bilagaana's" (Farmington Topix forum, October 2008).

The stereotypes portray Navajos as lazy, stupid, and inferior in every way to whites. One writer argued that American Indians originated in Asia and "this is not Native Soil," even going as far to say "the colonization of America is the best thing that has happened to Native Americans. . . . Bottom line is the native americans were not innovative, creative, courageous, and advanced enough to do what most europeans set out to do" (Farmington Topix forum, October 2008).

Within the forum there was unwavering denial of the history of oppression and injustice that Navajos have endured: "I get that there have been huge 'wrongs' in the past. However, I am willing to venture that your understanding of the wrongs done come from word of mouth, and not from actual research. . . . You need to realize that no one you encounter today created the oppressive issues that you are attempting to speak out against. We are all victims of our combined histories" (Farmington Topix forum, October 2008). A

Navajo forum member countered: "getting information from word of mouth is a concrete resource from my people who lived through it" (Farmington Topix forum, October 2008).

Numerous posts claimed Navajos were "behind the times" and stated that white Farmington residents were tired of being blamed for their ancestors' misdeeds. The majority of the posts depicted embedded racism, even though most steadfastly denied that Farmington is a racist town.

Within the Farmington Topix forum, debate was constant between whites and Navajos regarding racism in Farmington. Some Navajos wrote that the racism was undeniable, while most whites insisted that racism did not exist but was only in the imagination of the accusing parties. There was blatant and hostile denial, and even some Navajos agreed that they never encountered any racism in Farmington. The outright denial of racism is itself racist and hurtful, especially when a Navajo person gives clear examples:

> Years back I was on a government business trip to Farmington. I noticed to my right while stopped at an intersection waiting for the traffic lights to change, a family of natives with children also stopped at the intersection; along came a truck load of youthful looking white men and women waving with their middle index fingers to this family and shouting racial slurs. I was deeply saddened for this family with children. All of you who think racism does not exist in Farmington need some form of rude awakening. (Farmington Topix forum, October 2008)

A responder doubted the story and insisted that there were explanations for harassment. "Years back . . . how many? A town can change in 5–10 years. . . . It was not the whole town, it was a carload of young yahoos. Teens often do stupid things. . . . Wanna bet most of the load was drunk or drugged? Not that it's an excuse but people under an influence are generally stupid" (Farmington Topix forum, October 2008).

Some posts referenced the Chokecherry Massacre of 1974 and later hate crimes, but most respondents pointed to a select group, which they said was not representative of the whole town. Another forum member wrote, "my late uncle . . . (1974) who passed on in chokecherry canyon by three racist bred anglo youth . . . would still say 'Farmington is still a racist community.'"

The response: "He might. However, you are speculating because he does not have the ability to say anything. Besides, his experience with racism stopped in 1974 as the result of a HATE CRIME." Forum members were insistent that it was only "murderous teen-agers" involved in the Chokecherry murders: "The City of Farmington did not commit that crime. Three murderous teen-agers did. If there is racism taking place in Farmington, and I believe that there is, it is NOT the town but the PEOPLE that are committing the acts" (Farmington Topix forum, October 14, 2008).

One user summed up the racism, hate speech, and biased perspective on the Farmington Topix forum best: "Racism and intolerance is alive and well in Farmington. We see the closet bigot who sits and overtly expresses racism under the anonymity of a computer ID. The racial profiling by bigots who think the only drunks are Native in this community, and think that 'all' natives receive free service in schools, hospitals, and from the government" (Farmington Topix forum, October 2008).

The same types of racist comments were being made about Navajos on this forum as were made in the editorial section of the *Farmington Daily Times* in 1974, demonstrating an unceasing cycle of racism and violence against Navajos in Farmington. Throughout the years, even after 1974, the *Farmington Daily Times* editorial page has remained a place for vicious race-relations debate, and the paper has been accused of instigating racial hostilities on both sides (Brenda Norrell, Censored News Blog). But the anonymity of the Internet has made racist attacks more convenient and even more malicious than they might be in person, baring the racism in Farmington. The Topix forum for Farmington is now defunct, and in 2020 other social media platforms have become the primary hosts of hate speech in Farmington.

Stereotypes "justify hate crime in the mind of the perpetrator by providing him with the essential dehumanizing images of vulnerable individuals" (Levin and McDevitt 2002, 46). A person may find it easier to assault someone they view as less than human. In fact, in Barker's (1992) interviews, perpetrators of hate crime admitted that they viewed drunken Navajos as "subhuman." Stereotypes about Navajos continue to abound. Pernell Tewangoitewa's family had a difficult time filing a missing person report because the police thought he was "just another drunk Navajo," a perception that remains common even though only a small percentage of Navajos abuse alcohol. The Anti-Defamation League's Pyramid of Hate confirms that racist stereotypes are not harmless but fuel racial violence. Farmington's white privilege and racism, reflected in the racist stereotypes and comments about Navajos in the Farmington Topix forum, are also apparent in the interviews discussed in the following chapter.

eight

"Go Back to Your Hogan!"

Navajo Survivors of Hate Crime

The prevalence of hate crimes and racism in the historical record of Farmington and the Four Corners is undeniable, yet denial perseveres within the City of Farmington leadership and white citizens of Farmington. The historical and media data I collected and analyzed for this book provide substantial evidence of the prevalence of race-motivated hate crime, but I strongly believe that it is important to consider firsthand accounts of contemporary hate crime. My expertise as a Navajo scholar of American Indian studies allows me to use multiple data sets and rely on multiple analytical methods for a more comprehensive longitudinal study on hate crimes.

The Interviews

I conducted a series of semi-structured interviews, often allowing participants to lead the conversation on their experiences with racism or hate crimes. The participants seemed more at ease in less-formal interviews, where they could relay their experiences over coffee. This interview style, more reminiscent of the Navajo style of visiting with relatives, fit within Navajo tradition and takes into consideration the importance of oral narrative in Navajo culture. The interviews shed light on additional information that had not been gathered before regarding Navajo experiences with racism and racial violence.

Death is a taboo subject among traditional Navajo people, and I observed cultural protocol and did not speak the names of homicide victims. The topics of hate crime, racial violence, and racial discrimination can be emotional for many, and that may be why there were not more participants. Even though the interviews were at times emotional for some participants, telling their stories seemed to offer some measure of comfort and closure. At each interview, I felt that I would not have had the trust of the participants had I been non-Navajo. My knowledge of the community, familiarity with racism and racial violence in the Four Corners, and insider status were instrumental in this project.

Interview Analysis

I transcribed and coded the interviews in order to analyze the narratives according to theme, content, commonalities, and important events, as well as according to the connections and implications the narrative revealed regarding the research questions (Marshall and Rossman 2006). I asked these interview questions in the semi-structured interviews:

Where do you live? And how long have you lived there?
What do you go to Farmington for (job, shopping, school)?
What has been your experience with Farmington residents?
What do you think would improve race relations between Navajos and non-Indians in Farmington?
Have your experiences in Farmington stopped you from visiting?
Are you aware of the Navajo Nation Human Rights Commission?

Several main themes emerged throughout the interviews, including harassment, threats, intimidation, hate speech, racial violence, racist stereotypes about Navajos, educational disadvantages, and economic and cultural exploitation. Providing voice to previously untold events and incidents was imperative to the structure of this research project. It was important to allow individuals to tell their own stories (L. T. Smith 1999). Participants' statements are unedited as much as possible to preserve the integrity of the stories.

The codes and themes provided a general outline that was helpful for comparing the participants' experiences, but the narratives themselves provided a much more vivid depiction of the daily lives and experiences of Navajos who interact with Farmington and border towns. After I completed transcribing the interviews, I contacted the participants again to ensure that their stories and quotes were recorded accurately.

Place

The qualitative interviews focused on Farmington, New Mexico, and the Four Corners region. Because Farmington is located within San Juan County, I include the greater San Juan County in this study as well. The population of Farmington, which is located near the northern and eastern regions of the Navajo reservation, is approximately forty-five thousand.

As of 2020, the socioeconomic status of the Four Corners region is relatively low, with the median individual yearly income at approximately $26,000. Many of the residents work in the oil and gas industries and local coal-burning power plants. The majority of American Indians in Farmington earn less than $15,000 per year (United States Census Bureau). Few businesses are located on the Navajo reservation, so residents conduct their shopping and related business in Farmington. Additionally, employment opportunities on the Navajo reservation are scarce, so the unemployment rate is extremely high. Navajos who are employed either have jobs working for the tribe or work off the reservation.

As we have seen, the common narrative in Farmington and the Four Corners is that these areas are no longer racist. I believe it is imperative that this narrative, which is promoted by whites, be explored from the Native American perspective, asking Native Americans the fundamental question: does racism still exist in the Farmington and Four Corners area? In this chapter I rely on interviews I conducted to uncover the underrepresented and marginalized Native voice on this matter, as well as other concerns about the range of current hate crimes and racism in general.

I interviewed six brave Navajo individuals who identify as survivors of hate crimes: they were verbally or physically harmed by whites because of their race. I also interviewed two public figures. Several main themes emerged from the interviews: racist stereotypes against Navajos, hate speech, normalization of hate crimes among offenders and survivors, reinforced boundaries for Navajos to stay on the reservation, threats to survivors, avoidance of places where hate crimes occurred, racial violence, generational racism, and effects of hate crime. Most of the participants said white perpetrators harassed them with racial taunts or hate speech. The hate crimes the interviewees disclosed to me were primarily level 1 and level 2, and one level 3.

These courageous survivors and public figures shared their stories about racism in Farmington and surrounding towns. One woman in particular was adamant that she tell her story. It was a way for her to "fight back" and "do something" about what she experienced (Perry 2008). I will be forever thankful for and humbled by these individuals who bravely shared their stories with me and trusted me to share them to bring about change.

Hate Speech

In conversations with my Navajo friends and family, they disclosed to me their experiences with hate speech when visiting parks or other public places in Farmington. For instance, while a Navajo family was waiting to be seated at a Farmington restaurant, a white customer who was also waiting showed her disdain with the Navajo patronage and said that "there were too many savages" there and left the restaurant in disgust. Navajos have been mistreated by businesses and public places in Farmington for years (New Mexico Advisory Committee to the U.S. Commission on Civil Rights 1974, 2005; NNHRC 2009). This mistreatment typically occurs in the form of whites' anti-Indian hate speech.

Most people do not realize that they have experienced hate speech until after the fact. Hate speech is speech that offends, threatens, or insults groups based on race, color, religion, national origin, sexual orientation, disability, or other traits. But hate speech and incidents of harassment may not be deemed serious by law enforcement, and they are difficult to investigate.

However, hate speech and harassment have been shown to eventually escalate into violence or more serious forms of hate crime (Levin and McDevitt 2002; fig. 1). Hate speech must be identified, addressed, and confronted.

The Stories

I met and talked with a Navajo woman named "Sally" for an interview about race, racism, and microaggression. Sally is from the Navajo Nation but attended school in Farmington during the early 2000s. Sally described her unfortunate experience as a student at a predominantly Navajo high school in Farmington. She and her classmates frequently visited a park in Farmington after school and were harassed by Farmington High School students.

> We started hearing yelling. . . . it became clearer, and we noticed it was racial slurs. And the most prominent one we can remember is . . . "go back to your tipis," "go back to your hogans." These were kids that were our age. It's definitely been something that I've had to deal with randomly with the older people when I've gone to Farmington, but these kids were our age that were yelling these things to us. So we never really engaged in what they were saying to us. We ignored them. We would just sit there, and we'd sit there for half an hour to an hour and it was constant—the entire time we were there, but they would keep yelling. They would never approach us . . . It happened on more than one occasion . . . And after awhile it just became . . . normal to hear those things. We never really did anything or said anything about it. I think one thing we did say [to each other] was at least they got the house right [laughs] . . . hogan, but they did occasionally say tipi. And another one they used to call us is "redskins"—which has a very racial history. I thought that was pretty interesting. Later on, I found out about that whole thing. The history behind that "redskins" phrase. These kids that were our age were yelling that. I wonder if they know the history behind it. (Sally, interview, Window Rock, July 19, 2012)

The harassment clearly disturbed Sally, even years later. She mentioned that she and her friends still talk about the event, and how surprised they were at the attitude and harassment of the white teenagers. The white students who yelled racial taunts at Sally were students at Farmington High School, the same school that the perpetrators of the Chokecherry murders and other young perpetrators of hate crimes attended. Racism in Farmington is intergenerational.

Sally also spoke of how common it was to experience hate speech and harassment. She described incidents of both as occurring so frequently that such treatment became "normal" to her and other Navajos. When communities normalize covert racism, they also normalize overt racism. Respondents in Perry's (2008) research also reported that racist slurs and seemingly harmless racist incidents became normal to them. Victims may become desensitized to hate incidents, and indeed many of Perry's participants said they chose to ignore hate incidents rather than react. These incidents become part of the culture of the border towns where they take place and are just part of life for many of the local victims. In some cases Navajos "expected" to be harassed (Perry 2008). Normalizing hate at the smallest levels normalizes hate everywhere, which is why it must be addressed and dismantled everywhere if real change is to take place.

In another interview on the Navajo Nation, I met with another woman, "Jenny." Jenny is Navajo and she told a story of how her husband, who is also Navajo, encountered racism and hate speech. He was a contractor and at one time competed with white contractors for work. Jenny shared the racial taunts and threats her family received:

> You know the same contractor, he was telling my husband, you should go back to where you came from. You should do your contracting out there—on the rez. And just harass him [my husband] like that. But he never said anything. He pretty much just did what he had to do. So he got harassed and we even got calls at home, unidentified callers leaving messages like, "go home" and stuff like that, and even "I'm going to kill you" and stuff like that. . . . They left those kind of messages on our phone. So people even threatened him. . . . Every day he would tell me "this is where I'm going, I'll be at . . . if I ever get killed . . . these guys that might be behind it." He would give me a list of names of who he would be dealing with. So I kind of knew who he would be dealing with that day. (Jenny, interview, Shiprock, July 27, 2012)

Jenny and her husband experienced extreme threats of violence, which is common in hate speech. These threats still affected Jenny and her family members years later.

I interviewed a young Navajo man, "Billy," who was from the Navajo Nation but lived near Phoenix, Arizona. Billy wanted to participate in my interview process because he was friends with a white young man who committed an Indian rolling in Farmington. Billy described racial taunts during an assault he had survived, a brutal level 4 hate crime at a nightclub in Scottsdale, Arizona, long before our interview. He and two of his friends were violently attacked after striking up conversations with some white women. He and his friends did not know that there was a group of white men watching them, but the group began talking to other patrons derogatorily about the presence of the two Indian men, especially after Billy and his friend talked to the white women. Billy said of the incident: "The witnesses [of the crime] came to say that it was those two guys that were in the bar. And they were saying 'go back to the reservation, go back to the reservation. You guys don't belong here.' That's what they were saying. That's what the witnesses said [they heard], that 'go back to the reservation'" (Billy, interview, Tempe, February 14, 2012).

The group attacked Billy and his friend, inflicting serious injuries, especially to Billy's friend. Billy lost consciousness during the attack. Criminal investigators for Billy's case later revealed that the group of white men who attacked Billy and his friend were professional cage fighters. Justice was served in Billy's case, but like other survivors of racial violence, he will likely never forget his experience.

Billy's story demonstrates that hate crimes against American Indians can occur in urban areas such as Scottsdale, especially in states with a large Native American population. But because of its location adjacent to the Salt River Pima Maricopa Indian community, Scottsdale could also be classified as a reservation border town. Nonetheless, hate crimes against Native Americans can occur anywhere.

A significant finding that emerged from my data collection is that perpetrators of hate crime commonly say or yell "go back to the reservation!" before, during, or after they commit other hate speech or violence. As we have seen, Billy's experience is not isolated. "Go back to the reservation" can be classified as the racist anthem of hate crime perpetrators throughout the United States and even Canada. History, recent and current events, and firsthand narratives establish a clear pattern of whites telling Navajos to "go back to the reservation."

Jenny told me a story about harassment by her neighbors, who told her that she and her family did not belong in a predominantly white neighborhood in a small community outside Farmington: "Even there, where we live . . . they [white neighbors] are always telling us, 'you people are always moving from the west. You should move back.' We get harassed. Most of the old people that live in the area say 'oh, we've been here since 1959.' And I just laugh at that and say 'well, my ancestors have been here before 1959.' We just laugh. We just let them be. We don't retaliate in any way. We just mind our own business" (Jenny, interview, Shiprock, July 27, 2012). Jenny's narrative shows that the racism in Farmington and its suburbs is embedded and intergenerational. Her story demonstrates a racist perception that Navajos should be segregated from border towns and certain areas of those towns and reveals how whites continually resort to referring to their colonial past to justify hate speech.

Such commentary is used to delegitimize the Navajo presence and residence in the region. Such hate speech appeared in the *Daily Times* after the Chokecherry murders and again, later, in posts on the Topix forum. This proves that this form of hate speech is not only common but woven into the fabric of Farmington's culture. Farmington is segregated: The west side of Farmington is generally considered "the Navajo side." The grocery stores and businesses there cater to a predominantly Navajo clientele, and the majority of the people that live on this side are Navajo. I talked with a Navajo woman, "Mary," who lived in Farmington. Mary explained the segregation:

I know that my brothers and me had a habit of calling the Walmart that is further in [on the east side] the racist Walmart. There was an instance when, there were two women checking out and she was really nice to them and she gets to us she closes her light and walks away. Usually they tell you or serve you. . . . She flipped off the switch and she walked away from us. . . . That was another instance. We just knew that it was because we were Native. We were Navajo, because she very willingly served the two people ahead of us. Things like that would happen to us at that Walmart. To where, we started calling that the racist Walmart. We would hardly ever go there, we'd go to the one that's further out—on the west side. (Mary, interview, Farmington, June 21, 2012)

Mary's experience shows that racism affects her behavior; she avoided places where she had previously experienced harassment or discrimination. This is a significant finding that I think many privileged people do not see or experience. Hate speech, racial taunts, and harassment continue to affect Navajo survivors long after the occurrences. Most of my other participants also shared that they avoided the places where they had been subjected to harassment or assault. Additional impacts of racism may extend beyond the individual and include the family and community as well.

I asked Sally about the effects of hate speech she experienced as a teenager and whether or not she still frequented Brookside Park, where she had experienced hate speech:

No. (laughs) I drive by it a lot and I think about it a lot and think about those times. We were just kids and they were just kids. That is what is scary. The fact that population is increasing yearly . . . and the fact that these kids were growing up to be like that like goes to show that it goes down in generations. So I don't go there anymore. I can't remember the last time. I think I always remember that. That was the main thing that always popped out. . . . I get it [racism] everywhere. Especially in all parts of my life I would have to deal with that. Farmington is the most prominent city that I got it from. (Sally, interview, Window Rock, July 19, 2012)

Sally's narrative shows how she was impacted by the harassment. Her experience is much like that of Billy, the young man who was assaulted at a Scottsdale nightclub. Billy stated that he also avoided the location of his assault: "Yeah, I still go to Scottsdale. Matter of fact, I have a part-time job there, in Scottsdale. But don't go to that place no more . . . Cadillac Ranch" (Billy, interview, Tempe, February 14, 2012).

Mary experienced numerous instances of racism over an extended period of time. She stated that she had anxiety after going back to a restaurant where her family had been harassed when she was a child:

It is very hard for me to go into that place. It wasn't until five years ago, with this company that . . . they had their Christmas party there. And the thought of going to that place brought anxiety because, to me, the last time I remember being there it was a very uncomfortable situation. So when I went in there for the Christmas party . . . they have grown from then to now. There was a big difference, but that level of anxiety . . . just to walk into that building—and every time I'd go through town I would always see that building and it reminds me of that moment in time when that was uncomfortable. That was probably the most intense as far as [my experience with] prejudices here [in Farmington]. (Mary, interview, Farmington, July 21, 2012)

American Indians who experience racial violence or discrimination may also segregate themselves from white communities and avoid white people (Whitbeck et al. 2003). This self-segregation is a survival mechanism that nobody should have to rely on in the United States of America, yet American Indians and other people of color must do so for the sake of survival. Perry (2008, 103) argued that racial violence "reinforces social and psychological boundaries." There is an unseen boundary that American Indians are not meant to cross; when they step out of place, whites use racism and violence to put them back in line. Thus, segregation is reinforced, while whites continue to perpetuate their hate unchecked (NNHRC 2009).

Border towns like Farmington become a battleground for Navajos and other American Indians to fight for their right to merely belong. Since the first hostilities with whites, Navajos have constantly fought the physical and psychological boundaries imposed on them by white racism and the threat of violence. After the Long Walk, white policymakers removed Navajos from lands surrounding Farmington by creating physical boundaries, and the white residents kept them out using psychological boundaries. Hate speech maintains and reinforces white privilege, a psychological means to keep the colonized "in their place" (Perry 2008). Taunts also serve as a mechanism of hate crime, which includes intimidation and harassment. If unchecked, this mechanism is strengthened, and the hate only escalates (fig. 1).

Mary described the mistreatment she received from her supervisor. Mary tried to reason with her but could not change the racist mindset of her boss: "Every time I tried to give her a moment, like in a dysfunctional relationship—every time you try to make someone change and every time they disappoint you. It was always like that with her. But it's still that underlying prejudice—the way she treated me" (Mary, interview, Farmington, June 21, 2012). Mary experienced frustration even when she tried to discuss the workplace mistreatment with her white supervisor. Her narrative shows that prejudice and racism in the workplace is very much like an abusive relationship and affects victims similarly.

Explaining Hate Crime

Hate crime is a result of a multitude of motives, including stereotypes, jealousy, and retaliation over economic gain, when an oppressed group steps outside the status quo (Levin and McDevitt 2002). This has been consistent in regions where tribes have obtained casino wealth (Akee et al. 2015; Bennett 2018). Scathing criticism of the Navajo government, Navajo casinos, and economic development enterprises often appears in the *Daily Times*. The oppressed group is prohibited from exceeding not only physical boundaries but economic boundaries as well (Perry 2008).

The interviews show that the perpetrators of verbal assaults, hate speech, and microaggressions are adolescents, neighbors, coworkers, and employers. Billy discussed his family's friendship with a white perpetrator who I will call "James," who committed assaults against three Navajos. Billy said of James:

> He was just a good friend of my cousin's family. He grew up with Navajos. They played baseball together. As they grew up they still had contact with each other until this one incident that happened . . . but he [perpetrator] got involved in that group of white people that got a drunk guy. From what I heard it was an initiation that they had to do. . . . They grabbed a Navajo guy that was drunk, from what I understand they did something with some fireworks. I don't think the Navajo guy died. He [perpetrator] got in trouble for it. . . . He got caught. . . . I think word got around and they started bragging about it. Then he was sentenced to prison. I'm not sure if it was prison or jail. (Billy, interview, Tempe, February 14, 2012)

What is surprising about Billy's narrative is that even when a white perpetrator is friends with Navajos and familiar with Navajo people, he may still perpetrate Indian rolling against Navajos. Billy's narrative demonstrates that Indian hating, racism, and discrimination against Navajos are engrained in the white society of Farmington.

I found within the data that even more subtle forms of racism may be condoned by whites, who may not necessarily believe they are racist. Mary described the subtle racism and mistreatment she received from her boss. When Mary first started working for her employer, another Navajo coworker warned her, "'they're prejudiced.' And I didn't quite sense it. . . . Any opportunity for any career advancement, you're not going to receive that. It's never going to be presented to you" (Mary, interview, Farmington, June 21, 2012). In addition to being passed over for promotion and opportunities, she described the mistreatment as a more subtle form of prejudice.

> It was very hidden. . . . This is a different form of prejudice. This is a different form of intimidation. And it's hidden at a very professional level that is very discreet. And if you're pushed too far, you're going to be the one that's accused of being emotionally inappropriate or emotionally. . . . Let's just say I had to really maintain myself up until the last day I left. Because I felt that if I said anything or did anything it would affect the next job that I had, because she would be the one that they had to call for reference. Even though I trusted the people that I was going to work with. This was how this was going to affect my career—this is not right. And I'm like, just imagine how many other people that may not have the education that I have, because it's very hard—they may not have that. And they are going to continue being mistreated, taken advantage of, not ever being heard or respected. (Mary, interview, Farmington, June 21, 2012)

Mary described the last incident that took place as the most demeaning. The company she worked with had a vehicle that employees used for business purposes. The supervisor was constantly accusing her of making the vehicle "dirty" with her site visits to the reservation. The incident culminated when her supervisor removed all the items from the vehicle and placed them on her desk:

And apparently in her mind she said that the jeep was very dirty, and she was shocked to see—and took out everything in the jeep and put it on my desk. I wish I took a picture. I've done this job . . . and this is the respect you give me to put this trash on my desk. If I was the director I would have had a staff meeting, and say I found the jeep in this condition and make sure you maintain it. . . . I know she would not have treated the non-Natives that way. I know for a fact she would not have done that to them.

There was even non-Natives from other departments who would work with Natives and they would come to me and tell me something needs to be done. They would tell me you know some of these providers are doing jobs that they don't need to be doing. They're cleaning toilet bowls when they don't have to. Just because it's more of a convenience. It's kind of that two-for-the-price-of-one deal. Why pay somebody else when you can get them to do it—to do that job as well.

I really had to struggle with this because I could not understand where I could be working in this field . . . and then have trash put on my desk. There has to be a reason other than ignorance or rudeness, or maybe it was. (Mary, interview, Farmington, June 21, 2012)

Mary's experiences were upsetting and demeaning. She explained the racism she experienced as "subtle." These subtle but real instances of racism are perfect examples of a microaggression. Mary's experience is consistent with what others experienced in Farmington. Reports mention "improved race relations" but describe the more "subtle" forms of racism and mistreatment (New Mexico Advisory Committee to the U.S. Commission on Civil Rights 2005; NNHRC 2009). What is inspiring in her narrative, however, is how she was able to transcend discrimination in the workplace and move on to new and better opportunities, which tells of her resilience and strength.

Learned Behavior and Stereotypes

Indian hating and subsequent race-biased hate crime against Natives are learned behaviors. According to the data presented in previous chapters, racist attitudes are passed through the generations. While racists from past atrocities in Navajo history have died and disappeared, their legacies remain in modern culture and institutions. It is important to identify these roots in order to dismantle them. It starts by reeducating the youth.

Youth may engage in hate crimes for a variety of reasons. Some may participate in thrill-seeking hate crimes; they may be influenced by their peers or be outcasts in their own schools (Levin and McDevitt 2002). Some may view hate crime as a "recreational sport," as in Indian rolling. But in addition to Indian rolling, Farmington's white youth have participated in hate speech and harassment. Degrading others may make them feel better and even lift their self-esteem (Levin and McDevitt 2002). In Farmington this type of behavior is tolerated and even condoned. That this behavior has been normalized shows that the racism and racial violence committed against Navajos are intergenerational.

Navajo students in border town schools face racial discrimination and may be stereotyped as lower achieving. The following stereotypes are consistent with earlier examples. Jenny discussed racism in border town schools: "I had a stepson going to school there, attending Kirtland High School. . . . I could not believe what my husband was telling me. He went there to register his son and the people there at Kirtland said, 'oh he's a Navajo kid, if he can't handle this class we'll put him in this other easier class which he can handle.' Based on that, I said, 'I'm not sending my daughter to Kirtland.' I'm sending her to a different school" (Jenny, interview, July 27, Shiprock, 2012).

Kirtland is a small community about nine miles west of Farmington. In addition to stereotyping Navajo students, there had recently been a contentious issue between the Navajo school board members of Central Consolidated School District and the Mormon community in Kirtland. Jenny said the tension in the community

> was really evident last summer. I had my daughter enrolled in a swimming class at Kirtland swimming pool. And you could just really feel the tension between the Navajos and the Anglo people. You could really feel it. All the white people sitting on one side and all the Navajos on one side. This summer, I signed her up again and took her and everybody was just mellow. They weren't segregating each other. Even the kids seemed like they were getting

along. But I know I didn't feel the tension this year. Last year was really evident. (Jenny, interview, Shiprock, July 27, 2012)

This narrative illustrates the segregation that occurred between whites and Navajos after the conflict. Mormon parents organized a group called Children First, which sought to assemble Kirtland schools into their own school district, separate from the reservation schools. This group was initiated after the school district sought to close the Kirtland business office and move all administration to the school district headquarters in Shiprock. Immediately, Children First began spreading misinformation about Navajo preference in hiring policies, creating flyers and sending email about the dangers of moving all school district business to the reservation. One flyer read, "Do You Want Your Child's Next Teacher Chosen Because of Qualifications or Tribe of Origin?" (Children First, email, August 1, 2012). It was apparent that the main concern and reasoning behind the move to separate Kirtland from the rest of the school district was to avoid Navajo preference, even though most of the students attending Kirtland schools are Navajo.

Some staff members and teachers were involved with the Children First organization and even discussed these issues with their students. Navajo students who attended Kirtland Central "weren't supportive of Children First, and they wanted the Navajo culture classes to remain part of the high school curriculum" (Michael, interview, Farmington, August 7, 2012). A former Navajo student, "Michael," explained the outright call for harassment of the Navajo school board president this way:

Our school board president [who was Navajo] faced a lot of things—against members of the Kirtland community that didn't appreciate things he was doing. For example, I got this email that was floating around to the faculty and community . . . , and attached to it was this Children's First promotional flyer . . . citing their goals—and it had our board president's number at the bottom . . . saying you should call him and complain to him. And I thought, that's kind of taking it too far to put someone's number out there and use that for harassment. (Michael, interview, Farmington, August 7, 2012)

Most of the staff and teachers at Kirtland schools are white, particularly at the high school, where there is only one Navajo teacher who teaches the Navajo language. The Navajo government class is also taught by a white teacher. The former student I spoke with, Michael, did not agree with these staffing choices:

I really think there should be more Navajo counselors and staff. Because the majority of our student population is Navajo and the staff should reflect that to better serve our students. . . . I mean how empowering is that, to go to school every day and see someone of their own tribe teaching that, if that person can go on and achieve a high education and come back and work here to help our own people and help our own community, then why can't I do the same? And I think that is really empowering and motivating for a student to see that happen. So I know the Navajo Nation does that . . . Navajo preference and employment. I think that's really great. Because the Kirtland business office closed at our school district and everything moved to the Shiprock Branch, that Navajo preference and employment kind of came into play. Children First really, really, hated that because . . . they were practically saying that it would reduce the value of our students' education, to have more Navajo staff teaching our students.

They claimed that Navajos who are not qualified would be teaching our students, and that they wouldn't be taught well. And that the Navajo language and culture would be pushed on all students even if they didn't want to. None of that was true. The whole idea of the Navajo preference and employment . . . is that if two candidates apply for the same position and are both equally qualified then they are going to hire the Navajo. But that only comes into play if both candidates are equally qualified. So in no way are they going to hire the less qualified candidate just because they are Navajo. And for some reason Children First did not understand that. They were really hateful towards the Navajo culture and tradition and history being taught in our schools. And they're really against their students being taught by Navajo faculty. And that was really disturbing for me . . . for that group to have the nerve to say that.

They were pulling that out of the air because that's not what the Navajo preference employment thing was about. They were claiming that because Navajo tradition and culture would be taught in our schools it would continue to reduce test levels. Even though studies show that students who are bilingual do test higher, they do better in school. And that studies show that more Native students who have that self-actualization with their self-identity, they do better in school because they feel empowered because of that. Knowing who they are and where they come from, things like that. Having those cultural ties helps a Native student excel. I don't know if that's something that they couldn't understand—that it is beneficial. (Michael, interview, Farmington, August 7, 2012)

Michael credited having a supportive family immersed in Navajo culture and tradition as a factor in his success. It is no secret that off-reservation schools are rife with racism (Deyhle 2009, 1995), and Kirtland Central, where stereotypes regarding Navajo preference laws and low-achieving students proliferated, was no exception.

Another man I spoke with, "Joe," described his perception of Mormon theology. He explained that Mormons believed ethnic groups have dark skin because they had sinned, and if they accepted Mormonism they would become lighter and able to be saved. He argued that their religious views perpetuate racism, and that is reflected in the conflict between Kirtland Mormons and the school district (Joe, interview, Farmington, August 7, 2012).

Michael also described what he perceived while he was a student:

I think that mindset is still in there—that Mormons are better. And I remember once I started getting involved . . . and being around the Mormon students a lot more . . . and just excelling in all the student groups I'm in and as an individual. I happen to have white friends because that's who I'm with all day, and I'd hear comments [from other Navajo students] like, "You're just a white kid now, and you think you're better than us." . . . I never fell into the mindset that Mormons are better than Navajos. I guess I'm the Navajo that showed the other Navajos that that's not true.

Even among the Bilagaanas, they ask, "How'd you get into that [college]?" Well, I work hard. . . . Then they ask, "How are you paying for it?" They're really trying to find something to bring me down, to find a breaking point. They just can't believe that a young Navajo man has things figured out, knows what he's doing and knows where he's going. I always had this one Anglo teacher . . . he always put me down. Every day he would tell me . . . "when you go off to [college] you are going to fail. Oh, you're nothing." That's just him, I guess. I used to hear that every day. He used to irritate me. But I never let it get to me. So it made me want to work harder. It kind of reinforced the fact that it will be hard but I'm just going to work hard. That's what's gotten me through, that's what's gotten me everything I have. (Michael, interview, Farmington, August 7, 2012)

It is clear within this narrative that racism is rampant in border town schools. Fortunately, this young man was self-assured and confident, crediting his Navajo culture for his ability to withstand and rise above racism. Problems have existed in Kirtland with Navajos since after the Long Walk, when there were fights over the border in Kirtland. This racism and ill perception of Navajo students is prevalent in the school and addressed in the *Farmington Report* (2005). The report suggested hiring more Navajo staff, teachers, and administrators, but today Navajos remain underrepresented among staff at Kirtland schools. The NNHRC and Central Consolidated School District administrators should mandate trainings on Navajo culture and create a venue for students to complain about racism from teachers and administrators, without fear of repercussions.

In addition to racist stereotypes about Navajos being lower achieving and inferior to whites, other racist stereotypes, such as Navajos receiving unfair "benefits" from both the federal and tribal governments, also remain consistent. Mary explained how racist stereotypes about Navajo receiving government handouts are still prevalent:

There is this sense of ignorance with professionals that come from out of town that come to our area. That they have this mentality of "Oh, they're Navajo. They're one of the richest nations and they have all the provisions they need." So when you get a boss that hires you on, they feel like they are doing you a favor by hiring you on. And they don't quite have an understanding that . . . we're not rich, we don't get stipends for being Navajo or being on the reservation. I would have never put that together—It took me awhile until—I really had to step away from the program.

I was with a coworker who was non-Native, and we drove by NHA [Navajo housing authority] housing and she asked, "Why is that house . . . that house looks nicer than that house." She said, "They got trees, flowers, that house looks really nice." I said, "NHA is based on income, so that house right there— they are probably paying twenty-five dollars a month, whatever—or a hundred dollars a month. The other home is probably based on his income so of course that's a house he's trying to own." She said, "I thought all the houses were free on the reservation." (Mary, interview, Farmington, June 21, 2012)

Mary was shocked and dismayed about the persistent racist stereotypes regarding Navajos. This narrative correlates back to racist stereotypes mentioned after the Chokecherry murders and in the online Topix forum. These stereotypes remain current and prevalent and may increase the jealousy or envy of the white or non-Indian residents of Farmington and incite more racism, racial violence, and hate crime (fig. 1).

Activism

In the past, hate crimes have been committed against marginalized groups who advocate for their rights (Perry 2008), as during the protests organized by the Coalition for Navajo Liberation in 1974. Members received threats, and the media coverage focused more on the "troublemakers" and less on the actual heinous murders of three Navajo men. Protests and activism against the use of sewer water for artificial snow at the Arizona Snowbowl Ski Resort on the sacred San Francisco Peaks was said to have "polarized the community" in Flagstaff, a border town on the western side of the Navajo Nation (*Edge of the Rez* 2006). The use of sewer water desecrates a sacred site and violates the human rights of many American Indians. Amid this dispute, Navajos experienced increased discrimination in businesses and restaurants and police harassment. Even amid the potential increase in retaliatory hate crimes surrounding Native American activism, activism is a point of pride for many of the people I spoke with. Duane "Chili" Yazzie remarked that it was a "time of greatness" for the Navajo people.

Reluctance to Report

Navajo survivors of hate crime may not want to report the crime to police
for a variety of reasons, including fear of retaliation, distrust of police, and
fear of disbelief. A. R. Denham (2008), a scholar who studies healing and
trauma, discusses the silencing of traumatic histories in some instances.
In certain communities and families, members may not discuss traumatic
events because of cultural beliefs, or they may find these discussions too
distressing, painful, or uncomfortable to engage in. The Chokecherry Massacre, for example, is rarely discussed or mentioned among Navajos. Sally
reflected on why she didn't tell the school administration or any adult about
the harassment at Brookside Park in Farmington: "When we were kids we
didn't talk about it. Now we look back and we never really told anyone about
it. I think you know people don't talk about it. And yeah people don't talk
about it and at the same time the victims don't want to express their views
about it" (Sally, interview, Window Rock, July 19, 2012).

This reluctance to discuss hate crimes and racism is consistent with the
NNHRC's (2009) finding that victims did not want to report discrimination.
Another interviewee expressed her husband's concern about her participation in this study, but she was insistent on participating because she wanted
to do something about the racism and hate crimes in Farmington. Participating in this study became her way of telling her story about the harassment
and threats her family had experienced.

Victims fear that their allegations of hate crimes or racism will not be
believed. Within the analyses of hate crimes, we have seen that in many
cases the police refuse to classify a crime as a hate crime, so victims' distrust
is not unfounded. Most whites continue to argue that American Indians and
Navajos are "overly sensitive," even as they deny racism because they don't
want to acknowledge their own privilege. Even a Navajo Nation Council delegate, Lorenzo Bedonie, questioned the amount of racism in border towns:
"what percentage is real?" He also suggested that Navajos may be just "over
sensitive" (*Edge of the Rez* 2006). One Navajo woman argued that the "only
racism" and mistreatment she experienced as a city employee came from
Navajo people (Karen, interview, Farmington, July 23, 2012), yet she did not
have a clear understanding of racism, equating lateral violence with racism.

When Navajos deny racism, they demonstrate internalized colonization. Some Navajos choose to accept racism in border towns and say, "that's just how Farmington is," adopting a jaded attitude about the racism and hate crimes in Farmington. Mary explained her experience in the workplace:

> I wish I would had filed a complaint. But I filed a complaint before. I already met with the head director before. It appeared to have been acknowledged. But again everything went back to the same way. Was it worth the energy and the time it took to make a complaint? I was kind of fed up with the other Natives I worked with because I was like you want me to go forward and make a complaint, but I have . . . but when I look around, they are like, "We don't know her." I can understand that—they are going to take the safe route and not saying anything.
>
> No matter how much I stood up to her [white supervisor] or whatever, she was not going to take responsibility for anything. I could have been screaming at the top of my voice, she was never going to hear me. And that was just the way it was—it was like wow! (Mary, interview, Farmington, June 21, 2012)

Navajos may fear retaliation for reporting discrimination. At least three people I interviewed discussed that they were still upset about the harassment, racism, prejudice, and hate crime they experienced. Two said they wanted to participate in this research because they were not sure where to turn or they felt like something had to be done about the situation in Farmington. Other studies of Native Americans and hate crimes have not examined the long-term emotional, psychological, and spiritual effects of microaggressions and racial violence on Navajos (Whitbeck et al. 2004). These real issues must be identified and addressed to create paths of healing for victims and their families.

The narratives of hate crime and racism in Farmington make clear that sharing narratives of past violence and racism can be a mechanism for healing. We must keep these victims' stories alive so that racial violence will not be repeated. The people I interviewed might have been the only survivors who felt comfortable enough to share their stories, but by voicing their concerns and frustrations with racial incidents in Farmington, these individuals allowed us to better understand how incidents of racial violence and discrimination affect Navajos.

Narratives are a source of resiliency and survival. Denham (2008) cites that in ethnographies of one American Indian family, stories of historical trauma were the source of pride and inspiration. Indigenous methodologies and testimony are "a way of talking about an extremely painful event or series of events" (L. T. Smith 1999). All the people I spoke with ended our discussions positively. They mentioned how well they are doing in life after their experiences and moving forward as survivors. I was humbled by their strength and am grateful that I learned so much from them.

The formality of testimony provides "a structure within which events can be related and feelings expressed" (L. T. Smith 1999, 144) and which conveys the seriousness of the subject discussed and the weight it carries (Perry 2008; NNHRC 2009). Navajo people provided testimony about human rights violations they have experienced, including racial violence, at an NNHRC-sponsored meeting with the U.S. State Department in 2009. Although some were skeptical about whether or not State Department representatives would act on the violations, the testimony included discussion of racial prejudice and missing-persons cases that have gone uninvestigated (NNHRC Meeting 2009).

Remembering, which involves Indigenous people's and communities' recalling of a painful past, is another mechanism of healing. Indigenous peoples may use forgetting and silence as ways to preserve themselves and hide from the pain. Yet it is important for a community to remember trauma: "Both healing and transformation become crucial strategies in any approach which asks a community to remember what they may have decided to unconsciously or consciously forget." Holocaust survivors and their descendants have used remembrance as a mechanism to heal from trauma (Simon et al. 2000). There is a lack of education in public schools and in higher education about past genocide against American Indians and present hate crimes committed against American Indians. It is important to remember these events, even though they are traumatic, in order to transcend that trauma. Historical trauma is correlated with current racial violence. This was seen most clearly during the 1974 riot in Farmington, when cavalry from Fort Bliss appeared in the Sherriff's Posse Parade after the teenage perpetrators were sentenced as juveniles. The appearance of the cavalry was a reminder to Navajos that the painful past genocide was still occurring during as the Chokecherry murders. Even though only one of the participants mentioned the United States' historical mistreatment of American Indians, hate crimes committed against American Indians are rooted in colonialism, policies that resulted in cultural genocide, and a legacy of Indian hating. Ultimately, the racial violence demonstrates that Navajos are viewed as less than human and targeted for hate crimes. The next chapter discusses possible Navajo- and Native American–centered interventions and suggestions for community responses to hate crimes, especially those committed in Farmington and the Four Corners.

nine

"We Are Human Beings"

Recommendations for Seeking Justice and Healing

R acism and hate crimes committed against Navajos and Native Americans in Farmington and the Four Corners have persisted for more than one hundred years. The racial injustice in Farmington has taken a toll on Navajo lives physically, economically, and educationally. Chapter 8 discussed the numerous ways racism and hate crime impact and traumatize survivors and their families. The rampant racial conflicts, hate speech, and hate crimes will not go away instantaneously. Enacting real, long-term change will take time, energy, resources, and most importantly, commitment to identify, address, and confront these long-standing problems. In this chapter I present a series of recommendations, responses, tactics, and interventions that could aid in reaching this goal.

Interventions

Many of the people I interviewed disclosed that they did not want their children to face the same type of discrimination or hate crimes they had experienced in Farmington. One participant, while discussing a prejudiced supervisor, explained that racism is intergenerational: "I imagine it's like a seed, imagine what she said at home [about Navajos]. . . . I don't want my children to have to deal with this [racism]" (Mary, interview, Farmington, June 21, 2012).

The participants also offered suggestions for improving race relations, such as cultural sensitivity education in schools or cultural sensitivity education for professionals who interact with Navajos. They also discussed systematic racism. Jenny said,

> We wonder . . . how many other people have tried it [opening their own business] and the same thing happened to them, as happened to us. . . . My husband was talking about starting a foundation—where you teach the next group of entrepreneurs how to prevent stuff [hate crime] like that from happening.
>
> A local church had training on racism this past spring, and most of the people that attended were part of the Navajo Episcopal Church. People from Fort Defiance, Bluff, came. . . . We [Navajos] were the only ones that went. . . . The trainers were talking about how things can be improved in Farmington. And I was saying [to my husband], "Why are we here? The people across the river [whites in Farmington] are the ones that really need this. Where are they?" They're the ones that really need it more than we do.
>
> We had the training, but what's the next step? . . . We were talking about starting that foundation. . . . Would we get harassed again? Would we get blackballed? Would people believe us, other Navajos? Or would they say that we are just whining? (Jenny, interview, Shiprock, July 27, 2012)

Jenny recommended education as an important way to alleviate the race problem. Education and training are essential but would only work if the citizens of Farmington were open to learning. Many white residents have continuously denied wrongdoing and maintained that race relations have already improved, suggesting that there is no need for any work to be done. Issues of intolerance and hate crime must be brought to the forefront to resolve them and to demonstrate that victims' concerns are being addressed, yet it appears that there is a general lack of support and interest in doing this work in the area. As we've seen in the literature, most whites likely believe they have neither an individual nor collective racial problem with Native Americans.

Education about racial violence and past historical violence is essential to stop the cycle. As discussed, there is a code of silence around the topic of hate crimes and racial violence in Navajo border towns. Both whites and Navajos are reluctant to discuss these problems. Only one woman I spoke with, Mary, mentioned the previous hate crimes: "And then most of the time you'd hear history of things, you know. I think I was in college when I'd hear stories of locals hurting or injuring—of course they would refer to them as 'local drunks'—with shopping carts, and they just run them over with shopping carts, and it was kind of the teenage thing to do" (Mary, interview, Farmington, June 21, 2012).

This code of silence has done absolutely nothing to confront and change the current conditions. Time is overdue, and the cycle of racism must be stopped.

Speaking Out and Activism

Evidence suggests that victims may feel more empowered and vindicated when they speak out against level 1 and 2 hate crime and discrimination (Perry 2008). For example, several interviewees discussed how after experiencing racism and hate crime in the past, they now speak up when they are being mistreated and assert themselves in situations where they are confronted with racism. The act of identifying the problem is a powerful first step to confronting it. Such actions can lead to change. Victims may find power in direct verbal confrontation, as when Karina Rodriguez defended herself against a white woman's verbal attack in Phoenix in 2020. Some survivors of racial discrimination and violence have found power in direct action by confronting the racism head-on. Perry (2008) often discusses confrontation as a way of "fighting back" but does not mention the potential risk involved. Caution must also be used when confronting racism. Confrontation may lead to an escalation of an incident and even violence, especially since most brazen racists have proved to be violent, aggressive, and unpredictable white males.

In the current racial climate, confrontation can also be viewed by aggressors as their right to justify violence against victims. For example, in 2014, K. Chee, a Navajo man, was shot and killed by a white man, Kyle Quadlin, outside a Walmart in Chandler, Arizona. Quadlin allegedly made a derogatory remark to Chee's Navajo wife. Chee then intervened, and the incident escalated at the entrance of the Walmart. Video of the incident shows Quadlin making an aggressive posture toward the taller Chee. The two began to scuffle, and Quadlin drew a firearm from his pocket and shot Chee. Chee, a father and husband, was unarmed and died as a result of the gunshot. Chee's wife was not far from the incident. Quadlin, a young white man, had carried a concealed firearm into the Walmart and instigated the conflict with Chee and his wife. He later claimed that he had acted in self-defense when the two got into a "scuffle." Quadlin told police he shot Chee because he was "losing the fight," but video shows that he drew his firearm immediately, suggesting he had planned to shoot Chee. As of 2021, Quadlin remains free and was never arrested or charged with a crime (Leo Killsback and Cheryl Redhorse Bennett, *Navajo Times*, March 13, 2014). In the end, it is unclear if any response from Chee would have led to a different outcome, since Quadlin was out looking for a fight that day with a concealed gun in his pocket. It is yet another story of white terrorism and injustice in the United States.

Confronting racism certainly has its challenges. Fighting back must be done with caution, yet that does not mean Native Americans should sit back and accept racism, hate speech, and hate crimes. In the past, speaking out against racial violence has inspired individuals to join collectively and create social movements such as the Coalition of Navajo Liberation. Such groups may be an effective way to create support and safety for victims and families, and they can also bring about awareness. Duane "Chili" Yazzie, the former president of Shiprock Chapter, recalled the marches and activism during the Chokecherry Massacre. When I asked Yazzie if the marching helped to improve the situation in Farmington during the 1974 Chokecherry murders, he reflected, "I think that it helped. . . . Up until that time the mistreatment, discrimination, exploitation . . . by businesspeople was probably more pronounced, more open." He remarked on the improved race relations between Farmington and Navajos, "Things were quiet for quite a few years. We didn't hear of any outward mistreatment this whole time. I think people put those perpetrators on notice . . . that we we're not going to tolerate this." He also cited the Navajo economic impact in Farmington: "we know that the Native money going into Farmington represents 70 to 80 percent gross revenue there." Local businesses felt the impact of the marches: "toward the end . . . [white Farmington] businesspeople came to Fred and basically pleaded for us to stop because their revenue was greatly diminished" (Yazzie, interview, Shiprock, July 25, 2012). Clearly, the border towns depend on Native American commerce, and Native peoples could ignite change by choosing where to shop. Boycotts can be an effective intervention and should be revisited. They could potentially force Farmington and border town businesses to pay attention to allegations of racism and discrimination.

Despite the evidence that activism has also led to hate crimes, no change has been created without social movements. Oppressed people only make progress when they act against oppressors. In 2016 the water protector who demonstrated against the Dakota Access Pipeline faced numerous hate crimes and police violence. In 2020 a lower court ordered the pipeline to shut down, and then a higher court ruled that it can continue to pump oil. The controversy and fight over the pipeline remains. But the issue would not have been addressed at all if grassroots organizers had not brought attention to the matter. The stand at Standing Rock is just one of numerous direct-action movements that yielded the best possible result demanded by Indigenous peoples.

Just two years before the Chokecherry Massacre, on February 12, 1972, Raymond Yellow Thunder was murdered in White Clay, Nebraska, a border town to the Pine Ridge Indian Reservation. Yellow Thunder's murder instigated protests and outrage among American Indians and ignited the American Indian Movement (AIM; Deloria 1988). American Indians reported that they had always felt unsafe in Nebraska border towns, prompting AIM members and other activists to patrol the streets. The newly formed Indian organized community patrol gave a measure of safety and protection to the Native residents and Native visitors to the border town (Deloria 1988). Change occurs when people become participants in transformation. AIM's action brought national attention to a previously ignored racial injustice.

Similarly, when Navajo activists organized in 1974, their purpose was to bring visibility to racial violence and discrimination against Navajos and to demand justice. Persisting racial violence has been ignored and gone unreported in the mainstream media, which poses another set of problems as American Indians seek justice. We are reminded that in 1974 local media chose to denigrate the "radical" "troublemaker" Coalition for Navajo Liberation, and not focus their news coverage on the murder of Navajos. The media attention inadvertently shined a light on the issues Navajos were facing in

Farmington. The CNL was a driving force behind change. Its actions garnered the attention of the New Mexico Commission on Civil Rights and prompted investigation into racial discrimination. Many people, Navajo and non-Native, do not know about the activism in 1974 and the impacts of CNL. Navajos and Native Americans must continue to confront racial injustice.

Restorative Justice

Alternative forms of dispute resolution may be a way for victims of hate crime to seek justice and healing: "Restorative Justice is a theory of justice that emphasizes repairing the harm caused by criminal behavior. It is best accomplished through cooperative processes that allow all willing stakeholders to meet, although other approaches are available when that is impossible" (Restorative Justice). Some aspects of restorative justice may be appropriate to use in discussions of hate crimes with victims, families and communities (Coates et al. 2006). I am not advocating restorative justice between victims and offenders, but it may be a tool that can be used for victims to "talk out" their issues.

Restorative justice dialogue was used within the Cortez community after the murder of F.C. Martinez, a transgender Navajo youth, in Cortez, Colorado, by a Farmington man (Coates et al. 2006). The restorative justice dialogue and candlelight vigil were described as hopeful and healing, and at the vigil community members and Matthew Shepard's mother gave speeches. Whether or not it was truly toward healing is unknown, but it did provide some measure of comfort to the community.

In another effort following the restorative justice session, LGBTQ advocates assisted with the situation in Cortez and organized a workshop entitled Hurt, Hope and Healing: Our Community Responds to F.C. Martinez's Murder. Although the workshop did not solve the long-standing issues, it did open up dialogue within the community (Coates et al. 2006). The intent was not to bring Martinez's family and the perpetrator together but to focus instead on community healing.

In another effort, some people involved in the F.C. Martinez rallies also created the Four Corners Safe School Commission to "create an environment in which the seeds of hate do not flourish but rather are replaced by those of tolerance and mutual respect" (Coates et al. 2006, 13). The discussion of the F.C. Martinez case focused on their transgender identity. It is important to acknowledge that they were also Navajo, and the perpetrator was white and from Farmington. The focus of dialogue needed to also include all aspects of Martinez's identity. Although the Martinez case is an example of how restorative justice dialogue can be used to help a community heal and to promote change, the dialogue should have included more Navajos.

From the Navajo perspective, peacemaking is used to restore balance among individuals, families, and communities. Peacemaking has been used among the Navajo since time immemorial and may be another means to confront racism. A peacemaker in Shiprock, Dr. Larry Emerson, affirmed that it was possible to utilize peacemaking to work with victims of hate crime. Everything in the Navajo universe is interrelated and interconnected. In the Navajo worldview, "The Holy People journeyed through four worlds. In the course of their journey, they came upon many problems. . . . The problems had to be addressed and resolved before the journey continued . . . by the use of prayers, songs and offerings. . . . Another way to address the problems was talking about them in a controlled way. This talking out process became the Diné peacemaking process" (Judicial Branch of the Navajo Nation 2004).

The peacemaking process is elaborate and includes a "talking it out" session, which does not end until there is mutual agreement. The goals of peacemaking are self-healing, healing of disputants and their communities, and restoration of relationships among the participants. Traditional Navajo life revolved around concepts of harmony and balance among the people. The peacemaking process addresses the imbalance between the parties and seeks to restore that balance.

In instances of workplace discrimination or less serious hate crimes such as levels 1 and 2, peacemaking could be used for victims and offenders, if both parties were receptive. Billy, who was attacked in Scottsdale, told me that one of the men who attacked him wanted to apologize. But, understandably, Billy felt that the apology was insincere and too late. In situations such as Billy's, it would be inappropriate to bring perpetrators and victims together. But in other cases, according to traditional Navajo peacemaking principles, an apology in a peacemaking session could bring about some balance, depending on the wishes of the victim (Austin 2009).

The Navajo peacemaking framework has proven to be quite effective among the Navajos and in law practices and courts outside of the Navajo Nation. Navajo peacemaking has even been modeled internationally and in the United States in non-Navajo communities. Peacemaking could help victims to break their silence and talk about their experiences without the perpetrator there. Too many victims of hate crimes have been silent, disbelieved, or ignored. Peacemaking could address some of these issues in a committed effort to bring about balance.

Restorative justice might work with the victim after a period of time has passed after a hate crime (Coates et al. 2006). Peacemaking is not recommended instead of jail time for serious offenses but could be an option used in addition to punitive justice. In particular, peacemaking would be useful in schools where Navajo students have been targeted for harassment. As with the F.C. Martinez case, peacemaking could open up dialogue with the Farmington community to bring closure to victims and their families.

The Legal System and Policing

Native American Perpetrators of Hate Crime

According to FBI statistics, whites are the main perpetrators of hate crimes in the United States, though they are not the only culprits (Federal Bureau of Investigation). There are also American Indians who are violent offenders, but racially motivated hate crimes committed by American Indians are rare. In 2007, for example, two Navajo men were charged with committing a hate crime against a gay Navajo man. The alleged perpetrators denied the charge and insisted that the assault was opportunistic (the victim was in the wrong place at the wrong time) and fueled by alcohol. Both perpetrators were sentenced to jail with a hate crime enhancement.

In another case, discussed in chapter 7, V. Kee, a young Navajo man was kidnapped and branded with swastikas. Kee pursued legal action, claiming the attack was a hate crime and implicating three people: two whites and a mixed-race Navajo man. Prosecutors charged the three perpetrators with hate crimes, and they were convicted and sentenced (Schmidt, *Navajo Times*, August 25, 2011). But instances of American Indian–on–American Indian hate crime are rare in narrative accounts and the data.

Jurisdiction

All the hate crimes and racial violence investigated in this book have occurred in Farmington, New Mexico, or other border towns. Hate crimes committed against Navajos in border towns are under the jurisdiction of the city, county, and state. Even if a non-Native perpetrator committed the crime on the reservation, the Navajo Nation would not have jurisdiction to prosecute because *Oliphant v. Suquamish Indian Tribe*, 435 U.S. 191 (1978), prohibits tribes from prosecuting non-Natives in tribal court in many instances.

Since the *Oliphant* decision, two major pieces of U.S. congressional legislation have addressed jurisdictional issues in Indian Country. The Tribal Law and Order Act (2010) allows tribes to prosecute non-Indians in some instances and provides funding for tribal justice systems. The Violence Against Women Act Reauthorization Act extends jurisdiction over non-Indians in certain domestic violence instances in Indian Country and offers some promising remedies to protect Native women on the reservation. Though these two pieces of legislation address jurisdictional issues on the reservation, all the hate crimes I have uncovered and analyzed occur in reservation border towns or otherwise off-reservation. More work needs to be done at the off-reservation state and local level to investigate and prosecute hate crimes to pursue justice for victims.

Despite the lack of jurisdiction, Navajo law enforcement can still take steps to protect Navajo communities and citizens. In 2007, after Clint John was shot by a Farmington police officer, the City of Farmington contacted the Police Assessment Resource Center (PARC) "to evaluate the structure, procedures, and practices of its Citizen Police Advisory Committee. PARC was also asked to review the Farmington Police Department's files on the investigations of citizen complaints and its reports on uses of force" (Police Assessment Resource Center Farmington). PARC's recommendations centered on a Citizens Police Advisory Committee formed in 1995. The group had been relatively inactive, however, and PARC noted that in other areas, such as Los Angeles during the Rodney King incident, community advisory committees helped mitigate conflict between police and the community. PARC recommended that Navajos sit on the board, and that it become more visible to the public. However, the PARC report did not mention tribal sovereignty or jurisdiction, nor did it mention the addition of Navajo officers to the Farmington Police Department or the possibility of collaboration between the Navajo and Farmington Police departments. Navajo Nation police officers could potentially sit on a board or in an advisory capacity to the Farmington police (Jerome 2007).

Policing

Mutual aid agreement and cross-deputization of Navajo police and county and state police should be pursued. Cross-deputizing, which entails the deputizing of tribal police by state authorities, and state or local police by tribal police departments, is ideal where jurisdictional boundaries are blurred (Luna-Firebough 2007). Navajo Nation police are cross-deputized within San Juan County and McKinley County and certified by the New Mexico State Police. Recently, Navajo Nation police have begun efforts to cross-deputize in some Arizona counties. The problem, however, is that there are comparatively few Navajo police officers: only about one officer per thousand people compared to the national average of one officer per hundred or so citizens (Navajo Nation Police Department).

Cross-deputized Navajo police officers may be able to investigate racial violence in areas outside the city limits of border towns, where state and county police have jurisdiction. This would aid in cultural sensitivity and training. The *Farmington Reports* of 1975 and 2005 found that policing remains an issue and recommended that police recruit and train more Navajos as Farmington police officers. The reports also recommended border town police officers undergo Navajo cultural training, which should involve the NNHRC and Navajo trainers. Currently, the Farmington police utilize out-of-state, non-Navajo cultural competency trainers who do not train on Navajo culture (Gorman, interview, Window Rock, November 29, 2012).

Police Brutality and Crimes

The national average for hate crime reporting is 44 percent (Department of Justice). This figure may be even lower for Indian Country because American Indians view the police as potential perpetrators and are suspicious of them (Bennett 2018; Perry 2009a, 2009c). For example, in 2011 a Navajo woman accused a Farmington officer of assaulting her repeatedly. The woman filed a complaint with both the Farmington Community Relations Board and the NNHRC. Her lawyer stated, "My client—she is Navajo—really was seeking the support of her own people. . . . She wanted the backing of a Nation, which makes her feel stronger because she is going up against a police department. She feels small, she feels overwhelmed. And because we believe there is a pattern of discrimination by (O'Donnell) of harassing . . . pretty young Navajo or Hispanic women" (Piazza, *Daily Times*, November 28, 2011). Charges have not been filed in this case, but the officer was put on leave after the incident was reported.

In 2011 a San Juan County deputy assaulted Donovan Tanner (Navajo) with a flashlight. This incident was caught on camera, and an investigation was launched and a lawsuit was filed against San Juan County (Zah, *Navajo Times*, April 14, 2011). The deputy, Dale Frazier, was fired and then indicted. He pleaded guilty and was given probation. Tanner was awarded a $250,000 settlement from San Juan County (Associated Press, April 25, 2011): "The federal investigation revealed that on March 17, 2011, the defendant [Dale Frazier] used his department-issued Maglite flashlight to strike Tanner in the head, neck and body after encountering Tanner and his brother outside a bar in Farmington, N.M. Frazier struck Tanner two times in the head and neck with his flashlight while Tanner was on the hood of his police vehicle. Frazier stuck Tanner an additional three times with his flashlight while Tanner was on the ground" (NNHRC Press Release 2011).

Before 2006 several Navajos reported that Officer Shawn Scott committed police brutality on multiple occasions. Although Scott was cleared of any wrongdoing in the death of C. John in 2006, Scott had a questionable and alarming record as a police officer. He had previously shot a suspect in the hand as he was attempting to arrest them. In January of 2013, Scott shot and killed an unarmed Hispanic man. His record of police brutality mirrors that of other police officers who have shot Native Americans and people of color (Bennett 2018).

In November of 2012 a Navajo family filed a lawsuit against the Farmington Police Department alleging police brutality. The police were investigating a school break-in and pulled the family over with guns drawn.

The Navajo grandparents had three children with them. During the arrest, one of the children was recorded crying and praying to Jesus to protect the family from the officers (Boetel, *Daily Times*, November 29, 2012). Numerous other instances of profiling, mistreatment, and brutality at the hands of Farmington and San Juan County police officers have been reported (NNHRC 2009; New Mexico Advisory Committee to the U.S. Commission on Civil Rights 2005). According to the reports, Navajos cite police harassment on the west side of Farmington. It is well known to Navajos that there are more police DUI checkpoints leading to and from the reservation on the west side.

Navajo police being called in to respond to hate crimes might facilitate reporting of such crimes. Given the long history of police brutality in Farmington and San Juan County, it is not surprising that Navajos are uncomfortable and apprehensive when reporting incidents or filing complaints. Also, as demonstrated by the interviews in chapter 8, Navajo victims have valid reasons to be concerned that their allegations or complaints will not be taken seriously or be disbelieved (Mary, interview, Farmington, June 21, 2012; Jenny, interview, Shiprock, July 26, 2012). Police reform would be a start to changing the system but defunding the police to provide new intervention services instead may be a better solution.

Hate Crime Laws

As I have mentioned, I use the term *hate crime* throughout this book because the term itself demands response (Bennett 2018; Jenness and Grattet 2001). Additionally, hate crime law "sends a message to both the victim and the perpetrator" (Levin and McDevitt 2002). National hate crime laws are fairly new, considering how long the United States has existed, but these laws provide the only means for victims to seek justice. There is a lot of room for improvement in these laws, and the only way they can be effective is if victims, families, and oppressed people speak up and demand change. Hate crime laws are important to victims in that they may offer some measure of comfort and remedy. Hate crime laws also signal to perpetrators that law enforcement and the criminal justice system will take racial violence seriously and will not tolerate injustice (Levin and McDevitt 2002).

Hate crime laws vary from state to state. New Mexico's hate crime laws add another year to a sentence for first-time offenders and two years for second offenders. Three states do not have any hate crime laws that cover racial bias: Arkansas, South Carolina, and Wyoming. Congress passed federal laws in 2009, and these are now in place for when state laws are insufficient or nonexistent. Most notable are those that President Barack Obama signed into law, like the Matthew Shepard and James Byrd Jr. Hate Crimes Prevention Act (HCPA), which "gives the Department of Justice (DOJ) the power to investigate and prosecute bias-motivated violence by providing the DOJ with jurisdiction."

The HCPA also provides grants for prosecution of hate crimes, preventive education, and training police officers. The HCPA includes tribes in the language of the law, so they may also apply for and obtain federal assistance on investigation at the request of the tribal policing agency. HCPA clearly states: "At the request of a State, local, or tribal law enforcement agency, the Attorney General may provide technical, forensic, prosecutorial, or any other form of assistance in the criminal investigation or prosecution of any crime." The act provides $5 million during each one-year grant cycle. Tribes can apply for funding and elected tribal leaders must make this a priority.

The act indicates that tribes have hate crime laws; however, none are evident in any tribal code. Indian tribes are sovereign nations, and their elected leaders have the power to pass legislation that impacts their people and nation. As sovereign entities with self-autonomy and self-governance, American Indian nations must pass hate crimes laws that protect their members. As sovereign nations, American Indian nations can also establish relationships with federal law enforcement agencies and work with the federal prosecutors to charge non-Indians who commit hate crimes against Indians on reservations in federal courts. History has shown that American Indian nations have not always had the best relationships with federal agencies, but Indian leaders must begin prioritizing the needs and safety of their people by asserting their sovereign rights. Tribes can and should develop policies to strengthen tribal-federal cooperation. The complexity of criminal jurisdiction in Indian Country and the *Oliphant* decision's prohibition of tribal court prosecution of non-Indians has long prevented tribes from extending their sovereign power. But there is evidence that a new era is on the horizon: an era of strengthened and reinvigorated tribal sovereignty.

The NNHRC report (2009) revealed another significant issue related to hate crimes. Evidently, border town police departments revealed a shocking lack of motivation to investigate hate crime cases and missing-person cases. The HCPA could help alleviate these problems by providing another venue to report hate crimes, as it provides limited authority where local police and law enforcement are unwilling to act (Anti-Defamation League). The FBI has already been involved in investigating one instance of police brutality involving a Navajo man, Donovan Tanner, in 2011.

Advocacy

Communities both Indian and white should confront hate crimes and bring awareness and attention to them to strive for peace and justice. Non-Native communities have responded to hate crimes in a variety of ways. Some groups have tried interventions and have seen improvement, like the efforts initiated by LGBTQ activists after the death of F.C. Martinez in Cortez, Colorado. Advocacy on a much larger scale has proven to be quite effective, especially in the response to the rise of hate in the United States.

Advocacy groups such as the Southern Poverty Law Center (SPLC) were founded by civil rights attorneys in the aftermath of white terrorism in the South and have successfully used the legal system "to topple institutional racism" (Southern Poverty Law Center). The Southern Poverty Law Center's mission is to seek justice while fighting hate. The SPLC has had some measured success in lawsuits against organizations such as the Aryan Nation by asserting civil rights violations by these groups. Relatedly, the Anti-Defamation League (ADL) was founded to counter anti-Semitism, but it has been pivotal in drafting legislation and drafting model codes against hate crimes in general (Anti-Defamation League). The ADL has been instrumental in advocating for hate crime laws and provided a fact sheet regarding the new hate crimes law, HCPA. Native nations and Native communities can learn from these organizations and create similar organizations that serve

Native people. The SPLC and ADL have years of experience fighting against hate crimes, advocating for education, and lobbying for new hate crimes laws and would be great partners for Native American efforts.

Part of the strategy of non-Native organizations' advocacy efforts is to educate and bring awareness to hate crimes in order to prevent them. Other racial and ethnic groups have undertaken successful educational campaigns and awareness-raising initiatives. Perry (2008) argues for education at the school level, using the ADL's education on hate crimes as a model to curb racist attitudes and stereotypes that fuel negative perceptions of American Indian people. Education is desperately needed in Farmington. Additionally, the Southern Poverty Law Center has created educational materials for schools and communities and provides teacher training for responding to racism and hate crimes (Learning for Justice).

More locally, interventions need to be made at Central Consolidated and Farmington schools. If Indian rolling is still occurring, it's imperative to address racism and hate crime, especially at the high school level. There is also evidence that discrimination and hate speech are directed at Navajo students, and such incidents should be further investigated. The *Farmington Reports* (1975, 2005) suggested cultural education programs but did not discuss a strategy for implementing such programs. The Southern Poverty Law Center's educational strategy, which focuses on curbing hate and bias, not cultural sensitivity, should be recommended for schools in the Farmington area.

Native nations and Native American community organizations must be resilient and continue to educate about, confront, and bring public awareness to hate crimes. Spreading awareness and enacting change will require the Navajo Nation's continued involvement and response in addition to activism at the grassroots level. Efforts by Navajo activist group CNL brought unprecedented attention to racial injustice. It is doubtful that the Chokecherry murders would have drawn media attention if CNL activists and others had not been at the forefront demanding change and justice. Moreover, the Navajo Nation Human Rights Commission is the only American Indian human rights commission in the nation. Victims may file complaints at other venues, including the Farmington Community Relations Board or Equal Employment Opportunity Commission, but Navajo victims may feel most comfortable reporting to the NNHRC, just as they are often more comfortable talking to other Navajo individuals about racism and hate crime.

Native nations and Native people have recognized the power of their economic contribution to reservation border towns. Boycotting has been used by Navajo rights organizations as a tool used to demand change and push for racial justice. Navajos discussed boycotting again in 2006 to protest racism. The Navajo people provide a large amount of revenue to the reservation border towns; the NNHRC's report shows that Navajos spend millions of dollars in border towns. In fact, the MOAs that were sent to Gallup and Grants were readily signed, much to the surprise of the NNHRC (Gorman, interview, Window Rock, November 29, 2012). The city leaders acknowledged that they are economically dependent on the Navajo people and wanted the memoranda of agreements to continue and work toward better relationships. They also did not want to lose the Navajo revenue stream that pumps millions of dollars into their cities.

Although they are economically dependent on Natives, Farmington and many other border towns have shown that they are not safe places for Navajos and Native Americans. In 2011, city officials proposed to launch an advertising campaign that would allay Navajo concerns about racial violence in Farmington. Assistant City Manager Bob Campbell explained, "What we are looking at is how to change the perception that Farmington is a dangerous place for Navajo to visit. . . . What we would like to do is present some information that demonstrates Farmington is a safe place to be" (Associated Press 2011). This proposed marketing campaign about race relations was decided upon after a meeting with the NNHRC and discussion of the NNHRC report (2009).

Even though Farmington wanted to reassure Navajos that the city was safe, it is unclear how the city planned to ensure that guarantee, as it did not make any preparations to assure safety or address Navajo concerns. In my interview with Duane "Chili" Yazzie, I asked whether he though Farmington is safe for Navajos. He answered, "I would consider it safe for me. . . . If I am mistreated, I would say so and stand up for myself. But for grandma—who is not bilingual—there would be a certain danger there." Yazzie stated that elderly Navajos were particularly at risk for being taken advantage of and accosted in Farmington (Yazzie, interview, Shiprock, July 25, 2012).

Farmington must take substantial measures to demonstrate that Navajos will be safe in the city if it wants to continue relying on Navajo patronage. Officials could implement interventions at schools and train police to handle hate crime more appropriately. To date, the city's proposed ads have not been distributed, and it remains to be seen if Navajos have been avoiding Farmington. The city has a history of short-lived racial justice education programs or trainings with no follow-through, while hate crime and racism persist.

The Navajo Nation's relationship with Farmington remains challenged. In 2010 the NNHRC planned to organize a conference on race relations with the city. After many months of planning, the conference was stalled, postponed multiple times by the city. Ultimately, the conference did take place, but on a much smaller scale and with little city involvement. While the relationship with the city remains difficult at times, the continuing goal is to keep an open dialogue and use diplomatic measures to improve the relationship between Navajos and non-Navajos in Farmington (Gorman, interview, Window Rock, November 29, 2012).

Grassroots Organizing

In 2021 most Americans and the world have seen the power of grassroots organizing. The Black Lives Matter movement is certainly the prime example of effective grassroots organizing. Never has the message that Black Lives Matter made such an impact in American culture, society, politics, and legislation. The movement has transcended boundaries and cultures and will always remain a part of discussions among Americans. The movement spurred numerous sub-movements and other organizations to unite for the common goal of racial justice and equality. Some notable accomplishments of this grassroots movement include bringing national awareness to the unjust killings of George Floyd, Breonna Taylor, and numerous others, as well as aiding in voter protections and advocating for police reform legislation.

American Indian grassroots movements have also proven effective. The earliest and most well known is the American Indian Movement, which managed to bring awareness to numerous injustices and bring about crucial passages of key legislation. Most recently, the Idle No More movement brought the same type of awareness across the United States and Canada. Indigenous grassroots movements bring awareness to continued threats to tribal lands from resource extraction, like the Keystone Pipeline, which was shut down in 2021. In recent years, missing and murdered Indigenous women and girls have garnered national focus after years of advocacy and activism. Native Americans can and should also organize grassroots movements to fight against racial injustice.

CNL spearheaded a very effective grassroots movement that fought against racial injustice, even though most people do not know of the group. It was a force. I am certain that if the Coalition for Navajo Liberation had not formed in 1974, the Civil Rights Commission would not have come to Farmington. Undoubtedly, CNL and the Navajo community were instrumental in advocating for racial justice. They organized at a time when the Navajo Nation was not compelled to act strongly toward racial justice. Although CNL became inactive in later years, its legacy of true grassroots activism remains an inspiration. Native American organizing has been a catalyst for change in recent years. One such grassroots mutual aid organization, Indigenous Action, is based out of Flagstaff.

Indigenous Action has been providing support for the Native American unsheltered community in Flagstaff. The group recently supported an unsheltered relative who was attacked in a level 4 hate crime. Navajo organizer Klee Benally posted about the incident on social media and later urged the unsheltered relative to file a police report. The unsheltered community has long been ignored, even by the Navajo Nation. It is imperative that the Navajo Nation and other Native nations support unsheltered relatives because, in my research, they are the most at risk for hate crimes in reservation border towns.

Conclusion

As I write this conclusion, the entire world is enduring one of the most challenging times known in human history. For one, the COVID-19 virus is ravaging the world. Indian Country in particular has experienced dramatic loss as Native communities and reservations face another pandemic of genocidal proportions. COVID-19 has revealed that Indian communities remain vulnerable because of poverty, lack of infrastructure, and racial marginalization in the health-care system.

At the height of the COVID-19 pandemic, racism continues to rear its ugly head, and covert racists are quick to reveal their true selves. I mentioned in the introduction the hate speech by one white racist in Page, Arizona, a Navajo border town, in 2020, when Dan Franzen threatened to kill Navajos on sight, blaming them for spread of the COVID-19 virus. Unfortunately, that was just the beginning of despicable hate speech against Native Americans and Navajos during the pandemic. Due to a combination of factors including lack of running water, health disparities, and lack of funding, the Navajo Nation became an epicenter for the virus. The Navajo Nation took drastic steps to curb the pandemic that ravaged its citizens. Citizens of the Navajo Nation were asked to stay home each weekend and the Navajo Nation implemented an 8 p.m. curfew during the workweek. Again, malicious hate speech filled comment sections of news posts on Facebook. Online, many whites and Hispanics blamed the Navajos for the virus. I cataloged many instances of hate speech reported on social media. In Gallup a Navajo elder was accosted by a Home Depot manager. The vitriol spewed online included comments such as "stay on your reservation," and references to Navajos being "drunks" and "dirty" proliferated news commentary feeds. The same types of hate speech that Navajos had experienced during the Chokecherry murders (chapter 4) and on the Topix forum (chapter 7) had moved to Facebook and other platforms.

As I wrote this book, I also witnessed an increase in white terrorism in the United States, emboldened by the racist rhetoric of former president Donald Trump. I collected and analyzed data and wrote and edited this book during an onslaught of racial violence in this country, during a time that has been described as a period of the most racial violence the United States has experienced since the civil rights movement. I edited the manuscript while every media outlet showed footage of the killing of Ahmaud Arbery and of a white officer slowly killing George Floyd, who lay on a street pleading for his life. While I reread the accounts I collected of Navajo men being beaten and killed by whites twenty and forty years ago, 2020 was on its way to becoming the most violent year in recent history. I reviewed interviews I collected from Navajo survivors of hate speech as I watched thousands of white terrorists lay siege upon the U.S. Capitol, where two elected Native American women, Representatives Deb Haaland (D–New Mexico) and Sharice Davids (D–Kansas), worked to improve the lives of their constituents. For me, this book will forever be as associated with these events as with the events, stories, and people within its pages.

The murders of Philando Castile, Tamir Rice, Sandra Bland, Freddie Gray, Michael Brown, Ahmaud Arbery, George Floyd, and others show that not much has changed in the United States in terms of race, racism, and white terrorism. The killings of unarmed Black people have shown the world, not just the United States, the persistence of racial violence and the deep racial problems with the legal system that allows that violence to persist. Movements like #BlackLivesMatter, #SayHerName, and #SayTheirNames did not merely focus on awareness. They sought to find and promote long-term solutions for change and paved the way for new movements: defunding and dismantling the police.

During the 2020 movements, Native Americans in Minneapolis supported Black Lives Matter protesters, standing in the front line. Many were older AIM members and children of AIM members. The veteran AIM members reflected that the organization began when the police killed a Native American man. Unfortunately, solidarity wasn't uniform in all Native communities. In North Carolina some members of the Lumbee tribe clashed with and opposed Black Lives Matter protesters, but they are only one of many Native nations, and hundreds of thousands of Native Americans continue to stand against injustice. Yet racial justice is a work in progress, and this work also needs to be done in many Native American communities, especially in those pockets that hold anti-Black sentiment.

As I conclude this book, I cannot remind myself enough that this is a time of uncertainty but also a time of hope. The movement toward change is at a point where it cannot be stopped. Individuals and organizations must either reckon with their racist structures or be dismantled. Racism, hate speech, and hate crimes are on an unstoppable path to their own destruction.

After months of Black Lives Matter demonstrations, protesters toppled and destroyed Confederate monuments and some monuments to European colonizers, albeit sometimes meeting resistance. Statues of Christopher Columbus were toppled in Minneapolis and Baltimore, among other cities. These statues were described as being monuments to white supremacy. In the Southwest, statues to Don Juan de Oñate and Spanish colonizers were removed with much controversy. Statues to Junípero Serra in California were removed amid this change in consciousness. On the heels of monument toppling and protests, in the summer of 2020 the Washington Football Team finally relented to change its name.

The Washington Football Team's mascot and name has for years been an anti-Native slur. Previously, Dan Snyder, owner of the team, had adamantly refused to change the name. He often claimed the name honored Native Americans. In another example of shifts in cultural appropriation, Land O'Lakes quietly removed the Indian "butter maiden" featured on its packaging since 1928. We have seen how racist imagery and stereotypes contribute to racism and race-bias-motivated hate crime (fig. 1). They have also contributed violence against Native women (Bennett 2018). Slowly, these images are being questioned and removed. Images, caricatures, and racist stereotypes are no longer viewed as harmless relics of the past but are being seen for what they are: monuments to racism and white supremacy.

During 2020, in the Four Corners, people reignited a debate about a racist caricature displayed outside an art gallery in Durango, Colorado. The image of the smiling "chief" has been displayed in Durango since the 1950s, first outside a diner. Toh-Atin Gallery, a Native American art gallery in downtown Durango, later took over ownership of the "chief," and it has remained displayed there since. A petition was circulated on Change.org calling for the removal of the "chief." Durango is also home to Fort Lewis College, where I was an undergraduate student and which has a large population of Native American students. Back in the late 1990s, some students tried to start a conversation about racism and the "chief." It has been long recognized by the Native American community as an embarrassing relic of racism, a racist caricature of Native peoples.

In the commentary on the *Durango Herald*'s Facebook page, most people opposed to the removal were white or Hispanic. Many cited "tradition" or argued that "no one" was "offended" by the "chief." The nation has witnessed progress and admission that Confederate monuments are relics of a racist past. By contrast, public consciousness around racist images of Native Americans is more resistant to change. The *Durango Herald*'s Facebook comments illustrate prevalent racism, denial, and yet-to-be-made progress toward racial justice, especially in the Four Corners, where this type of racism against Native Americans has become normalized.

The people I interviewed for this book described incidents of hate crime, assault, hate speech, harassment, and intimidation committed against them. Most notably, they all experienced some form of hate speech. Some of what they described may not be classified as legal hate crime but is instead microaggression, or what I term level 1 and 2 hate crimes. Yet their narratives show that they were greatly affected by what they experienced. Still, despite the incidents, they persevered and wanted to speak out against the racism in Farmington and the Four Corners.

It was important for me, as a Diné/Numunuu researcher and member of the Shiprock community, to uncover stories and experiences that have not been previously recorded. In analyzing the various reports, forums, newspapers, and conducting the interviews, the common perception among whites and non-Indians is that Farmington and the Four Corners is not or is no longer a racist community. Racism in reservation border towns is traditionally, intentionally forgotten and denied, but the narratives within the interviews and posts on the Farmington Topix forum and other social media platforms illustrate that Navajos still face discrimination, mistreatment, racism, and hate crime in Farmington. Unquestionably more Native people have experienced hate crime but are unwilling or afraid to come forward. They may have adapted to the ill treatment or do not want to report, or they may even subscribe to the belief that hate crime and racism are in the past. This is why it is so important to uncover more stories of hate crime and racism: to demonstrate that it is ongoing and must be dealt with to provide safety to Native peoples who interact with border towns.

There is hope that different organizations will combine forces to end the cycle of racial violence perpetrated against Navajos. "We're neighbors, we're not going anywhere; let's try to get along. . . . But that's the hope. We just hold out on that hope that nothing as bad as what has happened happens again," Duane "Chili" Yazzie expressed (Yazzie, interview, Shiprock, July 22, 2012). The participants I interviewed were also optimistic that change is possible. The work of improving race relations and combating hate crimes against Native people in Farmington lies with future generations.

May 29, 2018, marked the twentieth anniversary of Pernell Tewangoitewa's disappearance and probable murder. His case has been marked as a cold-case homicide. I still think of Pernell when I drive past Chokecherry Canyon. I often wonder if he is buried in the vast desert wilderness. I think about the other Native American victims and survivors of hate crime and hope that there will be no more level 4 and 5 hate crimes committed in Farmington or the Four Corners. However, as a scholar of hate crimes and racial violence, I know that these crimes will persist if we continue to be complacent. I have uncovered here an undeniable historical pattern of hate crimes against Native Americans in the Four Corners. Since they arrived, white men have terrorized Navajos and Native Americans in the Four Corners. This terror must stop. I began this research before V. Kee was kidnapped and branded with swastikas in 2010. When I first heard of the hate crime against Kee, I thought to myself, *not again*. Hate crimes are incessant, and if we look at the pattern not only in the Four Corners but in the United States, they are only getting worse. Without serious interventions they will continue.

In the last few years there has been more attention demanded toward missing and murdered Indigenous peoples, particularly women. The movement to investigate the cases of missing and murdered Indigenous women and girls grew out of years of frustration and despair. In my research on missing and murdered Indigenous women and girls (Bennett 2018), I found that Native men are also victims of violence at particularly high rates. Change doesn't come unless it is demanded and fought for. For years I have taught a course called Crime in Indian Country. We spend a week studying hate crimes against Native Americans, and I teach students about the Chokecherry Massacre, the *Farmington Report* (1975, 2005), and the Coalition for Navajo Liberation. One Navajo student was baffled about why he had only learned about this history in my course: Why hadn't this incident sparked a civil and human rights movement in Indian Country? He likened the crime to the brutal lynching of Emmett Till, which became a catalyst for the civil rights movement. This book is a call to bring attention and justice to long overlooked and ignored race-biased hate crimes against Native Americans, with the hope that we will one day have justice for victims like Pernell Tewangoitewa.

References

Acoose, J. 1995. *Iskwewak—Kah' Ki Yaw Ni Wahkomakanak: Neither Indian Princesses nor Easy Squaws*. Toronto: Women's Press.

Acrey, B. 1988a. *Navajo History: The Land and the People*. Shiprock: Central Consolidated Schools.

Acrey, B. 1988b. *Navajo History to 1846: The Land and the People*. Shiprock: Central Consolidated Schools.

Akee, Randall K. Q., Katherine A. Spilde, and Jonathan B. Taylor. 2015. "The Indian Gaming Regulatory Act and Its Effects on American Indian Economic Development." *Journal of Economic Perspectives* 29, no. 3: 185–208.

Alvord, L., and E. Cohen Van Pelt. 1999. *The Scalpel and the Silver Bear: The First Navajo Woman Surgeon Combines Western Medicine and Traditional Healing*. New York: Bantam Books.

Associated Press. 2011. "Farmington Eyes 'Safe' Ads Aimed at Navajos." *Reznet News*. http://www.reznetnews.org/article/farmington-eyes-safe-ads-aimed-.

Austin, R. 2009. *Navajo Courts and Navajo Common Law: A Tradition of Tribal Self-Governance*. Minneapolis: University of Minnesota Press.

Bailey, Garrick Alan, and Roberta Glenn Bailey. 1982. *Historic Navajo Occupation of the Northern Chaco Plateau*. Tulsa: University of Tulsa.

———. 1986. *A History of the Navajos: The Reservation Years*. Santa Fe: School of American Research Press.

Barker, R. 1992. *The Broken Circle*. New York: Simon and Schuster.

Bazian, Hatem. 2019. "Islamophobia, Trump's Racism and 2020 Elections." *Islamophobia Studies Journal* 5, no. 1: 8–10.

Bennett, Cheryl Redhorse. 2013. *Investigating Hate Crimes in Farmington, New Mexico*. Tucson: University of Arizona.

———. 2018. "Another Type of Hate Crime: Violence against American Indian Women in Reservation Border Towns." In *Crime and Social Justice in Indian Country*, edited by Marianne O. Nielsen and Karen Jarratt-Snider. Tucson: University of Arizona Press.

Berkhoffer, R. 1978. *The White Man's Indian*. New York: Vintage.

Bighorse, T. 1990. *Bighorse the Warrior*. Tucson: University of Arizona Press.

Blout, E., and P. Burkart. 2021. "White Supremacist Terrorism in Charlottesville: Reconstructing 'Unite the Right.'" *Studies in Conflict and Terrorism*.

Buchanan, S. 2006a. "Indian Blood." *Intelligence Report*. Southern Poverty Law Center.

Buchanan, S. 2006b. "Violence against American Indians Is a Pervasive Problem." *Intelligence Report*, 124. Southern Poverty Law Center.

Chavers, D. 2009. *Racism in Indian Country*. New York: Peter Lang.

Coates, R., M. Umbreit, and B. Vos. 2006. "Responding to Hate Crimes through Restorative Justice Dialogue." *Contemporary Justice Review* 9, no. 1: 7–21.

Cook-Lynn, E. 2001. *Anti-Indianism in Modern America: A Voice from Tatekeya's Earth*. Urbana: University of Illinois Press.

Corntassel, Jeff, and Richard C. Witmer. 2008. *Forced Federalism: Contemporary Challenges to Indigenous Nationhood*. Norman: University of Oklahoma Press.

Daily Times. 2009. *San Juan County, New Mexico: A Photographic History, Volume II*. Piedmont Publishing.

Deloria, V. 1988. *Custer Died for Your Sins*. Norman: University of Oklahoma Press.

Deloria, V., Jr. 1997. *Red Earth, White Lies: Native Americans and the Myth of Scientific Fact*. New York: Scribner.

Deloria, V., Jr. 1999. *Spirit and Reason: The Vine Deloria Jr. Reader*. Golden: Fulcrum.

Denetdale, J. 2007. *Reclaiming Diné History: The Legacies of Navajo Chief Manuelito and Juanita*. Tucson: University of Arizona Press.

Denham, A. R. 2008. "Rethinking Historical Trauma: Narratives of Resilience." *Transcultural Psychiatry* 45, no. 3: 391–414.

Denzin, N., Y. Lincoln, and L. T. Smith. 2008. *Handbook of Critical Indigenous Methodologies*. Los Angeles: Sage.

Deyhle, D. 1995. "Navajo Youth and Anglo Racism." *Harvard Educational Review*.

———. 2009. *Reflections in Place: Connected Lives of Navajo Women*. Tucson: University of Arizona Press.

Dinebeiina Nahiilna Be Agaditahe, Inc. 2006. "Race Relations Report." Window Rock, Ariz.: DNA-People's Services, Inc.

Donaldson, L. 2006. "'Indian Rolling': White Violence against Native Americans in Farmington, New Mexico." PhD dissertation, University of New Mexico.

Drinnon, R. 1980. *Facing West: Political Theology and American Liberation*. New York: New American Library.

Drywater-Whitekiller, V. 2017. "We Belong to the Land: Native Americans Experiencing and Coping with Racial Microagressions." *Canadian Journal of Native Studies* 37, no. 1: 153–74.

Edge of the Rez. 2010. Directed, written, and produced by Lydia Nibley. Written and produced by R. Martin.

Erlich, H. 2009. *Hate Crimes and Ethnoviolence: The History, Current Affairs, and Future Discrimination in America*. Boulder: Westview Press.

Fanon, F. 1961. *The Wretched of the Earth*. New York: Grove Press.

Federal Bureau of Investigation. Hate Crime Statistics. http://www.fbi.gov/hq/cid /civilrights/hate.htm.

Feola, Michael. 2021. "'You Will Not Replace Us': The Melancholic Nationalism of Whiteness." *Political Theory* 49, no. 4: 528–53.

Flaherty, Anne. 2013. "American Indian Land Rights, Rich Indian Racism, and Newspaper Coverage in New York State, 1988–2008." *American Indian Culture and Research Journal* 37, no. 4: 53.

Foucault, Michel. 1982. *The Subject and Power*. Chicago: University of Chicago Press.

Furman, A. M. 1977. *Tohta*. Wichita Falls: Nortex Press.

Gantt Shafer, Jessica. 2017. "Donald Trump's 'Political Incorrectness': Neoliberalism as Frontstage Racism on Social Media." *Social Media Society* 3, no. 3.

George Washington Papers. 1783. Series 3, Varick Transcripts, 1775–1785. Subseries 3A, Continental and State Military Personnel, 1775–1783. Letterbook 7: January 3, 1783–December 23, 1783.

Gerstenfeld, Phyllis B., Diana R. Grant, and Chau-Pu Chiang. 2003. "Hate Online: A Content Analysis of Extremist Internet Sites." *Analyses of Social Issues and Public Policy* 3, no. 1: 29–44.

Getches, David H., Charles F. Wilkinson, Robert A. Williams, Matthew L. M. Fletcher, and Kristen A. Carpenter. 2017. *Cases and Materials on Federal Indian Law*. 7th ed. American Casebook Series. Saint Paul: West Academic Publishing.

Glaser, Jack, Jay Dixit, and Donald P. Green. 2002. "Studying Hate Crime with the Internet: What Makes Racists Advocate Racial Violence?" *Journal of Social Issues* 58, no. 1: 177–93.

Gomez, Christian. 2019. "Hate Hoaxes: Rise of Fake 'Hate Crimes': In the Trump Era, Leftists Have Repeatedly Created Hate-Crime Hoaxes to Try to Vilify Trump Supporters, Labeling Them Racist, Homophobic, and More—Trying to Stir up Animus." *New American* 35, no. 7.

Gonzales, Kelly L., Luohua Jiang, Ginny Garcia-Alexander, Michelle M. Jacob, Jenny Chang, David R. Williams, Ann Bullock, and Spero M. Manson. 2021. "Perceived Discrimination, Retention, and Diabetes Risk among American Indians and

Alaska Natives in a Diabetes Lifestyle Intervention." *Journal of Aging and Health* 33, no. 7–8: 18S–30S.

Grossman, Z. 2005. "Treaty Rights and Responding to Anti-Indian Activity." In *Sovereignty, Colonialism and the Indigenous Nations: A Reader*, edited by Robert Odawi Porter. Durham: Carolina Academic Press.

Harris, Cheryl I. 1993. "Whiteness as Property." *Harvard Law Review* 106, no. 8: 1707–91.

Heath, B., B. Street, and M. Mills. 2008. *On Ethnography: Approaches to Language and Literacy Research*. New York: Teachers College Press.

Hendricks, R., and J. Wilson., eds. 1996. *The Navajo in 1705: Roque Madrid's Campaign Journal*. Albuquerque: University of New Mexico Press.

Hill, J. 2008. *The Everyday Language of White Racism*. Malden: Wiley-Blackwell.

Horn, C. 1963. *New Mexico's Troubled Years: The Story of the Early Territorial Governors*. Albuquerque: Horn and Wallace.

Hswen, Yulin, Qiuyuan Qin, David R. Williams, K. Viswanath, S. V. Subramanian, and John S. Brownstein. 2020. "Online Negative Sentiment towards Mexicans and Hispanics and Impact on Mental Well-Being: A Time-Series Analysis of Social Media Data during the 2016 United States Presidential Election." *Heliyon* 6, no. 9.

Iverson, P. 2002a. *Diné: A History of the Navajos*. Albuquerque: University of New Mexico Press.

———. 2002b. *"For Our Navajo People": Diné Letters, Speeches and Petitions, 1900–1960*. Albuquerque: University of New Mexico Press.

Jenness, V., and R. Grattet. 2001. *Making Hate a Crime*. New York: Russell Sage Foundation.

Jerome, Richard. 2007. *Promoting Police Accountability and Community Relations in Farmington*. Los Angeles: Police Assessment Resource Center.

Judicial Branch of the Navajo Nation. 2004. *Peacemaking Manual*. Window Rock: Navajo Nation.

Kelley, K., and H. Francis. 1994. *Navajo Sacred Places*. Bloomington: Indiana University Press.

Kelley, K., and P. Whiteley. 1989. *Navajo Land: Family and Settlement and Land Use*. Tsaile: Navajo Community College Press.

Kelly, R. J., and J. Maghan. 1998. *Hate Crimes*. Carbondale: Southern Illinois University Press.

Khan-Cullors, Patrisse, and Asha Bandele. 2018. *When They Call You a Terrorist: A Black Lives Matter Memoir*. Unabridged ed. New York: St. Martin's.

Killsback, Leo. 2020. *A Sovereign People: Indigenous Nationhood, Traditional Law, and the Covenants of the Cheyenne Nation*. Lubbock: Texas Tech University Press.

Kiser, W. 2017. *Borderlands of Slavery*. Philadelphia: University of Pennsylvania Press.

Levin, J. 2007. *The Violence of Hate: Confronting Racism, Anti-Semitism, and Other Forms of Bigotry*. Boston: Pearson, Allyn and Bacon.

Levin, J., and J. McDevitt. 1993. *Hate Crimes*. New York: Plenum.

———. 2002. *Hate Crimes Revisited: America's War on Those Who Are Different*. Boulder: Westview.

Levin, J., and G. Rabrenovic. 2004. *Why We Hate*. Amherst: Prometheus.

Luna-Firebough, E. 2007. *Tribal Policing: Asserting Sovereignty, Seeking Justice*. Tucson: University of Arizona.

MacDonald, E. 1975. *I Remember Old MacDonald's Farmington*. Santa Fe: Sleeping Fox Press.

MacDonald, E., and J. Arrington. 1970. *The San Juan Basin: My Kingdom Was a Country*. Denver: Green Mountain Press.

Mankiller, Wilma. 2005. "Public Perception as a Sovereignty Protection Issue." *Kansas Journal of Law and Public Policy* 14, no. 3.

Marshall, C., and G. Rossman. 2006. *Designing Qualitative Research*. Thousand Oaks: Sage.

Matias, Cheryl E., and Peter M. Newlove. 2017. "Better the Devil You See, than the One You Don't: Bearing Witness to Emboldened En-whitening Epistemology in the Trump Era." *International Journal of Qualitative Studies in Education* 30, no. 10: 920–28.

Memmi, Albert. 1991. *The Colonizer and the Colonized*. Expanded ed. Boston: Beacon Press.

———. 2000. *Racism*. Minneapolis: University of Minnesota Press.

———. 2006. *Decolonization and the Decolonized*. Minneapolis: University of Minnesota Press.

McNitt, Frank. 1972. *Navajo Wars; Military Campaigns, Slave Raids, and Reprisals*. 1st ed. Albuquerque: University of New Mexico Press.

McPherson, R. 1988. *The Northern Navajo Frontier, 1860–1900: Expansion through Adversity*. Albuquerque: University of New Mexico Press.

Mihesuah, D. 1996. *American Indians, Stereotypes and Realities*. Atlanta: Clarity.

Native Americans: The Invisible People. 1994. CNN Special.

Navajo Community College. 1973. *Navajo Stories of the Long Walk period*. Tsaile: Navajo Community College Press.

Navajo Nation Human Rights Commission. 2009. *Assessing Race Relations in Navajo Nation Border Towns*. Window Rock: Navajo Nation.

Newcomb, F. 1966. *Navaho Neighbors*. Norman: University of Oklahoma Press.

New Mexico Advisory Committee to the U.S. Commission on Civil Rights. 1975. *The Farmington Report: A Conflict of Cultures*.

———. 2005. *The Farmington Report: Civil Rights for Native Americans 30 Years Later*.

Nockleby, John T. 1994. "Hate Speech in Context: The Case of Verbal Threats." *Buffalo Law Review* 42, no. 3: 653.

———. 2000. "Hate Speech." *Encyclopedia of the American Constitution* 3, no. 2: 1277–79.

Pearce, R. 1988. *Savagery and Civilization: A Study of the Indian and the American Mind*. Berkeley: University of California Press.

Perry, Barbara. 2002. "From Ethnocide to Ethnoviolence: Layers of Native American Victimization." *Contemporary Justice Review* 5, no. 3: 231–47.

———. 2005. "Putting Anti-Indian Violence in Context: The Case of the Great Lakes Chippewa of Wisconsin." *American Indian Quarterly* 29, no. 3/4: 590–625.

———. 2008. *Silent Victims: Hate Crimes against Native Americans*. Tucson: University of Arizona Press.

———. 2009a. "Impacts of Disparate Policing in Indian Country." *Policing and Society* 19, no. 3: 263–81.

———. 2009b. "'There's Just Places Ya' Don't Wanna Go': The Segregating Impact of Hate Crimes against Native Americans." *Contemporary Justice Review* 12, no. 4: 401–18.

———. 2009c. *Policing Race and Place in Indian Country: Over- and Underenforcement*. Lanham: Lexington Books.

Petrosino, C. 1999. "Connecting the Past to the Future: Hate Crime in America." *Journal of Contemporary Criminal Justice* 15, no. 22: 22–47.

Pezzella, Frank S., Matthew D. Fetzer, and Tyler Keller. 2019. "The Dark Figure of Hate Crime Underreporting." *American Behavioral Scientist*, 276421882384.

"Police ID Suspect in Hockey 'Hate Crime' against Native American Kids." 2015. *Talking Points Memo* (blog), January 29, 2015.

Prucha, Francis Paul. 1986. *The Great Father: The United States Government and the American Indians*. Abridged ed. Lincoln: University of Nebraska Press.

Redhouse, J. 2006. "Navajo John Redhouse: Farmington New Mexico Police Brutality." Retrieved from http://www.scribd.com/doc/53732743/Navajo-John-Redhouse-Farmington-NM-Police-Brutality.

Rushdy, Ashraf H. A. 2012. *American Lynching*. New Haven: Yale University Press.

Silva, Eric O. 2019. "Donald Trump's Discursive Field: A Juncture of Stigma Contests over Race, Gender, Religion, and Democracy." *Sociology Compass* 13, no. 12.

Silverman, Robert A. 2009. "Patterns of Native American Crime." In *Criminal Justice in Native America*, edited by Marianne O. Nielsen and Robert A. Silverman. Tucson: University of Arizona Press.

Simon, Roger I., Sharon Rosenberg, and Claudia Eppert. 2000. "Introduction: Between Hope and Despair: The Pedagogical Encounter of Historical Remembrance." In *Between Hope and Despair: Pedagogy and the Remembrance of Historical Trauma*, edited by Roger I. Simon, Sharon Rosenberg, and Claudia Eppert, 1–9. Lanham, Md.: Rowman and Littlefield.

Slotkin, R. 1973. *Regeneration through Violence*. Middletown: Wesleyan University Press.

Smith, G. 2005. "Theorizing, Transforming and Reclaiming Our Indigenous Selves." Presented at the WIPCE Conference, Hamilton, New Zealand.

Smith. L. T. 1999. *Decolonizing Methodologies: Research and Indigenous People.* London: Zed.

Spicer, E. 1962. *Cycles of Conquest.* Tucson: University of Arizona Press.

Sprinkle, Stephen V. 2011. *Unfinished Lives: Reviving the Memories of LGBTQ Hate Crimes Victims.* Eugene: Wipf and Stock.

Stannard, D. 1992. *American Holocaust.* New York: Oxford University Press.

Stein, Howard F., and Seth Allcorn. 2018. "A Fateful Convergence: Animosity toward Obamacare, Hatred of Obama, the Rise of Donald Trump, and Overt Racism in America." *Journal of Psychohistory* 45, no. 4: 234–43.

Steinfeldt, Jesse A., Brad D. Foltz, Jennifer K. Kaladow, Tracy N. Carlson, Louis A. Pagano, Emily Benton, and M. Clint Steinfeldt. 2010. "Racism in the Electronic Age." *Cultural Diversity & Ethnic Minority Psychology* 16, no. 3: 362–71.

Sue, Derald Wing. n.d. "Microaggression: More Than Just Race." https://www.uua.org/files/pdf/m/microaggressions_by_derald_wing_sue_ph.d._.pdf.

Title VII Bilingual Staff Lake Valley School. 1991. Oral History Stories of the Long Walk. Lake Valley: United States Department of Education.

Two Spirits. 2011. Directed, coproduced, and cowritten by Lydia Nibley. Independent Lens.

United States Commission on Civil Rights. n.d. *Discrimination against Native Americans in Border Towns.* Washington, D.C.

Valenti, JoAnn M. 1995. "Reporting Hantavirus: A Study of Intercultural Environmental Journalism." Presented at the Conference on Communication and the Environment, Chattanooga, Tenn.

van Dijk, Teun A. 1993. *Elite Discourse and Racism.* Newbury Park: Sage.

Wakeling, S., M. Jorgenson, S. Michaelson, and M. Begay. 2000. *Policing on American Indian Reservations: A Report to the National Institute of Justice.* Harvard Project on American Indian Economic Development.

Walker, Alice. 1983. *In Search of Our Mother's Gardens: Womanist Prose.* San Diego: Harcourt Brace Jovanovich.

Whitbeck, L., G. Adams, D. Hoyt, and X. Chen. 2004. "Conceptualizing and Measuring Historical Trauma among American Indian People." *American Journal of Community Psychology*, 33, no. 3/4: 119–30.

Wilkins, David E., and Heidi Kiiwetinepinesiik Stark. 2018. *American Indian Politics and the American Political System.* 4th ed. Lanham, Md.: Rowman & Littlefield.

Williams, Robert A. 2005. *Like a Loaded Weapon: The Renquist Court, Indian Rights and the Legal History of Racism in America.* Minneapolis: University of Minnesota Press.

———. 2012. *Savage Anxieties: The Invention of Western Civilization.* 1st ed. New York: Palgrave Macmillan.

Wyoming PBS. 2018. "No Dogs or Indians Allowed: Sheridan, Wyoming and the Miss Indian America Pageant." YouTube, July 11, 2018. https://youtu.be/4kYLq_LIhYg.

Index

activism: Chokecherry Massacre producing, 15, 71, 77–82, 88; on Chokecherry sentences, 81; for civil rights, 20; Farmington on "outside agitators" and, 88, 91; Farmington protested by, 6; hostility on, 80, 91, 120–21; by LGBTQ, 181; Navajos on, 95, 172; on pipelines, 43, 172, 185; Yazzie on, 164

ADL. *See* Anti-Defamation League

advocacy, 115, 181–84

African Americans, 34, 37, 53, 187; Black Lives Matter and, 3, 184, 188

AIM. *See* American Indian Movement

alcohol: abuse of, 31, 124, 126; Civil Rights Committee on treatment and, 93–94; Farmington and unsheltered population with, 73; *Farmington Report* (2005) on substance abuse and, 126–27; Level 4 and 5 including, 117; unsheltered relative population and, 31, 94; whites on, 88

American Indian Movement (AIM), 79–80, 87–88, 91, 172, 184, 188

American Indians: from Asia, 41, 46, 90, 141; *Daily Times* on "militancy" and

opportunism, 88–89; earnings by, 147; as fragile "vanishing Indian," 40–41; laws, legal status for, xiv; politics and, 42; research data collection on racism and, 11–13, 16; on treaty rights, 43; UCR data and, 24. *See also* Native Americans

American Indian studies scholars: on hate crimes, 10, 22; Indigenous theories and, 33–34; for intellectual foundation, 19–20; marginalization of, 4; on race, 33, 37, 39; on settler and Navajo relationships, 11; terminology by, 20, 22; on U.S. mistreatment, 4

Anderson, Larry, 80

animals: death and "bug smash," 115; hate crimes and kicking, 110; Indian Rolling as, 107; Long Walk and Navajo as, 58

Anti-Defamation League (ADL), 17, 22, 181–82; Pyramid of Hate by, 23–24, 144

anti-gay bias, 25, 175. *See also* Martinez, F. C.; Shepard, Matthew

About the Author

Cheryl Redhorse Bennett is an enrolled citizen of the Navajo Nation and descends from the Comanche Nation. Currently, Dr. Bennett is an assistant professor at Montana State University in Bozeman, Montana. Her area of expertise is in crime and violence against Native Americans and racial justice. She has published book chapters in *Crime and Social Justice in Indian Country* and is working on research that examines hate speech and Native Americans.